C.S. LEWIS

C.S. Lewis
A Philosophy of Education

Steven R. Loomis
and
Jacob P. Rodriguez

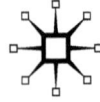

C.S. LEWIS: A PHILOSOPHY OF EDUCATION
Copyright © Steven R. Loomis and Jacob P. Rodriguez, 2009
Softcover reprint of the hardcover 1st edition 2009
All rights reserved.

Cover by Mark Epler and photograph by Steven Loomis

First published in 2009 by PALGRAVE MACMILLAN® in the
United States - a division of St. Martin's Press LLC, 175 Fifth Avenue,
New York, NY 10010.

Where this book is distributed in the UK, Europe and the rest of
the world, this is by Palgrave Macmillan, a division of Macmillan
Publishers Limited, registered in England, company number 785998,
of Houndmills, Basingstoke, Hampshire RG21 6XS.

Palgrave Macmillan is the global academic imprint of the above
companies and has companies and representatives throughout the world.

Palgrave® and Macmillan® are registered trademarks in the United
States, the United Kingdom, Europe and other countries.

ISBN 978-1-349-37311-6   ISBN 978-0-230-10058-9 (eBook)
DOI 10.1007/978-0-230-10058-9

Library of Congress Cataloging-in-Publication Data

A catalogue record of the book is available from the British Library.

Design by Integra Software Services

First edition: 2009

For David Loomis
For Michele

Contents

List of Sidebars ... ix

Acknowledgments ... xi

Introduction ... 1
   Reason and Nature ... 1
   Models of Thought ... 10
   Fear, Risk, and Models ... 13
   The Principle of Substitution ... 23
   The Outline of the Book ... 29

1 The Bloodless Institution ... 31
   The Importance of the Social Institution to C.S. Lewis ... 31
   The Idea of Proper Function and the Social Institution ... 36
   The Insufficiency of the Non-teleological Account of Social Institutions ... 42
   The Ontology of Social Institutions: A Preliminary Statement ... 45
   Growth and the Social Institution ... 56
   The Institution, the Substitution, and the Public Domain ... 57

2 The Ontology of Education as an Institution ... 67
   The Social Institution and the Model and Attribute of Growth ... 67
   Closed Growth as a Model of Thought ... 75
   Growth as an Attribute of Social Institutions ... 93
   Conclusion ... 99

3 The Epistemological Disabilities of Growth: How Expanding Markets Exchange Knowledge for Ignorance ... 101
   The Quest for Uniformity in the Mass Producing Age ... 105
   The Technical Image of Philosophical Naturalism ... 109
   The Irresistible Technique ... 115

4 Educational Sustainability and the Obsolete
   Man   127
   Man and the Expanding Domain of Nature   127
   The Choice – Decision Distinction   131
   The Division of Rationality from Reason   138
   The Sustainability of Education as an Institution   147
   Conclusion: With or Without the Tao   155

5 Reason before Nature: The Possibility of
   Education   159
   Nature, Education, and Freedom   159
   Knowledge is Supernatural   163
   Naturalism, Dewey, and the Central Offense of the Tao   173
   The Collective or the Body: A Reevaluation of the Social
   Contract and the Education Good   185
   Conclusion   194

Notes   197

Bibliography   211

Index   223

List of Sidebars

Sidebar	The Principle of Ontological Correspondence	48
Sidebar	The Principle of Reality Substitution	59
Sidebar	The Hegemony of the Categories—The Behavioral Objectives Model	81
Sidebar	The Culture of Educational Assessment	116
Sidebar	729 Times Closer to God: An Open Letter	121
Sidebar	The Insufficiency of Rational Choice Theory	135
Sidebar	The Synonymizers	165
Sidebar	The End of the Game: A New Unit of Analysis	181
Sidebar	Lewis on Equality	186

Acknowledgments

We extend warm appreciation to Michael Aeschliman, Julia Cohen, Samantha Hasey, Rachel Tillman, Jessica Edelman, Colin Harris (Oxford University), Christopher Mitchell (The Wade Center at Wheaton College), Dorothy Chappell, Joseph Weeres and our colleagues at The Eagle and Child for their kind assistance. We are also grateful to our respective colleagues and to our students for their energetic commitment to ideas. We also acknowledge the G.W. Aldeen Memorial Fund of Wheaton College which helped to finance part of this project.

INTRODUCTION

REASON AND NATURE

The book is about the philosophy of education. In it we have partnered with the mind of C.S. Lewis, working within the genius of his thought, to develop a new analytical framework for explaining the ways in which education falls into disequilibrium, thus stunting a society's prospects for human development and flourishing. In essence most of the book shows how an education system whose costs may soon exceed its benefits may nevertheless continue to expand. Our goal is to conceptualize and defend a vision of education that differs significantly from its present course. Knowing the cost of institutions presupposes some idea of the optimal social order (Tinbergen 1987; Rodriguez, Loomis, and Weeres 2007), and is vital before understanding just how completely the present course will move us toward that condition which Lewis called the abolition of man.

Before proceeding to set up our argument we offer an important caveat. The reader will need to keep in mind that, like Lewis, we are fond of nature and respect science, but we do not bow to their godlike ontological and epistemological status in our culture and within the Academy. That we would need to make this statement at the front of this book should signal to the reader that we are going to place into question two of the most powerful lines of thought in the world today: naturalism and scientism. But these two lines of thought by themselves do not gain their authority merely by their (ultimately inconsistent) tenets. Dozens and perhaps hundreds of books have been written to refute naturalism and scientism in the last 20 years yet both are as powerful as ever. Many are not aware that naturalism and scientism must be matched with another line of thought that activates their authority and sustains it over time. That is what this book will bring forth. We are offering a new, integrated theory of social institutions that explains a variety of social phenomena, including how education is theorized and practiced within the imposing background conditions of naturalism and scientism.

Our line of inquiry begins with the following axiom from C.S. Lewis's brilliant analysis in *The Abolition of Man* (2001a): the liberation of Nature's material growth occurs in proper proportion to the confinement of Reason. In the academic literature on institutions this axiom is a new understanding of the ontological and epistemological relations between the expanding domain of Nature (Lewis 2001a: 71), which fosters and is fostered by material (economic) growth, and the corresponding adjustments made to perceptions of Reason (Lewis 2001b: 39–51), a precondition for the social welfare, that is, the overall conditions of social reality.

By material or economic growth we roughly mean the total output of trade and the expansion of market structures. But we mean more than that. Growth is both a model of thought and a specific attribute of social institutions that affects the conditions of human development and flourishing. As a model and as a property, growth facilitates the enlargement of the size of market structures; it acts as a catalyst for universal information that advances an increase in the volume or quantity of production and trade; it brings about the universalization of rules, the standardization of activities, and serves as a hidden persuader of belief-forming practices. It is a rise in the scale of operations that is filtered through and supported by institutional rules, property rights, rights of access and use, customs, certain information sets, and so on. In a technical environment it also means the advance of the physical, the material, the tangible, and the quantitative over and above the nonphysical, the immaterial, the intangible or tacit, and the qualitative. Economic growth is to be contrasted with ideas about the social welfare, which represents that quality and condition of the social order, also mediated by institutions, that forms formal and informal political, social, and cultural arrangements, including rankings of alternative social states. We argue that the rising volume of trade, as envisioned by economic growth and which takes place within the context of institutions, alters information conditions, production probabilities, the set of preferences, the calculus of self-interest and interests for others, and the ideological construction of the social good. It even shapes and conditions the worldviews of participants, tying rationality to a least-cost direction of markets; it shifts the qualitative dimensions of the social welfare which affects human development and flourishing in important ways. Put simply, growth in the technical sense is an eliminative enterprise.

Our main argument pivots on the logic that there is an expanding disunity between Nature and Reason, one where economic growth stands as a proxy for the former and the social welfare a stand-in for the latter. At its core, the axiom represents the dividing of one domain of reality (Nature) from another domain of reality (Reason) and is predicated on the cost of information and knowledge represented by these two domains. The division acts as an agent of efficiency and order that creates thin simplifications to the edifice of human complexity, a move necessary for the technical expansion of social institutions and the State. Simplifications occur across the information base of social reality and are activated by reductions of reality to the material, abstractions made against the entity man, and worldview substitutions that regulate what knowledge and which models of thought receive institutional agenda. Over the long term the division holds weighty implications for education as an institution, not least is whether education itself is sustainable. Indeed, a central misconception about the character of the educational problem of society is due to an erroneous transfer of the habits of thought we have developed in dealing with the phenomena Nature and Reason. This has led to the unfortunate and false belief that education is a purely naturalistic enterprise. Almost the entire American, British, and European systems of education abide this belief through the lens of secularism. Nothing could be further from the truth. There is nothing in education—the institution, its processes, or its participants—that is a pure derivative of Nature or naturalism. Naturalism has no claim whatever on education.

What we must understand at once, even if this understanding is painful to our most cherished views about reality, is that Nature is a created and contingent institution, not a self-originating or self-perpetuating one; that in an expanding system or technical framework Nature displaces in the minds of many the eternal, self-existent entity of Reason—God. Nature is a particular (lower) institution that has been given the status of the (higher) universal. In making this "Nature before Reason" substitution, man elevates the created over the Creator. The motive for the substitution is an old one: power. "[W]hat we call Man's power over Nature turns out to be a power exercised by some men over other men with Nature as its instrument" (Lewis 2001a: 55). It is an ungrounded and illegitimate power. In a sense, Nature, or rather certain human views about Nature, liberates the human from having to take account of a superintendent, objective moral law. Yet, in the book *Miracles*, C.S. Lewis argues that the laws of Nature produce no events, no intelligence, no design, no purpose, no improvement, no ethics, which gives strong indication that it is a contingent order. Arguably, contingent order should know its ontological place in the universe. As he says (2001b: 93–94),

> they state the pattern to which every event—if only it can be induced to happen—must conform, just as the rules of arithmetic state the pattern to

which all transactions with money must conform—if only you can get hold of any money. Thus in one sense the laws of Nature cover the whole field of space and time; in another, what they leave out is precisely the whole real universe—the incessant torrent of actual events which makes up true history. That must come from somewhere else. To think the laws can produce it is like thinking that you can create real money by simply doing sums.

A social order at the sentient level of human beings is composed among other things of institutions. In the modern democracy the institutions a social order includes are, for example, education, law, language, morality, family, markets, government, and many other cultural, political, and economic institutions. In contrast to the manner in which the modern academic is taught to think, each of these institutions is to be considered nonnatural phenomena. There is nothing about Nature itself that could have produced them. Institutions are not contingent to Nature; they are contingent to the predicate Reason. Since the deepest philosophical problems of institutions are known only after recognizing these two basic facts we cannot hope to have a complete picture of the cost of institutions beforehand. We contend that when institutions operate outside of their proper function, when they fall into disequilibrium and become information poor, truncated, and disjointed, a cost is usually generated somewhere within them. This cost might show against a single individual, or perhaps multiple individuals, or even across that institution's span of affairs. What is not apparent to those who deny these two basic facts about social institutions is that when they separate from Reason they are likely working suboptimally and stand in need of some remedial correction. This is particularly true for the institution that we will examine in this book: education.

The axiom—the liberation of Nature's material growth occurs in proper proportion to the confinement of Reason—is also the beginning of an important and new institutional interpretation of C.S. Lewis's (2001a) astonishing *Abolition of Man* argument. *The Abolition of Man* is far more than an education book unique to its time (1940s) and place (United Kingdom). The book's subtitle, *Reflections on Education with Special Reference to the Teaching of English in the Upper Forms of Schools*, only serves as a case study for a much wider project. It is a book of perennial importance because its questions and arguments have to do with first things and touch the core of what it means to be human. It shows that the constitution of reality, the idea of objective truth and morality, the individual – collective problem of social choice, the nature and ordering of social institutions, the foundations and aims of education, the accurate use of language, the role of curriculum and instruction, the profound connections between education, the economy, and the social welfare all hinge on a proper conception of reality, humanity, and its education. By demonstrating the costs rising in the social sector, especially to humanity's sense of freedom, Lewis's book at its core is an argument for near-optimal conditions for human development and liberty.

In *The Abolition of Man*, Lewis delivers a brief, persuasively argued critique of the modern way that values are understood and are taught. Society expects children and adults (which children later become) to be guided by values, such as honesty, courage, justice, and compassion, as if these have objective validity. On the other hand, society signals in various ways that values are subjective, a matter of feeling and acculturation, a matter of instinct, solely a matter of a humanly constructed order over many generations of human thought. This pattern of moral education, Lewis believes, is not sustainable in one important sense and he foresees dire consequences if it breaks down. Education outside of the Tao (Lewis's term for universal moral law, including the historical Tao) will cease to be moral and cease to be education, as those terms are understood in their orthodox meanings. But the moral education of children is not the deepest part of the book. There are several levels on which the *Abolition* can be read. And aside from Michael Aeschliman's (1998) excellent work *The Restitution of Man*, ours is the first book to unlock the deepest levels of Lewis's argument.

Lewis first gave as three talks what would become the *Abolition* book in 1943. Lewis was invited to give the Riddell Memorial lectures at the University of Durham on February 24–26, 1943. The talks were to address "a subject concerning the relation between religion and contemporary development of thought."[1] By this time, Lewis had already given as radio broadcast talks (1942) what would become the book *Mere Christianity*, having also written the essay "On Ethics" (ca. 1942), which covered similar ground. Further, as Lewis-biographer Walter Hooper mentions, Lewis gave an address to Oxford University's Socratic Club on February 8, 1943, some 2 weeks before he would offer the *Abolition* argument at the University of Durham. The address at the Socratic Club was recorded in the *Socratic Digest* (No. 1, p. 23) and is cited here in full from Hooper's *C.S. Lewis: Companion and Guide* (1996: 330–331).

Mr. Lewis first demonstrated the existence of a massive and immemorial moral law by listing precepts from Greek, Roman, Chinese, Babylonian, ancient Egyptian and Old Norse sources. By this account of the immutable laws of general and special beneficence, duties to parents and to children, of justice and good faith and of the law of mercy, three illusions were dispelled: first, that the expression "Christian moral principles" means anything different from "moral principles"; secondly, the anthropological illusion that the crude and barbarous man is the natural and normal man; and, thirdly, that the great disease of humanity is ignorance and the great cure, education. On the contrary, it is only too obvious that while there is massive and immemorial agreement about moral law, there is also a massive and immemorial inability to obey it.

In considering the remedy for the cleavage between human nature and generally accepted moral law, Mr. Lewis first separated from normal humanity those faddists, whether Epicureans, Communists, or H.G. Wells, whose indefensible naivety forbade them to understand the actual condition of Man. The remainder of humanity would be divided into the ordinary mass of pagan mankind and Christians. Both these classes of men know the moral law and recognize their own inability to keep it. Both endeavour to deal with this tragic situation. The pagan mysteries and Christianity are two alternative solutions, and whatever falls outside these two is simply naïve. Now the *differentia* of Christianity, as against pagan mystery religions, lies in its survival, its historical core, its combination of the ethical and the sacramental, its ability to produce that "new man" which all rites of initiation premise, and finally its restraining effect upon a community under its domination.

To datum is the complete cleavage between human behaviour and the code of morals which humanity acknowledges. And Christianity is the cure for this particular disease. For "excellent instructions" we have always had; the problem is how to obey them. To ask whether the rest of the Christian Faith matters when we have Christ's ethics presupposes a world of unfallen men with no need of redemption. "The rest of the Christian Faith" is the means of carrying out, instead of merely being able to discourse on the ethics we already know.

Years after seeing the lectures into book form, Lewis expresses some well-earned pride in his work, writing to Mary Willis Shelburne on February 20, 1955: "[...] I'm so pleased about the *Abolition of Man*, for it is almost my favourite among my books but in general has been almost totally ignored by the public."[2] As it turned out, Lewis was prescient in his original *Abolition* argument. Perhaps because it was so well written, so fundamentally deep in its argument, it was not fully appreciated by the public during his lifetime. Yet there were readers who admired the book. Some years later, in 1959, Lewis replied to a letter from Dan Tucker, who had called Lewis a "good prophet" in constructing the *Abolition* argument:

The devil about trying to write satire now-a-days is that reality constantly outstrips you. Ought we to be surprised at the approach of "scientocracy"? In every age those who wish to be our masters, if they have any sense, secure our obedience by offering deliverance from our dominant fear. When we fear wizards the Medicine Man can rule the whole tribe. When we fear a stronger tribe our warrior becomes King. When all the world fears Hell the Church becomes a theocracy. "Give up your freedom and I will make you safe" is, age after age, the terrible offer. In England [in 1959] the omnipotent Welfare State has triumphed because it promised to free us from the fear of poverty. Mind you, the bargain is sometimes, for a while, kept. A warrior king may really save a tribe from extinction: the Welfare State, at a cost, has come nearer than any society ever did before to giving every man a square meal and a good house to eat it in. The fears from which scientocracy offers to free us are rational ones.... But we cannot trust the New Masters any more than their predecessors. Do you see any solutions?... I am you see, at my wit's end on such matters. Only a power higher than man's can really find a way out.[3]

Lewis is correct: "only a power higher than man's can really find a way out." While Lewis may have had moments of prescience into the future, delivering warnings to present and future participants of democracies (e.g., in the *Abolition, That Hideous Strength*), generally he saw himself as a man of the past. In a 1963 interview, Lewis was asked, "What do you think is going to happen in the next few years of history, Mr. Lewis?" Lewis replied, "I have no way of knowing. My primary field is the past. I travel with my back to the engine, and that makes it difficult when you try to steer. The world might stop in ten minutes; meanwhile, we are to go on doing our duty. The great thing is to be found at one's post as a child of God, living each day as though it were our last, but planning as though our world might last a hundred years" (1970: 266).

We focus in our book on the broader and deeper philosophical and economic issues raised by the *Abolition* text and the Lewis literature at-large, including his work *Miracles, That Hideous Strength,* and *The Weight of Glory*. Lewis foresaw certain implications in the widespread adoption of naturalistic ethics (so-called), but even more importantly he identified several causes of institutional growth as linked to the economic principles of scientific naturalism, on the philosophical spirit of developmentalism and its effects on a pattern of information trade-offs. Lewis repeatedly argued that naturalism, scientism and cosmic developmentalism could not be rationally defensible positions precisely because it rules out certain conditions of reality, certain categories of information and knowledge, such as the moral law and teleology, and does so while misunderstanding or miscalculating what it means to be fully human. We will call this confusion the fallacy of ontological awareness. Many writers have pointed out that there is a self-refuting quality to the naturalistic framework, not least is that to arrive at naturalism one is forced to deny all sorts of complex human qualities and properties, as for example, libertarian agency (Goetz 2000), the mind (Taliaferro 2000), the ontological status of properties (Moreland 2000), values (Hare 2000), and purpose (Craig 2000).[4] Yet the naturalistic framework, supported widely by economic and political growth, continues to role along in spite of its logical inconsistencies. We want the reader to know how and why this is the case, including the effects on systems of education.

We are examining a wide variety of issues raised by the *Abolition* book through the lens of philosophical economics. We use an institutional analysis, which simply means our method examines the logic of education as a social institution. Douglass North (1990: 3) has said institutions are "the humanly devised constraints that shape human interaction." But they are not merely humanly devised, and some institutions (e.g., Nature, the moral law) are not at all humanly devised. Indeed, we regard institutions as integral features of the productive base of the economy; they form the capital assets of society and function to guide the allocation of scarce resources; they are ontological entities within which organizations exist and function and individual's work, play, and live. As Samuel Bowles (2003: 48) phrased it, "Institutions influence who meets whom, to do what tasks, with what possible courses of action, and with what consequences of actions jointly taken." For purposes of this book, we distinguish the term institution from the term organization. North's comment to Geoffrey Hodgson delineates this distinction: "[O]rganizations...are special institutions...but for my purposes organizations are to be separated out from institutions" (Hodgson 2006: 19). So it is with our argument: we are distinguishing between organizations and institutions.

Our philosophical lens focuses the background theories, institutional frameworks, information conditions, knowledge structures, and models of thought that set the conditions of production and exchange in education. Because all social institutions are nonnatural phenomena, we must not reduce our method to a framework of inquiry that is broadly committed to naturalistic principles. This would be to commit a fallacy of category. The logic and structure of our thinking should adhere to long-known truths and first principles: the truths and things by which any knowledge is possible. And in order to understand the direction of education in the twenty-first century—and comprehend the deepest arguments of Lewis in the *Abolition*—an awareness of how institutions create and sustain social, cultural, economic, and political facts that constrain or enable forms of human activity is required, especially as prices attaching to models of thought, belief-forming practices, and the practical affairs of education as an institution.

Using theoretical and applied ontology, our methodological emphasis is on critical realism and truth as correspondence (Chisholm 1996; Alston 1997). Critical realism is the general idea that there exists a mind-independent reality and that knowledge refers to things as they really are, while leaving space for corrections to those understandings over time (David 2002). Likewise, a realist account of truth claims is that beliefs, statements, and views are about—and should be weighed against—real reality, not reality as we might prefer it to be. The philosophic category of ontology allows us to open or reopen a set of important but long-ignored (at least in education and in economics) first questions.[5] Questions concerning the nature of man, his reality, and his development, from which the aims of education are derived, take logical priority over the manner of acquiring and grounding knowledge, what curriculum to have, as well as methods for imparting it.[6] These important but secondary matters must follow the ontological questions.

Thus a social institution's underlying ontic commitments and its epistemological structure is always of utmost importance to its performance. And the institution's influence on human reality is indigenous both to the information environment of theory (e.g., how the architecture of reality is viewed and explored), and to practice (e.g., how education is conducted and lived). The institution itself is a locus of worldviews and models of thought. As such it acts as a hidden persuader by exerting downward and outward causal forces that can affect a participant's set of dispositions, choices, and agency (Hodgson 2003). Through its information economy it affects the social environment of belief and action (MacIntyre 1999). Through its incentive structure and pricing system the institution locates a pathway for all rational participants (Olson 1971).

On very general terms, in order to know how or know in what direction to order and structure the institution of education, from what information base to operate, what range of curriculum to impart, what production conditions to emphasize, what decisions to make, what plans to set, what degree of spontaneous order to preserve, and so on, one would need to know what exists, what man is, who he is, know his final ends or purposes, have a conception of the ideal direction and proper function of his becoming and developing, know how institutions impact his existence and agency, and have a general idea about the kinds of knowledge and social structures necessary for sustaining his development, flourishing, and freedom. Simply put, while social institutions are ultimately contingent to Reason they function on a human substratum. Whatever the human being is, the social institution must give due consideration to him and her and structure its operations to optimize the human condition. The optimization process is a direct consequence of the overarching model of thought prevailing within the institution, which, we argue, should be informed by Reason.

Models of thought

This book examines the dominant model of reality under which education—its production and consumption—today operates. We begin by noting that the model of reality underwriting the education process is a principal determinant of the nature and realization of the education good: the development and flourishing of the individual human being; her knowledge, skills, experiences, talents, gifts, intelligences, virtues, understandings, and wisdom. Models of reality, like worldviews, get "everything in without a clash.... We see how everything links up with everything else" in human thought and action (Lewis 2007: 11–12). Models tend to develop from a desire to understand human thought and action, the attempt to find a solution to the fundamental problems of the individual and social welfare, to solve the perplexities of human existence and all social evils, to understand the world and man's place in it—how to live, what to be (Berlin 1999). Models are intentional human constructions or frameworks built to make sense of and even resolve tensions arising from a shared fear of survival, personal or institutional risk, and the individual – collective social situation, including the problem of social choice (Arrow 1950, 1963, 1974).

The problem of social choice is the idea that there are liberty tensions arising from claims, dispositions, actions, and goods pursued by individuals and those allowable by collectives; that from any given social environment emerges the complex challenge of aggregating dissimilar individual preferences. The social choice problem seeks to reconcile individual convictions and preferences largely by signaling a rational direction across the social sphere. Reconciliation between disparate factions is predicated on the costs of human exchange. Social institutions mediate the content of the signal, the signal of the rational path, in the form of rules and other information. Contract theories of society and the State, help to resolve the inherent cultural tensions between competing factions and interests, individuals or small groups pursuing their own ends and the diverse means to achieve them, as well as a society's ordering of scarce resources and collective goods. The contract stipulates certain rights and obligations recognized throughout society and culture. Stipulations are either formal (e.g., constitutions, statutes) or informal (e.g., custom, tradition, ceremony), but they are nearly always institutional.

So, for example, how to form a viable education system in a society entails a series of questions and procedures concerning the means and ends of production and, ultimately, on who decides, on what principles and criteria ground those decisions, as well as the nature of the trade-offs made under conditions of scale and scarcity. As Kenneth Arrow (1963: 103) says, "the true grounds for disagreement [in social choice] are the conditions which it is reasonable to impose on the aggregation procedure." For example, the imposition principle can be achieved coercively, as through Arrow's dictator (1963) or C.S. Lewis's conditioners (2001a), where one individual or a small group of individuals (e.g., an oligopoly or oligarchy) decides for the rest, thus constraining forms of individual freedom in radical ways. Yet social choice may also be achieved with minimal levels of coercion, as through the precarious informational environment of expanding institutions (we will talk more about this shortly).

Antecedent to *how* the social choice set is constituted, and long before the practice of education occurs, are the theories and philosophies of life and models of thought and how these background theories, philosophies, and models account for reality, existence, relations, knowledge, values, purposes, actions, and the nature and purpose of social institutions, divine or human.[7] The most controversial questions in economic, political, and educational philosophy have to do with what parts of reality receive agenda, what information and knowledge to exclude from the calculus of social choice and social contract. For example, John Rawls (1971) did this for a certain conception of social contract with a hypothetical mechanism called the "veil of ignorance," under which people may reflect on and develop their respective choices relative to the indeterminacy of life's lottery in the allocation of resources and opportunities. Models of thought (or worldviews) move this process along. The basic decision for the theorist and her students is whether the model should move in the direction of information conservation (a closed model) or information liberation (an open model). But it is also a question of great care and some humility in the application of models to individual cases. Hayek makes an observation of fundamental importance to our study. From his essay "The Theory of Complex Phenomena," Hayek (1967: 34) writes:

One of the chief results so far achieved by theoretical work in these fields seems to me to be the demonstration that here individual events regularly depend on so many concrete circumstances that we shall never in fact be in a position to ascertain them all; and that in consequence not only the ideal of prediction and control must largely remain beyond our reach, but also the hope remain illusory that we can discover by observation regular connections between individual events.

Hayek goes on to argue that theoretical models cannot make precise predictions of concrete instances of complex phenomena. "Economic theory is confined to describing kinds of patterns which will appear if certain general conditions are satisfied, but can rarely if ever derive from this knowledge any predictions of specific phenomena" (p. 35). Traditional approaches to economics tend to use static, mathematics-driven models that try to make such predictions (Beinhocker 2007). These models of thought trim the information base to analysis by substituting for complex, dynamic, and adaptive phenomena (an open system) a noncomplex and nonanomalous environment (a closed system). They tend to depend upon naturalistic assumptions of human reality that bear little affinity to complex reality. This is, of course, the classic mistake of a method (an epistemology) driving a reality (an ontology). Educationists often make this same error. How one knows and how one justifies knowing is important, but is secondary to what one knows directly if critically about reality.

Understanding models of thought was important to C.S. Lewis, as it should be to all institutional participants with stewardship responsibilities (this means all of us). This is so chiefly because a model helps to structure beliefs, ideas, social relations, and attempts to smooth out the tensions and transitions between the means and ends of life. "Every Model is a construct of answered questions. The expert is engaged either in raising new questions or in giving new answers to old ones. When he is doing the first, the old, agreed Model is of no interest to him; when he is doing the second, he is beginning an operation which will finally destroy the old Model altogether" (Lewis 2007: 18).[8] Along with Lewis, fellow Oxonian Isaiah Berlin (1996: 7)[9] notes the significance of models on the concepts and categories of human life:

The great system-builders have in their works both expressed and influenced human attitudes towards the world—the light in which events are seen. Metaphysical, religious, scientific systems and attitudes have altered the distribution of emphasis, the sense of what is important or significant or admirable, or again of what is remote or barbarous or trivial—have profoundly affected human concepts and categories, the eyes with which men see or feel and understand the world, the spectacles through which they look.

Fear, risk, and models

Models of thought help humanity cope with exogenous and endogenous fear. What we do not ordinarily bear in mind is that fear can be expensive. Fear is a cost borne by an individual or society of individuals when he or they are uncertain about an event or state of affairs. Let us take a contemporary example. On the idea of global climate change, Kenneth Arrow (2007: 1) posits that while futurity and uncertainty require formal discounting in an economic cost–benefit model, he goes on to write, "we are much better off to act to reduce CO_2 emissions substantially than to suffer the consequences of failing to meet this challenge."[10] North (1990: 126) writes that uncertainty in an economic sense is "a condition wherein one cannot ascertain the probability of an event and therefore cannot arrive at a way of insuring against such an occurrence." This is driven as much by a search for security as by the attenuation of fear.

Fear can stimulate as much as it can inhibit; it can enhance the human experience by fashioning a correct or sound subject – object relation as between man and himself, man and man, man and the institution, man and Nature, or God and man. Fear can also threaten these relations, or create other ones in human experience, as under Arrow's dictator, or human imagination, as for example with Lewis's demons Wormwood and Screwtape. At its fundamental intensity fear manifests at the cosmological level—upon realization of one's ontological contingency to all manner of material and immaterial forces and entities, known or unknown, in the universe. Resolution to that form of fear has garnered the attention of model builders for centuries, from Plato to Nietzsche, from Augustine to Marx. Indeed, the search for security has been a powerful stimulus for many fields, including economics, philosophy, and education. Berlin (1999:77) again notes that,

> Plainly one of the most powerful of philosophical stimuli is the search for security—the infallible knowledge of incorrigible propositions... no matter how dry, dull, uninformative such propositions may turn out to be, or how difficult to formulate, all our [philosophical] efforts and austerities will be most richly rewarded if we really secure unassailable certainty at last, reach islands, which may be small and arid and isolated, so long as they constitute dry land in an uncertain and uncharted sea.

The quest for certainty has driven the development of technical solutions and methods across a range of institutions in order to umpire risk, place bets, and work out bargaining solutions to the problems of information and competition for scarce resources. Mathematical models are a particularly good example because like law, which is itself a measure and rule of human conduct, mathematics as an institution provides a technology of distance, a legible, rule-bound structure for quantifying social reality. By displacing the local and particular, statistics minimizes the need for intimate knowledge and trust (Porter 1995: ix). Knowledge and trust shift to the impersonal, to the detached, and to the statistical norm. In short, knowledge and confidence shift to the technical institution whose legions of experts work to tame chance (Hacking 1990).

The fields of psychiatry and psychology are another example of taming variation. As a revolutionary movement, "psychology provided an independent, scientific legitimation of the Progressive agenda and a set of categories and measurements for efficiently ordering children and assessing school systems" (Tomas, Peck, and DeHaan 2003: 356). For example, the Diagnostic and Statistical Manual (DSM-IV) categorize and define for clinicians and mental health experts the range of "normal" behavior and mental states by defining disorders and the abnormal. These are created categories that signal irrationality outside of a mean. Consider the philosophical assumptions of this statement from the manual (1994: xxvii):

The specified diagnostic criteria for each mental disorder are offered as guidelines for making diagnoses, because it has been demonstrated that the use of such criteria enhances agreement among clinicians and investigators. The proper use of these criteria requires specialized clinical training that provides both a body of knowledge and clinical skills.

These diagnostic criteria and the DSM-IV Classification of mental disorders reflect a consensus of current formulations of evolving knowledge in our field. They do not encompass, however, all the conditions for which people may be treated or that may be appropriate topics for research efforts.

The purpose of DSM-IV is to provide clear descriptions of diagnostic categories in order to enable clinicians and investigators to diagnose, communicate about, study, and treat people with various mental disorders.

The DSM-IV defines the rationality and irrationality, normality and abnormality of mental heath on the basis of *consensus* about categories and statistical aggregates. But think for a moment about a liberty-loving teenager in a school, one who is not an anarchist or a crude libertine but whose commitments and actions operate in dispersion from the mean. This is a teenager who does not always walk with the crowd. The teenager is less compliant than other students, has a difficult personality, and is identified with (2), (3), (6), and (7) below. Consequently, he receives an official label by a school psychologist: Oppositional Defiant Disorder (ODD; DSM-IV 1994: 91). This label can follow him throughout his school years. He is considered abnormal, his views about freedom lie outside of mainstream thought (the mean). However, let us stipulate that in reality he is expressing early resistance to the violence of aggregation set forth in the hyper-standardization of the compulsory education system (though as a teenager he cannot quite articulate it in this way). He is less compliant within the institutional setting for reasons that have to do with his value system and the emphasis he places on liberty, autonomy, and personal responsibility. He is a difficult person because he merely wishes to protect the individual human prerogative to oppose the crowd when, say, it is hostile to reason.

Diagnostic criteria for 313.81 Oppositional Defiant Disorder
A. A pattern of negativistic, hostile, and defiant behavior lasting at least six months, during which four (or more) of the following are present:

(1) often loses temper
(2) often argues with adults
(3) often actively defies or refuses to comply with adults' requests or rules
(4) often deliberately annoys people
(5) often blames others for his or her mistakes or misbehavior
(6) is often touchy or easily annoyed by others
(7) is often angry and resentful
(8) is often spiteful or vindictive

Note: Consider a criterion met only if the behavior occurs more frequently than is typically observed in individuals of comparable age and developmental level.

On one reading of Lewis's accounts of attending school, his autobiography and letters to his father during the time he was in school, one might conclude that a young Lewis might well have been diagnosed with ODD, had the category then existed, simply by disagreeing with sadistic adults, refusing to comply with certain rules, exhibiting annoyance with school bullies, and harboring some resentment for the way authorities proceeded with education at his school. Indeed, most of the biblical prophets would certainly today be diagnosed with ODD; they operate outside of the Gaussian curve. We can imagine John the Baptist in this predicament. We suspect British psychologists would have used the label against the new Americans, or perhaps Nazi psychiatrists would have employed the label against Polish Jews at Warsaw.

What is important to recognize is that the distinctly *human* power to determine normalcy and define abnormalities is an effort to define rationality, which is an effort to reduce societal risks by creating conditions for assent and raising costs against dissent. Buried within such categories is a method of control. While societal control over human pathologies is not in itself a bad or a harm, the chief problem is that the definitions of normalcy and abnormality and others like them do not tend to originate from an observer-independent source like the moral law; definitions do not link to concepts like proper function because they do not hold, generally speaking, to an objective human teleology. Yes, the moral law is subject to human interpretation but not in an absolute sense. As C.S. Lewis (2001a: 1–26) says, the interpretation of our emotions and moral sentiments is accurate to the degree it conforms or fails to conform with reason. Modern positions of psychology or psychiatry do not ask questions about what man was intended to be in light of Reason. Rather, definitions come about by creating cost-lowering, stability-seeking categories like ODD as a way to restrain defiance against a social order. The label is so malleable as to apply to anyone or any people seeking to preserve a cost-elevating modicum of freedom. It is a way to lessen the risk of activating certain parts of human nature that might threaten the social order, hence might threaten human (collective) progress.

Consider too the various attempts to find a mathematical way to conquer risk. A fundamental principle of competitive markets is that a trade-off exists between risk and reward. As a general rule, the greater the risk one is willing to take, the greater the potential return on one's investment. Conversely, the lower the investment risk, the lower the return. The quest to master risk in markets has loomed as an insurmountable obstacle. The discovery and use of sophisticated mathematical formulas in the late 1990s, e.g., the Black–Scholes hedging strategy, was thought to have given financial institutions the ability to protect against market turbulence by putting a price on uncertainty. The main service of these mathematical models consists in having imposed an order of certainty on what before had been outright uncertainty. The uncertainties of a market crash, or even the next hurricane, tornado, and earthquake, can be priced and divided into marketable pieces and sold to someone who is willing to bear that risk in exchange for a future stream of payments. Thus risk implies the pursuit of an actuarial determination of the likelihood of an event in order to insure against its outcome. It is the ability to put a price on uncertainty, which is the essence of financial engineering. The management of mortality in the insurance industry is another example of technical solutions and statistical methods created to control variation (unknowns).[11] The use of such models to value and hedge securities, to calculate "acts of God," or even place bets against death is an exercise in estimation; it sets in motion an initially self-reinforcing but eventually self-defeating process. It is a self-defeating process because, as the Merton–Black–Scholes "trillion-dollar-bet" of the late 1990s demonstrated, the unpredictable exercise of human agency is not mathematically determinate. Though persuaded, prodded, and beguiled, the human will remains free in diminishing degrees as human agency constricts relative to the proportions and price factors of the expanding domain of Nature.

In education, the uncertainty of exchange among participants generated by the growing disunity between educational attainment and the acquisition of knowledge and skills represents institutional risk that is resolved by a turnover in the rules of production (centralization and standardization). This process socializes risk. The general, institutional method for reducing uncertainty about the value of the education credential (diploma) is to obligate consumers to purchase more schooling, thereby adding scarcity value to the credential. By graduating to higher levels within the education pyramid individuals attain relative separation from the masses. The primary way students reduce uncertainty of the value of their property right is by adding scarcity value to it. This is where the power of the institution comes in as an efficiency instrument. Institutional arrangements to a large extent determine what is produced and how it is produced. The institutional structure of education secures agreement on matters of final knowledge through a prescribed allocative process that removes the possibility of alternatives that endanger the stability of the system (lowering risk). Since the stability of things depends (in part) on scale, there is a compelling basis for the belief that the desire to stabilize education, that is, to narrow the scope and range of human activity to manageable proportions, to central control, has in reality become an obstacle to human progress and flourishing. While risk and uncertainty are lowered, the institution of education becomes a source of deprivation of certain opportunities. The preservation of individual options gives way to the impositions of preferred options of the formal hierarchy and rule set. The diversity of individual preferences is traded off to the preferences of educational priorities. In other words, to provide stable forms of education in certain institutional arrangements is not necessarily to expand liberty. The efficiency movement of education (1900–1930) is a prominent example, where myriad business schemes were foisted on the schools including the principles and mechanisms of scientific management (Callahan 1962; Tyack 1974). The reason was to bring legibility and certainty to a complex set of processes for control over the chaotic situation (uncertainty).

On the cosmological level, uncertainty has caused an inward turn, with many economically developed Western societies and their institutions formally or informally placing bets against God's existence in the form of secularism. These wagers have fundamentally influenced the position of the individual relative to his fellows and social institutions, e.g., education, science, and the State. Evidence of this is the deterministic framework and methods of scientism so prevalently used across social institutions, and which presuppose a particular kind of naturalistic human destiny. It is the anthropocentric turn described by philosopher Charles Taylor (2007: 301) in these terms:

> Living in a disenchanted world, the buffered self is no longer open, vulnerable to a world of spirits and forces which cross the boundary of the mind, indeed, negate the very idea of there being a secure boundary. The fears, anxieties, even terrors that belong to the porous self are behind it. This sense of self-possession, of a secure inner mental realm, is all the stronger, if in addition to disenchanting the world, we have also taken the anthropocentric turn, and no longer even draw on the power of God. Power, reason, invulnerability, a decisive distancing from age-old fears, of which we still have some sense, not only from history, and not only from the yet unenlightened masses, but also because they resonated somehow in our own childhood; all this belongs to the sense of self of those who have made the anthropocentric turn. And there are strong satisfactions which attend this.

In the history of models the cost of cosmological fear has attenuated in two principal ways. First is the original position relative to the necessary being, God, his transcendent nature and attributes. These are the first questions, principles, laws, virtues, and obligations emanating from the divine in order to understand ultimate things and one's place in the universe. The turn toward God occurs when the contingency of being, relating, thinking, feeling, and acting is realized and centered within the composite nature of the necessary being, an uncaused eternally existing being.

A second way to resolve cosmic fear is a turn toward man and his stochastic creative capacities, often motivated by the denial of fear or its concealment. Denial involves merely ignoring questions related to transcendental contingency; basically, these questions do not reach agenda. They are blocked from the list of items through formal and informal institutional processes (abstractions, reductions, and substitutions) and divisions (the division of information, the division of rationality from reason). The material, non-transcendent realm is all there is; physical death is the end of life; the pursuit of happiness is the pursuit of rational, material self- or collective interests; and so forth. Denial places a cost against human teleology. It precludes whole sectors of knowledge, including questions about the nature and purpose of man: man in proper function, man as he was intended to be in the cosmos.

Yet it is the concealment of fear—and the social welfare costs buried within that concealment—which is perhaps the most powerful way that individuals and societies in modernity cope with cosmological fear. Prospects for material success, including the scientific management of the environment, education, politics, economics, food production, health care, and even the manufacturing of the new man (e.g., eugenics, cloning, embryonic stem cell research, and organ farming), repress and veil material, social, and spiritual risk. We might call this widely applied movement an updated version of Taylorism (Taylor 1911), even as applied to the spiritual domain, "transporting into our spiritual life that same collectivism which has already conquered our secular life" (Lewis 2001c: 160). In this regard, "cosmic developmentalism" is at the same time both a legitimating force for social "progress" and a force wielded for delegitimating God. Lewis (1986: 63, 64) notes several of its progressive characteristics.

What I call Developmentalism is the extension of the evolutionary idea far beyond the biological realm; in fact, its adoption as the key principle of reality. To the modern man it seems simply natural that an ordered cosmos should emerge from chaos, that life should come out of the inanimate, reason out of instinct, civilization out of savagery, virtue out of animalism. This idea is supported in his mind by a number of false analogies: the oak coming from the acorn, the man from the spermatozoon, the modern steamship from the primitive coracle. The supplementary truth that every acorn was dropped by an oak, every spermatozoon derived from a man, and the first boat by something so much more complex than itself as a man of genius, is simply ignored. The modern mind accepts as a formula for the universe in general the principle "Almost nothing may be expected to turn into almost everything" without noticing that the parts of the universe under our direct observation tell a quite different story. This Developmentalism, in the field of human history, becomes Historicism: the belief that the scanty and haphazard selection of facts we know about History contains an almost mystical revelation of reality... [where] the very standard of good is itself in a state of flux.

The concealment of God is thought to open all human options to chance, and chance must be controlled because it creates fear and uncertainty; it must not be allowed to jeopardize visions of common progress and collective conceptions of moving forward. On the one hand, the expanding domain of Nature, accompanied by naturalism and scientism, increases personal insecurity and societal uncertainty. For it was during the shift in models of thought at the Enlightenment, the sources of safety, rights, and obligations became dislodged from absolute values originating in God and repackaged in secular form. Fear and the minimization of risk created a natural appetite for unity; a new basis for binding the social situation into a contract; and a spirit of developmentalism—progress from lower to higher, from worse to better—was the result. "With such people I argue, for I do not share their basic assumption. Believers in progress rightly note that in the world of machines the new model supercedes the old. From this they falsely infer a similar kind of supercession in such things as virtue and wisdom" (Lewis 2001c: 82). Unity once bound up in the intellectual tradition of reasoning and spiritual noumena, such as values, was split and then *transposed* to a new unity bound in natural phenomena, its reference system and categories, and its method of rational inference. This is Lewis's (2001c: 91–115) "transposition" argument used backward. Lewis's original argument is roughly this: the spiritual or divine realm "transposed" onto and into the natural realm; the higher informs the lower, the richer adds to the poorer, the sufficient gives to the insufficient, the noncontingent to the contingent. It is the foreword of more knowledge and final causes into the sphere of less knowledge and efficient causes. "Transposition occurs whenever the higher reproduces itself in the lower" (p. 103). Developmentalism reverses this relation, where the lower reduces the higher, ultimately denying the existence of anything "higher" or "richer" than Nature itself. The idea is that things everywhere are getting better; that change means development and improvement; that Darwinian mechanisms are thought to be sufficient accounts for human values, the character of social institutions, and any knowledge whatever (Rosenberg 2000).[12]

Yet it is the loss of information that increases the opportunity for a formal substitution, a grand unifier, a Great Myth of progress established through the growth instrument and the institution Nature. This is so because progress fundamentally depends upon the notion of growth (moving forward implies endowed capacity and bigger structures), and growth ushers in an integrated social reality, increasing the saliency of the State and multistate federations (e.g., the United Nations Education, Science, and Culture Organization, International Monetary Fund, World Bank). The secular State and political, economic, and cultural institutions gain legitimacy by socializing risk and portraying the naturalistic turn as both costless and redeeming progress. The quantification of social reality—the sharp rise of social science and statistical assumptions, and particularly their use by the State for surveillance—nudges this process along by transforming chance into regulative magnitudes. The technical apparatuses of the State usher quantification into public policy—capturing knowledge through numbers; creating, systematizing, and reinforcing artificial social categories; employing technique to measure social entities—all for the purpose of developing an appearance or feeling of certainty in the face of risk. Lewis (2001a: 60) was outspoken on the combustibility of this arrangement: "the manmoulders of the new age will be armed with the powers of an omnicompetent state and an irresistible scientific technique: we shall get at last a race of conditioners who really can cut out all posterity in what shape they please."

Crosby (1997) correctly suggests that the technical model of quantification has been with us since before the thirteenth century, though it became much more effective as advances in technology increased capacity for market surveillance. By reducing the nature of the subject and object relation to the minimum level of knowledge required by its essential definition, both subject and object may be calculated, manipulated, experimented on, torn from proper unity and transposed into artificial entities. It is the ability to make a new man by altering categories and typologies. Hacking (1990: 3) comments on the making of people: "Categories had to be invented into which people could conveniently fall in order to be counted. The systematic collection of data about people has affected not only the ways in which we describe our neighbour. It has profoundly transformed what we choose to do, who we try to be, and what we think of ourselves."

What is important to recognize is that statistical category, mathematics, positive law, and the actuarial processes of probability are inflated features of the interlocking domain of Nature, Nature as a technical institution, which seek to resolve chance in the impersonal universe. By themselves these technical methods are neutral as procedures for acquiring knowledge; they are but one source of information. When inflated, as by a technical model, these procedures form a new determinism created by social construction. Growth in the technical model becomes an active and resolute propagandist. The technical model itself becomes self-determining in closed parameters, not open to higher transposition, one where means drive ends, where values are expurgated from facts, where costs are thought to tend toward zero (Ellul 1964).[13] Fear is resolved by looking at security a different way: *crede quod habes, et habes* (believe that you have it, and you do).

In spite of the obvious power of technical models of thought, the moral law does not disappear. It continues to set nontrivial ethical demands on institutional participants and social institutions. The stress in our book is on the active negotiation of error in social structures (see the complementary work of MacIntyre 1999), which requires a strong, not a weak will; it requires rationality and reason working in unison. In other words, it requires the proper function of mature human beings. The moral law makes these assertions by demanding that social institutions stand in right relation to the individual, and individuals to institutions. This is the principle of ontological correspondence. On this basis, when error or distortion becomes intolerable—that is, too much injustice to ignore, too much of what we take for granted about the past and present is being ignored or destroyed—models are often rejected as being too unfaithful to the reality of human life (Berlin 1969). For example, an economic or social construct often idealizes an insufficient form of man, one that technical models use to enlarge the range of prediction and the control of risk. It does this by reducing the nature and scope of man, narrowing categories over the information base available to social choice. In fact, the fundamental goal of neoclassical economic science is to narrow, not enlarge the composite nature of man (Caldwell 1982). This is what makes it a dismal science. The information base constricts conceptions of agency in order to mathematically calculate probability distributions. This information embargo is thought necessary for generating conditions of predictability so essential for (secular) progress and the allocation of scarce resources. Milton Friedman (1966: 4, 7) offers a classical account:

Positive economics is in principle independent of any particular ethical position or normative judgments. As Keynes says, it deals with "what is," not with "what ought to be." Its task is to provide a system of generalizations that can be used to make correct predictions about the consequences of any change in circumstances. Its performance is to be judged by the precision, scope, and conformity with experience of the predictions it yields. In short, positive economics is, or can be, an "objective" science, in precisely the same sense as any of the physical sciences. Of course, the fact that economics deals with the interrelations of human beings, and that the investigator is himself part of the subject matter being investigated in a more intimate sense than in the physical sciences, raises special difficulties in achieving objectivity at the same time that it provides the social scientist with a class of data not available to the physical scientist. But neither the one nor the other is, in my view, a fundamental distinction between the two groups of sciences.... The ultimate goal of a positive science is the development of a "theory" or, "hypothesis" that yields valid and meaningful (i.e., not truistic) predictions about phenomena not yet observed. Such a theory is, in general, a complex intermixture of two elements. In part, it is a "language" designed to promote "systematic and organized methods of reasoning." In part, it is a body of substantive hypotheses designed to abstract essential features of complex reality.

There is an important truth on the other end. Methodological abstraction can eliminate too much information, too much of reality, too much identity, too many variables, too much that is vital to the human experience. This can lead to an incompatibility within the social institution between the production function and the nature of the good itself. Means conflict with the ends of production such that ends, not means, must yield. The fallacy of abstraction involves a category error when locating a complex being and complex goods (e.g., human education) into a single, legible scale, represented by a less complex reality. Much of the State's apparatus, and social science itself, depends upon the a priori abstraction. Abstraction is selected in order to reconcile the complexities of human nature, decision making, and values to the new social order. For example, the function of Hayek's (1940: 125–149) infamous "quantity adjuster" is to conduct this preproduction reconciliation work: to simplify reality by feeding abstractions into the "equation-machine" resulting in a quantification of reality and better control over where to cast our lots. In other words, social or economic progress occurs relative to the price system of information. The abstraction is a methodological device that lowers the cost of information on an inherently cost-generating entity: the individual human being with libertarian agency. Over time, we see persons differently, seeing them in a new but inferior way.

The principle of substitution

Processes of abstraction do a great deal of philosophical work for naturalistic models of thought. Information loss from abstraction augments reduction and substitution. Information abstracted from human reality endorses a reduction of human beings to the statistical mean, to arbitrary norms of thought and behavior. Free will, for example, becomes controllable variation. The solution to the control of variation lies in the creation of a space of abstraction or probability space. Abstraction, reduction, and substitution do not occur in a tight, predictive sequence. In some cases they occur simultaneously.

In other cases, a large event is enough to set off a worldview substitution, which is followed by abstractions and reductions. In other cases, the progressive and incremental use of abstractions and reductions lead to a shift (a substitution) over time. There is no set pattern, no linearity. What is clear, however, is that the technical growth model of thought engenders these three phenomena; wherever the technical logic of growth exists, these related phenomena will exist at some level, in some dimension, in some meaningful connection.

Lower for higher substitution tends to run all the way down. The philosophic aim is to reduce qualitative distinctions to measurable and regulative dimensions in order to lower the price of certain categories of information, categories that enlarge the scope and scale of material progress. It is this type of information, born from naturalism and extended across social thought by developmentalism, positivism, and scientism, which facilitates economic growth outside of C.S. Lewis's moral framework (Lewis 2001a: 18). Material growth outside of the moral framework of the Tao requires these reductive mechanisms in order to trade off one kind of reality for another kind, including particular conceptions of knowledge and views of man. The substitution aligns information on the basis of least cost. Because they are inherently information-sensitive entities, institutions like education incrementally nudge their frameworks and philosophical commitments relative to the cost of information. Any substitution that maintains or accelerates the shift toward a lower-cost (less expensive) environment is welcome. Any information or knowledge that might interfere with it is, over time, removed from formal agenda.

Thus in the history of human risk, fear and its related costs are dealt with in two general ways: (1) the turn toward man (humanism) and Nature and (2) the turn toward God (or the gods) or Reason. Anthropologists and religious historians have now studied this phenomenon for decades. Eliade (1987: 14–15) recognizes the tensions created by the two spheres when he says, "*sacred* and *profane* are two modes of being in the world, two existential situations assumed by man in the course of history.... [These] modes of being depend upon the different positions that man has conquered in the cosmos; hence they are of concern to the philosopher and to anyone seeking to discover the possible dimensions of human existence" (emphasis in original). It took several centuries after Christ before the Christian Church became a leading social institution in the West and East (we will have nothing to say about other religions in this work). The Church attempted to mediate social existence on paradoxical biblical principles, e.g., human free will working in concert with God's sovereign will. In the secular sphere, the later part of the Enlightenment made clear that the link between the State and Nature was inviolable. The State and its institutions acquired capacity to generate large volumes of information and statistical data within its borders, information that informed managers of the State (government) about its subjects and which fostered the expansion of its power. The State no longer required religious ideas of human nature in order to manipulate human behavior in a certain direction; it could do so by merely adjusting the information conditions to social choice. This is how personal and societal values are altered by the dynamics of growth. Because the rule structure of markets forms over a long period of time, the values sustaining that rule system get deeply embedded in the society. But under expansion that rule regime itself becomes frayed and eventually abandoned. This, in turn, puts pressure on individuals and society itself to abandon previously held values. The key question in all of this is whether these personal and societal values have any intrinsic tie to human nature or whether they are principally a function of economic growth and the rules that sustain that growth. On this point, we join Lewis in recognizing that the intellectual and moral virtues originate from the mind-independent Tao, which has for its aim human nature.

These two institutions, the Church and the State, have been competitors for many centuries and are institutional proxies for the more fundamental institutions (entities) Reason and Nature. Indeed, the contest goes back as far as Augustine and *The City of God* (see Plantinga 1996). At first, Church and Reason may seem an odd juxtaposition in light of modern thought; faith and reason are widely thought to be incompatible if not opposites. This idea has been the great success of the Myth we spoke about earlier, built up by Hume and others and counterattacked by Lewis in his work *Miracles* (see also Earman 2000). But this is a wrong-minded view; in reality this is not true. Reason (God) is not only the author of faith, without which faith would never exist and nothing much else would either. Further, reason as an endowed human faculty cannot completely conform to Reason without faith. Thus faith and reason have a symbiotic relation whose aims include the education goods wisdom, knowledge, and understanding. We might look on it as an alignment of heart and mind: faith an attribute of the heart and reason one of the mind. Yet when all is cut away the information properties of the expanding State coincide with those of the expanding domain of Nature and a powerful symbiosis between the two evolves.

What will be clear in this book is that competition between the two models is really a conflict between ultimate ends and between the means to achieve those ends. It is also a contest between two rival institutions. Lewis (1970:118) remarked that Church and State are not compatible institutions; their respective claims are dissimilar. For example, in an ideal form the Church seeks community, where individual identity is preserved; while the State tends to seek collectivity, where individual identity is not preserved.

Where the tide flows increasingly towards increasing State control, Christianity, with its claims in one way personal and in the other way ecumenical and both ways antithetical to omnicompetent government, must always in fact... be treated as an enemy. Like learning, like the family, like ancient and liberal profession, like common law, it gives the individual a standing ground against the State. Hence, Rousseau, the father of totalitarians, said wisely enough, from his own point of view, of Christianity, ["I know nothing more opposed to the social spirit"].

Models of reality within these two spheres—the sacred and the secular—developed in large measure to calm cosmic tensions, minimize contingency, and construct and lay out plausible worldviews concerning reality, man, knowledge, and the purpose of education. More practically, models seek to generate conditions of clarity, certainty, and predictability by establishing sets of general and procedural rules, customs, values, and existential and concrete modes of being and acting in the world. These bring levels of rationality, control, and direction in day-to-day planning and exchange across society, culture, and their institutions. When models of reality operationalize as working frameworks, they lead to commensurate political, economic, and religious visions. Visions, in turn, lead to a set of social processes and policies that either unleash or constrain costs in the nature and pursuit of goods or harms (Sowell 2002: 67–98). In some cases, such as under the technical model of growth, information costs can rise in one direction (against the social welfare) and lower in another direction (economic development). Social institutions have direction in their information economy where some ideas, experiences, and things are embraced and others discarded.

By leading with questions about the nature of being and reality, such as the relation between Nature's material growth and the confinement of Reason, we are advancing a line of thought within the Lewis tradition which shows what the expanding institution of education is doing and why it is doing it, shows certain effects impacting human beings (individuals and communities), shows path dependencies, offers pattern predictions, delineates the costs of information, and provides moral warrant sufficient to arrest and reverse institutional direction by focusing on the truth of things. Lewis was keen to comment on this last point, where he implied that the processes of contesting movements and models of thought is as old as thought itself.

Models of thought are often contested at one time or another. Intellectual life is conflict, disagreement, and challenge. It takes a lot of work to understand the dynamics of contests across the philosophies (see Collins 1998). What is clear from the general pattern of reform movements is a that moral rebound occurs when people begin to realize that a model removes too much human experience, that is, abstracts from reality too much what is central to what it means to be human. The abstraction imposes too heavy a price against individuals and communities and causes a counter-model of thought, old or new, to initiate. Errors of abstraction, reduction, and substitution in models of thought impinge on human identity and are usually discovered and corrected over time. The three-fifths of a person compromise in the U.S. Constitution is a fitting example. Yet it is important to recognize that errors and distortions of this kind are not easily or always apparent under the technical growth model. Instances of harm are not likely to be clear; they are less likely to be obvious in the technical institution. Activities in areas such as cloning, biotechnology, forced prisoner organ donation, mistreatment of the young or the aged or of animals, and mistreatment of the environment are not always transparent, especially when material goods brought about by utility and progress are foremost in view. It is often the case that the "good" of industrial agriculture and the genetic modification of foods create production efficiencies that allow for greater reliabilities in acquiring food, despite a loss of genetic plant diversity. Looking at the human as a scientific object, e.g., the creating and killing of human embryos, has fostered the capacity of medicine to move toward studying disease solutions. In the technical institution, trade-offs are rarely counted against the social welfare.

It is clear enough, then, that under the all-reconciling institution of Nature the human being is regarded as a mere natural object. The view removes certain barriers that allow the social sphere to expand on technical principles. But new statistical categories, classifications, and typologies, so common now as thought to have always existed, allow for the manipulation of social data that reduce, and even eliminate, conflicts between ultimate ends and their means. It curtails deviation, individuality, and freedom in the interest of the general welfare; it locates (reduces) particular beliefs, feelings, values, and volitions of an individual life to the rationality of the collective. This rationality once separated from Reason satisfies the craving for risk-reducing uniformity in the social system. Getting the rules right becomes a big deal; it signals the correct path, the most efficient direction. Lewis (2001c: 31–32) yet again anticipates the move brilliantly:

> Almost our whole education has been directed to silencing [of the] shy, persistent, inner voice [desiring heaven]; almost all our modern philosophies have been devised to convince us that the good of man is to be found on this earth. And yet it is a remarkable thing that such philosophies of Progress or Creative Evolution themselves bear witness to the truth that our real goal is elsewhere. When they want to convince you that earth is your home, notice how they set about it. They begin by trying to persuade you that earth can be made into heaven, thus giving a sop to your sense of exile in earth as it is. Next, they tell you that this fortunate event is still a good way off in the future, thus giving a sop to your knowledge that the fatherland is not here and now. Finally, lest your longing for the transtemporal should awake and spoil the whole affair, they use any rhetoric that comes to hand to keep out of your mind the recollection that even if all the happiness they promised could come to man on earth, yet still each generation would lose it by death, including the last generation of all, and the whole story would be nothing, not even a story, for ever and ever.

What we are describing in this book is a complex institutional process of both the delegitimation of the old and the legitimation of the new. Under the principle of substitution, imperfect man can be made perfect by altering his preferences, thus guaranteeing the security of normative social values and their efficient compatibility. The moral law (the Tao) is substituted for Nature, not Nature as she was originally, but a technical form of Nature. And the institutional properties of scale, scarcity, and cost that cut across all social institutions like education are ameliorated in a final, friction-free synthesis. Chance is resolved by institutional order, positive rules replace an old and irrelevant (or ambivalent) God, and the individual person is substituted for the new social order.

The process of reversing a powerful movement or model of thought like this one—that is, "reversing" in the sense of "a kind of thought which attempts to reopen the whole question" of what is real or true—is a newer procedure than merely altering or even arresting the model's likely trajectory (Lewis 1979: 11–12). It is new particularly to modern thought, where the progressivist notion of "we can't go back, we must always press forward" survives as an unquestioned assumption. The technical growth model, operating within the antecedent of naturalism, unifies all models of thought represented by modernity;[14]

it acts as a synthesizer of worldviews, data, and people. For liberty to survive, reverse it we must: "There is nothing progressive about being pig headed and refusing to admit a mistake. And I think if you look at the present state of the world, it is pretty plain that humanity has been making some big mistakes. We are on the wrong road. Going back is the quickest way on" (Lewis 2001d: 29).

The outline of the book

Perhaps the most interesting threat to the central social concerns expressed by C.S. Lewis in the *Abolition of Man* is what takes place after the social institutions are fully integrated under the technical growth model. The expanding domain of Nature, which is really the conquering of man and his domain, achieves a separation of man from his original identity. Aquinas wrote that "The principal ends of human acts are God, self, and others, since we do whatever we do for the sake of one of these" (1988: Ia IIae, q. 73). These ends in their full sense are no longer in view under the institution Nature; self and others reduce to the instrumental axis of social cooperation available under naturalism and developmentalism (see Skyrms 1996). The consequences of that shift for man and his education are devastating. We have developed five chapters to explore the problem in light of education.

The first two chapters set out the deeper logic, categories, and implications of the relations between Nature and Reason, economic growth and social welfare. At stake here is not only the sustainability of formal education, important as that is, but prospects for human development, reliable dimensions of liberty, the advance of the social welfare, and the proper function and very identity of humankind itself. As Lewis noted, whether the human is sustained or abolished, whether he flourishes or falters depends almost entirely on answers to first questions in the philosophy of social institutions.

Chapter 3 sets out the epistemological parameters of growth, how expanding markets exchange knowledge for ignorance, and how the growth framework is sustained by the quest for uniformity. Chapter 4 discusses how the educational enterprise under the technical growth network is sustainable after a process of divisions occurs, including the division of rationality from reason. Finally, in Chapter 5, we focus on plausible resolutions to the problems set forth in earlier chapters: the very possibility of education.

Chapter 1

The Bloodless Institution

The Importance of the Social Institution to C.S. Lewis

C.S. Lewis was anything but naïve concerning the power of the social institution (SI). As a churchman, Lewis came from theological and intellectual traditions that cut across the antithesis between collectivism and individualism, because of which he could say, "The Church will outlive the universe; in it the individual person will outlive the universe" (2001c: 171–172). It was from this ontology, formed by reason and faith, honed in the rigorous climes of Oxford and Cambridge Universities, that Lewis could order and frame the normative relations between the individual and the group, between first-order SIs and second-tier ones.

Touching on the development and flourishing of humans, Lewis displayed keen insight into the problem of social choice (e.g., Arrow 1963). It was not so much the formal and mathematical aspects of the theory, but the deep-seated ontological nature of the human being in that vexing twentieth-century dilemma that concerned, roughly, the nature and scope of the choices of the individual relative to a collective or larger social entity (e.g., the organization, institution, state) in the allocation of scarce resources, rights, duties, goods, property, etc. There is in recent centuries an expanding technical tradition and logic whereby the individual gives significant ground to the group as the outcome of an aggregation procedure. In today's world, no less than in Lewis's, the collective is thought to have greater weight and value than the individual, and the collective, not the individual, is thought pivotal to social progress.

Lewis's long-standing suspicion over the uniformity of thought embodied by collectives was well worked out by the time he wrote "Screwtape Proposes a Toast" (2001e), first published in 1962, a year before his death and added as an appendix to *The Screwtape Letters*. In it he gives a bruising account of the ideology of equality as tied up with democracy. Democracy, according to Lewis, at some stage inverts to mean collective order at the expense of individual identity and freedom. Lewis's character Screwtape offers the means by which collectivism instantiates against the individual human being. The principle of equality extends beyond the political notion and across all being, making people "Normal and Regular and Like Folks and Integrated" (200). Justice and fairness come to mean sameness. The institution itself becomes an integrative agent of equality, setting up the criterion of rationality in a democracy as a reversion to the mean (not excellence but the average), resulting in a denial of variation, the dissent from real human diversity, in every instance.

> Conformity to the social environment, at first merely instinctive or even mechanical—how should a *jelly* not conform?—now becomes an unacknowledged creed or ideal of Togetherness or Being like Folks.... What I want to fix your attention on is the vast, overall movement towards the discrediting, and finally the elimination, of every kind of human excellence—moral, cultural, social, or intellectual. And is it not pretty to notice how *Democracy* (in the incantatory sense) is now doing for us the work that was once done by the most ancient Dictatorships, and by the same methods? You remember how one of the Greek Dictators (they called them "tyrants" then) sent an envoy to another Dictator to ask his advice about the principles of government. The second Dictator led the envoy into a field of corn, and there he snicked off with his cane the top of every stalk that rose an inch or so above the general level. The moral was plain. Allow no pre-eminence among your subjects. Let no man live who is wiser, or better, or more famous, or even handsomer than the mass. Cut them all down to a level; all slaves, all ciphers, all nobodies. All equals. Thus Tyrants could practise, in a sense, "democracy." But now "democracy" can do the same work without any other tyranny than her own. No one need now go through the field with a cane. The little stalks will now of themselves bite the tops off the big ones. The big ones are beginning to bite off their own in their desire to Be Like Stalks. (191, 201–202)

Being British, where queuing is a national hobby, and with Keynesian economics on the march during the 1940s and 1950s, Lewis's insights were radical for the day, joining contemporaries Aldous Huxley and George Orwell (Eric Blair) in the dystopian literary genre. As suggested, the example of *Screwtape*, and his many other works, fiction and nonfiction, only signaled the prominence Lewis assigned to education as an institution. Lewis was deeply worried about SIs, such as education, becoming a means by which unfreedom for the individual obtains.

Lewis was by all accounts a gifted educator and his sharp perception into the theory and practice of education simply cannot be ignored. He raised too many definitive and cognate questions concerning the ontological status of persons and their social entities. Indeed, SIs figured prominently in Lewis's ontology. In his essay "Membership," Lewis puts a fine ontological point to the assertion: "There will come a time when every culture, every institution, every nation, the human race, all biological life is extinct and every one of us is still alive. Immortality is promised to us, not to these generalities" (2001c: 172).

What is characteristic across Lewis's writings is a coherent conception of the institution, one that subordinates the institution's functions and purposes to those prescribed by the overarching institution we know as the moral law, what he called in the heralded book *The Abolition of Man* (2001a) the "Tao," inclusive of the historical Tao but tethered to moral law. In his important if unknowing contribution to social choice theory, Lewis set out an impressive explanation of what happens within social reality when institutions like education grow into disequilibrium, when they disfavor the individual and his or her respective agency, liberty, and values for collectivist aspirations. The quest to master Nature through technique, whether now, in the contemporary world, or for all posterity is at the fore of the developmentalist spirit that draws Lewis's ire. That disequilibrium lesson, which affects the practical affairs of teachers and their students at the school, is as relevant to the twenty-first century as it was for the twentieth. The lesson that C.S. Lewis has for us as human beings is perennial.

The moral law is the overarching or supreme, observer-independent institution that sets rough, imprecise limits on the activities of SIs as well as on individual human beings. The moral law is both a constraining institution that seeks to prevent abuse as well as an enabling one that promotes conditions for justice and flourishing. At various places in Lewis's writings, including in *Mere Christianity*, he refers to the moral law as the law of right and wrong, the law of right behavior, and the law of human nature, and even compares the moral law to a sheet of music: "The Moral Law tells us the tune we have to play: our instincts are merely the keys" (2001d: 10). The moral law exists as a guide, a kind of Sherpa showing the climber various and reliable ways up the mountain. It also exposes the risks associated going up or down a wrong path. But like the Sherpa, who does not coerce the climber to climb, the moral law does not, because it cannot, compel the SI toward proper function, toward equilibrium, toward justice.

An institution doesn't just happen into a healthy state of affairs. That takes specific, concrete individual human beings of moral wisdom and agency (e.g., leaders, statesmen, philosopher-kings, reformers, mandarins, ordinary folk) to steward an institution toward just ends and proper means. What the moral law can do is to demonstrate to reason and to conscience the correct way to proceed, and show the social welfare costs from individual – collective disequilibrium. It can persuade individuals to act within its economy by demonstrating that such action is consistent with being fully and properly human and showing the practical benefits for doing so. In this regard, the moral law is necessary for justice. In appealing to reason and conscience, the moral law reminds humanity what it means to be human, what one owes to himself and to his neighbor (George 2001), and what is impeding the quest for just relations (Lewis 2001d: 69–75). Fortunately, Lewis says, humans are constituted in such a manner that reason, when not dormant and when connected to Reason, helps to send him or her to the correct authority. In the present instance, it is the moral law that is the correct authority, and conscience as the internal reserve, where the whole of the man is engaged (Lewis2001c: 65), urging him to obey that authority (Lewis 1995: 27).

Setting institutional parameters necessitates the prohibition of some activities, such as maltreatment of human beings, as well the prescriptions of other activities, such as maintaining or enlarging the fitting range of liberty for an individual to develop and exercise native talents and diverse gifts. Because of the kind of immortal entity that individual human beings are, it is right to say they are logically prior to the SI in the ontological ordering of social reality. Lewis observed, "[i]f individuals live only seventy years, then a state, or a nation, or a civilization, [or an institution] which may last for a thousand years, is more important than the individual. But if Christianity is true, then the individual is not only more important but incomparably more important, for he is everlasting and the life of a state or a civilization [or an institution], compared with his, is only a moment" (2001d: 74–75). Elsewhere, in *The Weight of Glory*, Lewis stresses this same ontological ground.

There are no ordinary people. You have never talked to a mere mortal. Nations, cultures, arts, civilizations—these are mortal, and their life is to ours as the life of a gnat. But it is immortals whom we joke with, work with, marry, snub, and exploit—immortal horrors or everlasting splendours.... And our charity must be a real and costly love, with deep feeling for the sins in spite of which we love the sinner—no mere tolerance or indulgence which parodies love as flippancy. Next to the Blessed Sacrament itself, your neighbour is the holiest object presented to your senses. If he is your Christian neighbour he is holy in almost the same way, for in him also Christ *vere laitat*—the glorifier and the glorified, Glory Himself, is truly hidden. (2001c: 46)

The school, the college, the learning organization, the accrediting firm, the media, and the wider institution of education, all are inferior and subordinate entities relative to the immortal individual human being. This is certainly different from how we are taught to think of organizations and SIs. We are usually taught that the claims of society are greatest, that the human being is a natural object, surrendering the distinction between persons and objects, and that SIs are involved in the technical production of happiness (utility maximization). Yet Lewis's conception of reality is at odds with the technical path of social theory, which tacks with the collective direction and is sewn into the ideology of institutional expansion, every part predicated on the whole, every move an effort to improve and not merely adapt. The fundamental premise is that mere Nature is all there is, but it is enough to sustain all human effort, enough to demand our loyalty, and enough to avert our defection. It is from this background position about reality that C.S. Lewis could articulate in straightforward language the dual approaches to moral education.

Hence the educational problem is wholly different according as you stand within or without the Tao. For those within, the task is to train in the pupil those responses which are in themselves appropriate, whether anyone is making them or not, and in making which the very nature of man consists. Those without, if they are logical, must regard all sentiments as equally non-rational, as mere mists between us and the real objects. As a result, they must either decide to remove all sentiments, as far as possible, from the pupil's mind; or else to encourage some sentiments for reasons that have nothing to do with their intrinsic "justness" or "ordinacy." The latter course involves them in the questionable process of creating in others by "suggestion" or incantation a mirage which their own reason has successfully dissipated. (2001a: 20–21)

Lewis's was a full-bodied teleological account of education as an institution. It hinges on two unified realities: the nature of external reality and the nature of man.

THE IDEA OF PROPER FUNCTION AND THE SOCIAL INSTITUTION

Perhaps the cardinal questions regarding institutions as entities is whether they are entities that operate below or above Nature, whether an SI is moving toward or away from proper function in the context of C.S. Lewis's Tao. Lewis's ontology sees Nature as the "first sketch." "Nature is mortal; we shall outlive her. When all the suns and nebulae have passed away, each one of you will still be alive. Nature is only the image, the symbol; but it is the symbol Scripture invites me to use. We are summoned to pass in through Nature, beyond her, into that splendour which she fully reflects" (2001c: 43–44). Nature by itself is insufficient to give us ultimate purpose or final causes; it would seem implausible that it can provide an orientation sufficient to define the proper function of a non-natural entity. Yet it is no doubt tempting, to the technical mind of the social engineer, to define "proper function" within the Normal distribution (the statistical curve). This is the idea of marrying the principle of proper function to what it is that SIs do, in the technical environment, not what they ought to do. Yet this error of category occurs when the technician confuses or equivocates the term "mean", locating it in the sense of a statistical mean (the distribution) instead of the Aristotelian sense of a mean, that is, an excellence of relation between extremes of excess and deficiency as defined by the moral law. The former is based on descriptive validity (what the SI *does*); the latter is centered in the normative validity of virtues and justice (what the SI *should do*). Since Nature and naturalistic methods cannot be the final criterion on which SIs (as non-natural entities) are evaluated, it can say little to the normative validity of virtues and justice; it cannot define for an SI what is or is not "proper" function.

The notion of proper function is used with some frequency in the biological sciences and physical organisms; physical systems in Nature do entail the notion of proper function. Consider the eye. The eye is more likely to function properly when the cornea's outer covering and the internal lens allows the eye to focus the image; when the pupil and iris coordinate the amount of light entering the eye; when the retina's translucent "screen" accurately receives the projected image and the optic nerve sends along a set of undistorted electrical impulses to the brain. While assigning purpose, design, and proper function to artifacts is without controversy, this is less certain for physical organisms (e.g., see Amundson and Lauder 1994).[1] However, Alvin Plantinga correctly notes, "The bulk of mankind [...] has applied the notions of purpose and proper function to natural organisms, and has done so without any confusion or incoherence at all: for most human beings have thought that natural organisms and their parts *are*, in fact, designed [...] From a theistic point of view, human beings, like cathedrals and Boeing 747s, have been designed; we might say they are divine artifacts" (1993: 197).

What the general idea of proper function means to the SI, on minimal terms, turns on the normative (teleological) term "proper." Because the majority of social science has for some time traded off normative analysis for descriptive analysis, it will have nothing to say on the matter we are about to discuss. The term "proper" means the designated range of being, knowing, and doing by which an entity, like an SI or an individual human being, tends toward an equilibrium state according to that entity's design plan (its purpose, its *telos*), where it is not in conflict with what it ultimately means to be human. Put simply, the entity works the way it ought to work given certain truths of reality. For example, an otherwise healthy human body operates in an equilibrium range of 97.3°F and 99.1°F, "and this system's thus regulating temperature (by way of perspiration, shivering, adjusting metabolism, and expansion and contraction of blood vessels) no doubt confers a [sic] sep on its owner" (Plantinga 1993: 207). Or consider that law has a designated range of operations proper to its functions. Frederick Bastiat (2004: 6) wrote about its distortion:

But, unfortunately, law by no means confines itself to its proper functions. And when it has exceeded its proper functions, it has not done so merely in some inconsequential and debatable matters. The law has been used to destroy its own objective: It has been applied to annihilating the justice that it was supposed to maintain; to limiting and destroying rights which its real purpose was to respect. The law has placed the collective force at the disposal of the unscrupulous who wish, without risk, to exploit the person, liberty, and the property of others. It has converted plunder into a right, in order to protect plunder. And it has converted lawful defense into a crime, in order to punish lawful defense.

There is a part-to-whole link between knowledge centers and culture, arguing that philosophical questions must precede and inform scientific ones in order to have proper functioning of SIs.

The health of a culture, like the health of the body, consists in the harmonious functioning of its parts. Science, philosophy and religion are certainly major parts of European culture; their distinction from one another as quite separate parts is certainly the most characteristic cultural achievement of modern times. But if they have not been properly distinguished, they cannot be properly related; and unless they are properly related, properly ordered to one another, cultural disorder, such as that of modern times, inevitably results. (Adler 1940; see also Rader 1941)

An SI tends toward proper function when it is in state S, where S represents minimally needed desiderata:

(a) the SI does not conflict with the moral law (Lewis's Tao)
(b) the SI has no significant information malfunction or distortion (whatever information necessary for the knowledge and production of the good is present and amply so)
(c) the SI offers a congenial knowledge environment that harbors the truth about human beings
(d) the SI optimizes decision-making conditions in a climate of liberty
(e) the SI entails independence from the rigidly interlocked jurisdiction of the chain of spatiotemporal Nature, by which a proper range of individual – collective freedom obtains
(f) the SI achieves the complex good(s) in view according to its design or purpose

The SI in state S tends to foster a hospitable exchange environment for human development and flourishing (an approximate equilibrium). In this environment, education tends toward optimization (all things being equal). State S is the SI's ontological parameter, the nonviable area of market relations that places outer limits on scale, the scope and context of rules, certain forms of information, and the exchange conditions. The ontological and epistemological conditions are aimed at truth or the truth-relation and the capacity-building nature of human development, individually and in community. These are not quantifiable or tightly legible conditions, but they are exculpatory. Proper function is minimally the idea that SIs work within a dynamic but bounded range of criterion and parameter. The conditions themselves are often known heuristically and numinously, in the imperfect give and take of cultural and economic processes, in the individual strivings of life and its pursuit of truth, beauty and goodness, in spiritual and moral discernment, in wisdom and the good judgment of common sense, in theoretical and practical reasoning.

We must admit something quite painful to some of us and perhaps obvious or necessary for others. In the human realm there can be no perfect ordering of SIs, no precise equilibrium point. In the state of proper function equilibrium is elusive, particularly in the type of world we presently occupy. Again, Arrow (1963) showed that the emergence of a dictator could solve the choice problem, at the price of the individual. The game theorists and Rawls, Habermas, and others have made similar efforts trying to resolve the one and the many problem. Not one of these theories can reliably preserve individual liberty. Lewis (2001a) showed that the emergence of an elite ("conditioners") could provide a corrupted form of equilibrium and solve the choice problem, at the cost of humanity. And we showed how equilibrium tends to obtain when expanding institutions divide information, with a resulting loss of freedom (Rodriguez, Loomis, and Weeres 2007). But these are no sound equilibriums because the costs to achieve them require a vicious trade-off of the individual human being and his freedom. The ideal or utopian state is never reached in this life because we live in an environment that has two competing tensions: scarcities of resources (including information) on the one side and human self- and group-interest on the other. C.S. Lewis knew this and suggested that the social choice problem could not be handled until the moral condition of the human being was addressed.

Unless we go on to the second thing—the tidying up inside each human being—we are only deceiving ourselves. What is the good of telling the ships how to steer so as to avoid collisions if, in fact, they are such crazy old tubs that they cannot be steered at all? What is the good of drawing up, on paper, rules for social behaviour, if we know that, in fact, our greed, cowardice, ill temper, and self-conceit are going to prevent us from keeping them? I do not mean for a moment that we ought not to think, and think hard, about improvement in our social and economic system. What I do mean is that all that thinking will be mere moonshine unless we realize that nothing but the courage and unselfishness of individuals is ever going to make any system work properly. (2001d: 73)

Yet an ideal does continue to exist in our minds. It haunts our human faculties, which bear witness, and furnishes reasons why we as a species give attention, energy, and resources to solutions. Generally speaking, reason tells us what is wrong even if we have difficulty in positing solutions; it is the realization that we have gone too far and removed too much of reality. If Lewis is correct, institutional theory, as an initial step, should legitimize the external superintending source we call the moral law.

Therefore, we can understand proper function criteria as the application of moral law to SIs. The first two proper function criteria, (a) and (b), are minimal liberty curtailments (restrictions). These two criteria ensure that utility (pragmatism) as a criterion is prevented from becoming central to complex production activities. In our and Lewis's open and dynamic model, SIs are free in their creative activities as long as they do not conflict with (a) and (b). The next four, (c)–(f), are responsibility criteria. These are conditions that each SI has a duty to generate (offer, attend to, etc.) in light of the first principles of theoretical and practical Reason. For example, an SI has the responsibility to harbor or permit pursuit the truth about things, especially human beings, including averting inflationary constructivism and propaganda (e.g., from marketing persuaders, political parties, and the like). Set up on these tenets, ontological parameters, (a) and (b), as well as a few minimal obligations, (c)–(f), exist for SIs in virtue of their responsibility to the human as the *imago Dei* (image of God).

Enter the attribute of growth. Because growth means the enlargement of structures and is an attribute (a relation) that social entities like institutions can have, its mode of being is neutral until activated by a model of thought. The question is, what model of thought will govern an SI like education? Inside a properly functioning SI, growth is constrained by first principles of theoretical and practical Reason and does not create significant distortions and disequilibriums between the individual and collective, between economic expansion and the social welfare, between universal and particular information, between facts and values, between rationality and reason. We call this the open or transcendent model of growth because it is open to and governed by the observer-independent reality of the moral law (Lewis's Tao). It is this law that governs or regulates the sound exercise of an institution's means and ends.

An SI that operates with some credible equilibrium in (a)–(f) would be an institution moving toward proper function. To know with some level of assurance whether an SI is functioning properly is to know whether human beings themselves have the freedom to achieve proper function within the domain of the institution. This is not a question-begging problem; the two are in a relation of reciprocity and may be judged on either end of that relation. As Aristotle once said, it is the opportunity for the human being to realize one's intellectual and moral virtues and capacities, which are likely to occur at different levels and degrees for different people. This is not a quantitative analysis but a qualitative discernment. In other words, it is to know whether the institution extends an optimal range of agent sensitivity to persons in their proper development and flourishing (Hodgson 2006: 16). Relations between the institution and the individual human being find a plausible degree of reciprocity: the institution accounts for the composite nature of man (the individual), including the composite range of knowledge and knowing. Yet both the individual and the institution are subject to the same moral constraint; the individual owes to the SI moral conduct (e.g., the free rider problem) and vice versa.

Let us consider a couple of counterexamples to determine if the initial conception of our theory holds. We have maintained that unrestricted (closed) growth tends to violate each of the desiderata (a)–(f). A suboptimal institution is functioning at the sub-natural level. It is doing harm to the human, either by omission or by commission. Consider the problem of slavery as an institution. If the minimal criteria for the proper function of the SI are (a)–(f) then it would appear that slavery would be an institution that violated at least (a), (c), and (d). We get to that conclusion by asking: did slavery as an institution promote a hospitable exchange environment for human flourishing? Did slaves flourish as human beings under that institution? Did the institution foster individual decision making in a climate of liberty? Slavery may have been a highly efficient institution (a disputable point), but in no sense, even an Aristotelian sense, did slavery as an institution promote the slave's flourishing (a human being's identity and proper function is not reducible to their role within an institution). Let us consider a second challenge. Could an institution satisfy the points (a)–(f) concerning proper function and yet be an example of an improperly functioning institution? These desiderata are of course minimal criteria. An SI that meets these criteria is *more likely* to be in or moving toward proper function than an SI that (a) is violating the moral law; (b) is distorting the information environment; (c) is misrepresenting what human beings are, their purposes, etc.; (d) is constraining decision making in illiberal conditions; (e) is ontologically and epistemologically closed; and (f) fails to achieve the complex good.

It is very important to notice that SIs exist as nonnatural phenomena and operate above Nature when their attributes secure an environment conducive to human development and flourishing. All of this brings us to what we know by conscience and intuition: that when an institution functions within the demands of the moral law, such an institution is more likely to be in the range of or moving toward proper function. In contrast, the institution underwritten by the technical growth model threatens individual moral agency, induces a compartmentalization of life, envelops the public and private spheres, splits rationality from reason, divides and insulates forms of information, and leads to the phenomenon of divided selves where elites regard human beings as mere institutional furniture (Taylor 2007). In this setting, institutional participants are unaware of their responsibilities beyond those assigned to them by their institutional roles "all snug beneath the Conditioners" (Lewis 2001a: 68). Role-playing within an institution becomes a proxy for human identity where one's humanity narrows to be within the parameters set by the role.

The insufficiency of the non-teleological account of Social Institutions

A most discouraging trend in economics and political theory concerns the non-teleological study of institutions.[2] From a time in which institutions were largely ignored, through an era in which it was thought that institutions were mere constraints on otherwise beneficent behavior in markets, to an era in which it was thought that the purpose of institutions was to promote economic efficiency, we now seem to be firmly in a time in which it is understood that institutions are the very substratum of economic and social action (e.g., North 1990, 1991; Williamson 1987). What we forget, and what Lewis's work reminds us, is that the substratum of institutions and all economic and social action is the human being. SIs are, in one sense, human dependent, and what the human being *is* cannot be taken for granted in or separated from social analysis. We can in fact derive a teleology of SIs from what man is and was designed to be.

However, there is a strong materialist (naturalist) objection to the teleological view for what will be obvious reasons.[3] Consider the institutional work of John Searle, particularly where he applies a bare-bones background ontology to the theory of institutions: "The truth is, for us, most of our metaphysics is derived from physics. ... It is a condition of your being an educated person in our era that you are apprised of these two theories: the atomic theory of matter and the evolutionary theory of biology [...] We live in a world made up entirely of physical particles in fields of force" (1995: 6–7). This allows Searle to reduce all social reality into a naturalist (materialist) ontology: "Our aim is to assimilate social reality to our basic ontology of physics, chemistry, and biology" (41). Searle writes that

> [o]ne of Darwin's greatest achievements was to drive teleology out of the account of the origin of species. On the Darwinian account, evolution occurs by way of blind, brute, natural forces. There is no intrinsic purpose whatever to the origin and survival of biological species. We can, arbitrarily, define the "functions" of biological processes relative to the survival of organisms, but the idea that any such assignment of function is a matter of the discovery of an intrinsic teleology in nature, and that functions are therefore intrinsic, is always subject to a variant of Moore's open question. (16)

From this background metaphysics—a closed, natural system—Searle then extrapolates this to the status of functions within SIs: "Functions are never intrinsic; they are assigned relative to the interests of [human] users and observers" (19). For Searle, collective intentionality is reducible to the sense-perceptible world, one predicated on a naturalistic structure of reality. Now, Searle must hold this belief about institutions—their function and status ultimately reducible to Nature—because he is a rational man, and one central characteristic of rationality is consistency (coherence). His metaphysics demands that SIs derive their status functions, indeed their very existence, solely from the mind-dependent situation of users and observers. Many times this is the case, as we will point out. However, it is not always the case. Searle's position might also be viewed as inconsistent, for if there is no design or purpose to biological life, and man is merely biological life, then the mind of man has no design or purpose either, being reducible to brain events (e.g., random electrical, chemical impulses). In our judgment, accounts of the mind as agent require (even if implicitly) a more complex and purposeful account of life. What is important to observe is that Searle's theory ultimately reduces SIs to Nature. But how can this be? Nature itself is an institution but it is not a self-caused one. Where Lewis's theory offers a final cause, Searle's theory does not and would seem to have a regress problem.

Consider Lewis's moral law argument in the *Abolition*. The Tao is an institution that does not derive its status functions, deontic powers, etc., from human users and observers. The moral law is not human or observer dependent in that sense; it exists and does what it does, brings what it brings, represents what it represents, *for* human beings. But in no way is it dependent upon them. The moral law is a basic feature of external reality, one which we cannot not know, and which we must presuppose to make sense of any being, knowing, or doing.

What happened to the Tao (the moral law) as a governing institution is explicable through history, economics, and sociology, but not metaphysics. And history, economics, and sociology cannot tell us that the Tao does not exist. Social theory *can* tell us how the moral law disappeared from public discourse. Basically, the social situation shifted once information costs were elevated against the Tao, and all that it represents. It lost its status function in the view of the State and state institutions (or, the other way: the State stripped the status functions from the Tao). It was thought to have become (or was always) observer dependent, the reduction to sentiment, emotivism, or subjectivism, even when, as Lewis points out, it did not lose its ontological objectivity. As Lewis mentioned in the book *Miracles*, we have a situation wherein the human being and the world she knows, so it is claimed, are reducible to mere Nature and its processes of cause and effect. This is an incoherent position made worse by applying it to institutions. What is nonetheless interesting to note is that Searle's theory of institutions does match his materialist conception of human beings and their reality (as far as this is concerned, his theory is consistent), but it is entirely inconsistent with regard to the reality that SIs are in fact nonnatural phenomena. They are not products of biology or the brain (or synapses within the brain); they are not fields of force. Biology (adaptive physical life systems) or brain (neurophysiology) cannot create SIs. Social institutions are not constitutive properties of material things.

It is imperative to a plausible theory of SIs that the individual human being and the moral law become the criterion for the evaluation of all their activities: for the individual not as an aggregate, not as a statistical mean, not as utilitarian calculus might hold, but more in the deontological sense that each individual person minimally ought to be treated as an intrinsically valuable end, as an I and as a Thou (Buber 1970; Lewis 2001a: 79), not in the I – It or I – Them relation. This would seem to imply that social theorists, including educationists and economists, are ethically obligated to account for the individual human being in their theories, including the deeper human attributes (common or differentiated), complexities, and purposes than their method can at present tolerate. This is a famous methodological problem for economists and many educationists. To ignore human ontology before constructing institutional ontology can be a fatal error in theory building, particularly if the substance-attribute assumptions about human beings are left wanting a greater accuracy to reality.

Perhaps the most critical philosophical debates revolve around the ontology of reality and the human person. Most economists writing on institutional theory will avoid at all costs bringing metaphysics into the discussion. This is just another way that the technical model trims the information base. A whole host of fallacies derive from separating human ontology from institutional ontology, but the fallacies are concealed by the information structure developed within the institutional setting. Institutions under rising scale thin the complexity of human ontology thereby marrying a distorted facsimile of human nature to the utility function of the SI. Alas we get an organizing principle far out of sync with what human beings are and what they were designed to be. The problem is as much method as it is structure.

Arrow (1974: 17) acknowledges the problem of method when discussing limits on narrow conceptions of rationality in the choosing of ends. Many scholars approach social theory from trade-offs basic to social cooperation, not those that align with an objective- and desire-independent sphere such as the moral law, but where the individual must sing in tune with the collective (facilitated by the institution). In order to get them to yield, individual human beings must be compartmentalized into some fraction of their true complexity and identity: the desire-dependent passions (Hume), utility functions (Bentham and Mill), preference orderings (Richter), usefulness (Dewey), fitness (Spencer and Simon), and general self-interest (Smith). Veblen (1950: 232–233) may have said it best in describing the hedonistic conception of man to be "a lightning calculator of pleasures and pains, who oscillates like a homogenous globule of desire of happiness under the impulse of stimuli that shift him about the area, but leave him intact." The preference for the technical procedure tends to abstract and demote the human to a slice of his or her actual identity. When this happens, the loss of information is irretrievable. Development becomes diminishment and freedom becomes enslavement.

Yet the analysis of institutions will reliably fall into incoherence if we continue to insist on seeing them as merely instrumental rather than as teleological. The proper teleological rendering of institutions, and not its absence, brings coherence to their existence and relations. The purely instrumental view distorts the human situation, as in the relationships between Nature and Reason, between the one and the many, between economic growth and the social welfare, between schooling and learning. If we want to make any genuine progress toward understanding the nature and role of SIs in culture and society, if we endeavor to understand the relation of institutions to the individual, we must come to understand (1) the purposes that different individuals and collectives ascribe to particular institutional arrangements and how these affect social choice and (2) realize that institutions are in fact nonnatural entities bound to an inescapable relation with the moral law (the supreme institution).

The ontology of Social Institutions: A preliminary statement

By now it should be evident that we offer unambiguous conceptual guidance to the study of education as an institution. Our analysis of education might apply to nearly any SI whose purposes and goods are as complex as those of education: public or private, political, economic, or cultural. In the present growth environment—the early part of the twenty-first century—where it is thought that expanded access, trade, and exchange will offer impressive global gains in goods and services, we show the reader how to link our original economic theory (Rodriguez, Loomis, and Weeres 2007) with the weighty philosophical and economic issues set forth by C.S. Lewis in his *tour-de-force* book *The Abolition of Man* and other writings.

Basically, what we are putting forth in this work is a new integrated theory of SIs, and especially a new way to account for education as an institution. But we must begin at the beginning, and that beginning originates with an ontological explanation of SIs, including most of all education. We give a preliminary statement of it here and will more fully develop that statement as the chapters unfold.

In recent years, scholars across a large number of disciplines have come to recognize institutions as integral features of the productive base of human activity, as underlying determinants of the long-term growth of economies, and as important to the condition of the social welfare. It is now widely accepted that all markets—economic, political, and cultural—are constrained by institutional rules and procedures that reflect their efficiency and the range of choice in production and exchange. In other words, everyone agrees that institutions matter. All over the world people have been trying to come up with an integrated theory of institutions. That is, they have been trying to identify a common set of factors that motivate the behavior of all SIs. The thinking is that such a theory would help us get a better handle on how the economy works and how political institutions function, and it would help us better understand the requirements for improving the social welfare, including in the field of education. In our original work we identified information and scale as key factors that link the interaction of institutions across markets and, in so doing, we have taken a major step in the development of an integrated theory of institutions.

Let us be clear from the outset: both persons and social entities like institutions operate within a "model" or "framework" of thought (Taylor 1989). Understanding the model is a key to understanding the deeper logic and agenda of SIs. In *The Discarded Image*, Lewis articulates the power of the model as deeply influencing the human mind in every age: "But there is a two-way traffic; the Model is also influenced by the prevailing temper of mind [...] each reflects the state of that age's knowledge" (2007: 222). Like a worldview, a model of thought is a way of seeing reality and structuring things. A model or framework of thought represents, among other things, a logic of relations, and the content and patterns of information and knowledge that have various dimensions such as quality and quantity, breadth and depth, volume, rigidity, as well as influencing forms of practice, including how people go about their daily lives. Institutions as social constructs help to regulate these dimensions of information and knowledge through a composite network of general and procedural rules[4] and set of categories. Information and knowledge are the lifeblood of SIs, and the better-functioning (more humane, but perhaps less efficient) SIs have goods (and the means to achieve them) that are complex and tend to appropriate a rich information base and knowledge environment. A bloodless institution is one whose information and knowledge environment has been divided and depleted. The SI in this state is an accessory for human errors in category, logic, reason, and ethics.

Central to institutions are formal and informal rules and conventions that help to umpire individual and collective relations, action, production, and exchange (North 1990, 1991; Searle 2005; Bowles 2006; Rodriguez, Loomis, and Weeres 2007). The nature of how rules and conventions are constituted and what it is that they constitute, what they presuppose about reality, what status functions they confer, what they enable or disable as options, what institutional facts they condition or create, depends significantly on prior background assumptions about reality. Assumptions do not only represent the model and the interpretative framework of human thought, as well as the character of the structural network that pressures institutional direction and performance; they also have practical characteristics such as gatekeeper functions, preventing some information from coming in while keeping other information away from deliberation.

It is almost too obvious to mention, but the belief-forming practices of individual human beings usually do not occur in a vacuum. As Donne said, no man is an island. Much of what we believe relies on a knowledge base developed by others (e.g., the academic traditions and disciplines). Knowledge acquisition and decision making is more likely than not to take place within the context and framework of the institutional environment. Addressing how that ontological situation influences the epistemic environment is unavoidable. Institutions act as "hidden persuaders" that influence (but do not necessarily determine) belief patterns of participants in ways that may not be entirely obvious (Hodgson 2003). It behooves the scholar and the student, then, to carefully examine and consider the institutional environment within which education occurs in order to arrive at some credible conception of educational processes that match, or do no harm to, plausible ends of humanity.

It should be clear by now that institutions matter greatly as social existents. Functioning on behalf of civilization (society and culture) and the individual human being, they mediate the multifaceted development, delivery, and acquisition of various human goods. The SI's proper function is well defined, at least in part, by the nature and intricacy of goods pursued (signaling its teleology), the processes and freedom to achieve them, and whether institutional activities and the facts that they create actually promote the aims of human development and flourishing. While it would be foolish not to recognize their instrumental nature, it would likewise be imprudent to disregard the teleological account of institutions. For them to function properly, we simply must know why and for what purposes they exist. It is a methodological error to assume their existence without giving a nod to their ontology.

Neglecting the teleological relation between individual human beings and their SIs is like discounting Plato's argument in *The Republic* between the nature and moral health of the city-state as measured against the character of the individual citizens comprising it, or vice versa. It would be like saying that New York, Los Angeles, Mexico City, Tokyo, and Nairobi do not in some significant way represent or reflect the people comprising it, or that the people do not reflect their cities and SIs. Working out plausible market or political solutions to problems within Mexico City or Los Angeles requires a vast amount of information and knowledge about the people, cultures, histories, and their institutions (political, economic, educational, etc.). Ignoring this principle would also be to ignore, for example, the important traditions of legal institutions embedded in culture, such as whether a Romanic, civil law or whether an Anglo, common law governs a city or state.

Sidebar: The Principle of Ontological Correspondence

Plato conceived the principle of ontological correspondence in *The Republic*. He did so by drawing a relation of reciprocity between the kind of people occupying a city and the kind of city in which people dwell. Plato put these words to Socrates in response to Glaucon:

Do you know, I said, that governments vary as the dispositions of men vary, and that there must be as many of the one as there are of the other? For we cannot suppose that States are made of "oak and rock," and not out of the human natures which are in them, and which in a figure turn the scale and draw other things after them?

Yes, he said, the States are as the men are; they grow out of human characters.

Then if the constitutions of States are five, the dispositions of individual minds will also be five? Certainly. (1986: 293)

Socrates, Glaucon, and Adeimantus then move on to discuss five types of city regimes and, correspondingly, five types of souls (Book VIII; 543–570):

City	Soul	Character	Leader	Distortion
Aristocracy	aristocratic	just and good	philosopher	too much order
Timocracy	timocratic	contentious	soldier	power
Oligarchy	oligarchic	pursuit of wealth	wealthy	materialism/inequality
Democracy	democratic	pursuit of equality	commoner	too much freedom
Tyranny	tyrannical	pursuit of power	tyrant	restriction of freedom

Each of these cities and corresponding human souls necessitates some trade-off or other. These trade-offs are well known to readers of Plato and we will not pursue them here. We pause only to note that some external authority is required when addressing the problem of social choice. That authority can either originate from within the moral law (the Tao) where one is ruled "by divine wisdom dwelling within him" (self-rule under the weight of Reason) or "by an external authority" that is an SI of the market and government (1986: 358). In Plato's view, the ideal or properly functioning city strives for friendship, justice, and the cultivation of higher goods. In other words, in striving for the goods of justice, etc., a properly functioning city strives for a plausible equilibrium, though as we have shown an equilibrium is never per se reached. On this view, the purpose of education, as an SI, becomes the propagation of an orderly and just society where wisdom attains the highest level of political virtue.

> **Sidebar (Continued)**
>
> Lewis's principle of correspondence was more basic, more fundamental than Plato's version. Man inside of the Tao looks different than man outside of the Tao. In reality, the Tao serves as a touchstone for human development and flourishing. Without it, some form of secular humanism or developmentalism will inevitably distort and in some cases become the enemy of the human, as it does in unjust cities. Lewis noted that "if any one age really attains by eugenics and scientific education, the power to make its descendents what it pleases, all men who live after it are the patients of that power" (2001a: 57). The distortion of the human is not difficult to see within nineteenth- and twentieth-century history and across sectors of human knowledge.

Education "as an institution" is comprised of those collective fields and organizations of human activity within society and culture whose purpose is to transfer or create knowledge, skills, ideas, worldviews, beliefs, practices, experiences, values, and information. Education is the pursuit of learning. Individual schools are a classic example of formal organizations operating within the broader institution of education for these purposes. So are universities and colleges, park districts, corporate training programs, think tanks, institutes and foundations, the family, media, religious and civic organizations, and, as Plato suggested long ago, law.[5] Individual educational organizations like schools and universities comprise a part of the larger institution of education. They synthesize fields of knowledge, academic traditions, and a range of relevant skills in order to advance an idea of social preservation and progress across time. Hence the overarching function of the school or university is to—within scarce resources to do so—inculcate knowledge, skills, experiences, etc., such that the culture and civilization are preserved in a manner that human beings reach some approximation of proper function (as Plantinga says, according to their design plan). As Lewis (1939: 81) noted in the essay "Our English Syllabus," "higher" education is concerned chiefly with learning and the pursuit of higher levels of knowledge (with or without students' participation), and the schools are principally focused on students receiving an education, producing the "the good man and the good citizen."

The full level of development that so concerned Lewis, whether in schools or the university, is increasingly difficult to achieve within the expanding institution of education. The reason for this is evident once we notice that the institution divides two types of information from the production process, each being necessary for successful education production. The trading off of local/individual information and concerns for standardized and legible (collective-oriented) information under central authority is an aggregative consequence of individual choice orderings under institutional expansion. The interaction of scale and information must favor the collective over the individual under conditions of scarcity. Because collective valuations are thought less expensive than the valuations of the individual, the effect is to downgrade or lower the estimate of the individual's purposive character and role in production and resource allocation.

Yet it bears repeating that the one and the many problem that lies at the heart of institutional activity surfaces on two grounds: a scarcity of physical and human resources and the struggle to account for diverse values in the competition to secure access to those resources (Arrow 1963, 1974). The critical thing to know is that as institutional expansion occurs, as its scale increases, the SI that frames that growth must control costs to scarce resources. The fact that resources are scarce means that as the scale goes up, an institution must concentrate on common characteristics—similarities—and not on things that tend to differentiate, as these are barriers to expansion. In other words, it must move in the direction of lower costs, from more to less variation, toward simplicity and legibility, and to do so must adopt standardized rules and methods of production. Many simple goods (automobiles, hamburgers, gardening tools, etc.) can undergo this standardization process without much loss in quality (we realize that certain exceptions apply at the margins: a Lexus is not a Ford). But not all goods conform to these requirements. For certain goods, like those of education, the levels of complexity and variation cannot be depleted from production without loss of quality. Lewis recognized this tension in concluding comments about his first school.

What is the moral of this? Not, assuredly, that we should not try to make boys happy at school. The good results which I think I can trace to my first school would not have come about if its vile procedure had been intended to produce them. They were all by-products thrown off by a wicked old man's desire to make as much as he could out of deluded parents and to give as little as he could in return. That is the point. While we are planning the education of the future we can be rid of the illusion that we shall ever replace destiny. Make the plans as good as you can, of course. But be sure that the deep and final effect on every single boy will be something you never envisaged and will spring from little free movements in your machine which neither your blueprint nor your working model gave any hint of. (1986: 26)

This is a significant challenge for an education system. Ends have traditionally been correlated with higher, not lower levels of quality. A higher-quality education system will seek to optimize opportunities for individual development and minimize impediments to that development. The plans must not be so standardized as to lose the complexities and spontaneities of the exchange. This is simply another form of disequilibrium. Put in other terms, higher education and the schools start off with stewardship liability in the development of institutional thought along the normative lines we suggest in this book. We join with C.S. Lewis in noting that the moral condition of the social welfare, as well as the preservation civilization and ideal forms of democracy, depends on a true and just ordering of SIs. Education is one of those overarching institutions responsible for safe-harboring the social welfare, for a reliable, generational renewal of civilization and democracy. Its quality is of paramount importance.

Institutions, of course, are not necessary in a world of complete or perfect information (North 1990: 6). Short of that state of affairs called heaven, where perfect information would seem to reign, human beings presently live in a world of incomplete information, and the range of human capacities for knowing complete reality is quite constrained. Therefore, institutions matter and are a necessary component of social reality. In terms of collective action (Olson 1971), they help people to access information and to realize goods and services that they could not individually. They referee and reconcile the philosophical and economic complexities of social reality, including the millions of decisions made by participants. The ethical relationship of their means to ends is of utmost concern to us, chiefly because of the temptation to abuse the work of institutions. Machiavelli's formula of maximizing *virtu* (power) and minimizing *fortuna* (luck) looms large in the technical model. To catch us from error in moments of temptation and weakness, MacIntyre advises, "Always ask about your social and cultural order what it needs you and others not to know" (1999: 328). This exercise will bring to reason what may have gone wrong and how to fashion agenda to correct it.

When an SI is working suboptimally, when it is doing harm, when it falls out of proper function, it disadvantages the individual human being in important ways. It creates conditions that neutralize the individual as a valued being in himself, denigrating important qualitative properties necessary for maturation as well as to substitute one reality for another. The very practical result of this substitution occurs daily in schooling. Instead of diagnosing individual students in a classroom and their specific needs and talents, the teacher adjusts her work on principles of scientific management, a way to cover and assess the curriculum at least cost, in order for her class to reach the test-score bar placed before them. The law of the instrument, the test, supersedes other, more qualitative, factors of education. Indeed, the "bloodless" institution is a posture whereby the formal and informal conventions that shape human interaction evolve from prior philosophical commitments (worldviews, models of thought, frameworks, paradigms, etc.) that are in fundamental conflict with—and insensitive to—what it means to be fully human. When this happens, the loss of symmetry between the SI and the individual human being causes a situation that ultimately distorts the means and ends of institution's activity, including underlying premises for sustaining production of the good. Lewis writes about the price that is "exacted for analytical knowledge and manipulative power, even if we have ceased to count it" (2001a: 70).

We do not look at trees either as Dryads or as beautiful objects while we cut them into beams: the first man who did so may have felt the price keenly, and the bleeding trees in Virgil and Spenser may be far-off echoes of the primeval sense of impiety. The stars lost their divinity as astronomy developed, and the Dying God has no place in chemical agriculture [...] But that is not the whole story. It is not the greatest of modern scientists who feel most sure that the object, stripped of its qualitative properties and reduced to mere quantity, is wholly real. Little scientists, and little unscientific followers of science, may think so. The great minds know very well that the object, so treated, is an artificial abstraction, that something of its reality has been lost. (70–71)

In a situation of this nature, degrees of harm to individuals and communities are not only possible but also probable. Harm can manifest in what does not occur as much as what does take place. These include forgone learning opportunities, the underdevelopment of reading or thinking skills, an incomplete knowledge of mathematics and science, a diminished understanding of history and civics, and the failure to realize the liberty-sustaining intellectual virtues of the trivium: grammar, rhetoric, and logic (Sayers 1947/2007).

However, the set of distortions running throughout an institution's means (it's production functions) is often hidden or concealed from direct apprehension by participants by a number of subtle mechanisms. For example, under the powerful presuppositions of naturalism, growth as a model of thought conceals reductionistic and false premises about human beings. By treating men as material, by rigging rationality to instrumental (utilitarian) views of human persons, the technical solution obscures the more important reduction of the human on terms of mere Nature. It is the reduction of the human to the material sphere, reducing it "to the level of 'Nature' in the sense that we suspend our judgments of value about it, ignore its final cause, and treat it in terms of quantity," that gives power to the "manmoulders" of this and future ages (Lewis 2001a: 69).

In the essay "Learning in War-Time," C.S. Lewis (2001c: 58) wrote, "[g]ood philosophy must exist, if for no other reason, because bad philosophy needs to be answered." Equally, we must attend to the ontology of the SI precisely because initial false premises can lead either to false beliefs or even to sound (but wrong) beliefs, though a rational belief made under false premises will inadvertently lead people deeper into error.[6]

The SI influences the formation of beliefs on the price factors of information. Some beliefs are just more expensive to hold than others in certain environments. Expanding SIs also shape the incentive structure surrounding social choice, often giving preference to a collective direction of thought. Indeed, Kenneth Arrow's impressive work recognizes what perhaps is the core problem of civil society, that is, how to reconcile individual and collective preferences within the limits of human cooperation to do so. We put forward the unorthodox idea that the economic system already succeeds in securing direction in production (the aggregation of dissimilar preferences) *without* a dictator, that is, without appealing to a sense of obligation beyond consent. Our theory of institutions (2007)—as well as Lewis's (2001a) underlying information theory in the *Abolition*—plainly shows that the way to overcome the social choice impossibility is through a narrowing (or dividing) of the available information under institutional expansion (growth). Accordingly, the division of information is on net balance a cost-increasing mechanism in that it leads to the progressive loss of particular information and, with it, individual or local liberty.

What often goes unrecognized is that the standard, empirical, inductive method of social analysis is incapable of accessing the first principles of theoretical and practical reason necessary to have a basic set of questions for inquiry. This is a problem going back to David Hume and others and we will give some account of it in Chapter 3. But without first principles, the individual – collective problem that lies at the heart of educational, social, political, and economic theory is barely a technical problem of resource allocation, solvable through mathematical modeling (e.g., game theoretic, neoclassical models) and various scales of efficiency. It is a mechanical, positivist (Caldwell 1982) alternative to complex, on-the-scene human judgment (*metis, arête, phroenesis,* and *sophia*) where "quantity adjusting" (Hayek 1940) attempts to solve the tricky problems of resource allocation in production (e.g., in planning and exchange). This of course includes individual – collective problems in education.

The reason such models and methods of thought have so obviously been effective and widely used is that they tend to mitigate the information costs of analysis and social ordering. The expeditious rise of social sciences since 1860—matching key revolutions of industry, management, and warfare—is an indicator of successful mechanical attempts at cost containment. Yet the history of bringing human beings into a scientific, quantitative framework goes back much further, as early as the thirteenth century if not before (Crosby 1997).

The target or aim for all belief, presumably, is not simply coherence, not mere rationality. We would not be intellectually virtuous if mental satisfaction rested only on the criterion of belief compatibility (coherence). As properties of the good life, coherence and rationality are important, even necessary to belief-forming practices. But they are, we can without reservation hold, insufficient for reaching optimal human performance. To be rational is not the same thing as to be reasonable. In fact, there are two kinds of truth relations that belief, in a teleological sense, should target. These correspond to the respective purposes of the two faculties. For the present, we will use the shorthand version: truth is always about something, reality is that about which truth is. The aim of "reason" is truth as correspondence (matching up) to the way things really are, whereas the chief aim of "rationality" is coherence (consistency) between beliefs. Reason (*intellectus*) is the higher and rationality (*ratio*) the lower part of the mental faculty. (This of course is not a spatial higher or lower.) Reason is more often concerned with final truths, causes, and ends; rationality more so with instrumental truths, efficient causes, and means. Reason is the ability to reliably umpire what is real or not real by thinking accurately. And here is the rub: if rationality is divided from reason (as we show in Chapter 4), and then set above reason as pivotal, one can instantly make out the great potential for moral error. We might simply point out that many of Stalin's followers were among the most rational institutional actors in the twentieth century. Together they lined up their beliefs and belief-forming practices on the criterion of Stalin's subjectivism. However, no one who is sane could call Stalin or his followers "reasonable." The risk here, when this division occurs, is that the individual human being becomes indifferent to ends, affected only by his assent to the means to achieve whatever ends have been assembled. Consequently, public or private life is proportionally weakened and reducible to the roles that one plays, and generally takes for granted the hand dealt at the table of life.

Growth and the Social Institution

We are giving some preliminary thought to the institutional phenomenon of growth or expansion and we do this in two senses. In the first sense, growth is a "model of thought" that sets general information parameters around social thought: what collectively gets valued, what receives or does not receive agenda in the way of specific beliefs, dispositions, attitudes, decision making, the distribution of goods, etc. In other words, growth as a model of thought sets collective limits to rationality, binding the activity of making decisions to the model. Second, growth is also a specific "attribute" of SIs during the expansion of trade. As an attribute, growth greases the information environment of the institution, seeing to it that the right information, rules, values, relations, and exchange conditions are permitted and supported.

It may be helpful initially to picture the SI as a sort of traffic cop that regulates the flow of exchange between the individual and larger culture and society, for example, education. As an extension of that cop's authority, growth is the expanding domain of authority. The traffic cop (the SI) operates ethically when operating from within the larger moral law (the supreme institution with legitimate jurisdiction). He is more likely to operate unethically when operating outside of the moral law. Behind the cop is the institution of law.

There is way in which the traffic cop analogy does not hold. The traffic cop is a visible, tangible, symbolic coordinating authority, standing amid traffic in uniform, with badge, gun, and whistle, and gesturing (signaling) to specific, concrete individuals in cars to proceed this way or that way, to go forward, to stop, or to turn. We are not saying that the SI is a personal authority. It is not. Rather, the SI is an impersonal, less visible authority that empowers the traffic cop's authority in law, giving him the authority to signal information and the discretion of sanction in cases where those signals are misinterpreted or intentionally violated. The legal code is impersonal authority (Arrow 1974: 63–79); the traffic cop is a personal authority whose agency originates from the legal code.

Because personal authority cannot be everywhere (scarcity and cost prohibit a traffic cop on every corner), impersonal authority, that is, the SI, takes on greater prominence in terms of becoming an efficiency and surveillance instrument. The expanding impersonal authority, in a closed system, only survives on the division of information mechanism, which helps to indicate the correct pathway by removing the individual and local contexts and aggregating the preferences and activities of millions of actors; what follows is that decision-sets are reduced to choice-sets (see Chapter 4). When the closed growth model marries impersonal authority, efficiency and surveillance become key attributes of a larger firm (e.g., Walmart), the State (e.g., United States, China), and multistate international financial institutions or political organizations (e.g., World Bank, United Nations).

THE INSTITUTION, THE SUBSTITUTION, AND THE PUBLIC DOMAIN

Institutional growth in its manifold varieties—economic, political, and cultural—has become the proposed solution for many, if not most, of the world's most pressing problems. Poverty, corruption, and disunity of practically every kind are problems invariably seen as having a solution in which growth plays or can play a leading part. Growth in trade is seen as a progressively positive force in society, a movement toward zero costs, or a way to define social progress to material (economic) gain.

In its status as a model and as an attribute, growth is morally neutral until it violates objective and normative principles of the moral law. As we have maintained, the moral law exists as the supreme or overarching institution that both protects and guides the human to right means and ends. The term "guide" is not meant to signal that an externality passes by and whispers, "Let me give you every reason why you should take that path." Instead, we mean by "guide" the broad range of morally reliable decision-sets that is appropriate to a given set of circumstances. This is why time-tested traditions are important. We *know* the relative decision-set through our epistemic faculties. Conscience, memory, intuition, and reason are among the faculties necessary for knowing. But when growth is permitted to take no notice of the moral law, costs are raised against both individuals and the overall social welfare, even though economic expansion proceeds unabated. Costs tend to rise on two levels: within the possible conditions of human exchange and development that fail to occur and in those conditions where harm is done to the human being in the transactions that do occur. Lewis saw this trade-off very clearly.

> I believe a man is happier, and happy in a richer way, if he has "the freeborn mind." But I doubt whether he can have this without economic independence, which the new society is abolishing. For economic independence allows an education not controlled by Government; and in adult life it is the man who needs and asks nothing of Government who can criticize its acts and snap his fingers at its ideology. Read Montaigne; that's the voice of a man with his legs under his own table, eating the mutton and turnips raised on his own land. Who will talk like that when the State is everyone's schoolmaster and employer? Admittedly, when man was untamed, such liberty belonged only to the few. I know. Hence the horrible suspicion that our only choice is between societies with few freemen and societies with none. (1970: 314)

Once growth is activated within an institution, in the technical model, it morphs into one of the institution's principal attributes. It does this through a process of substitution. Lewis thought we should understand these substitutes: "[The] first thing I do is to try to find out what I know about substitutes, and the realities for which they are substituted, in general.... For a gramophone record is precisely a substitute, and an orchestra the reality. But owing to my musical miseducation the reality appeared to be a substitute and the substitute a reality" (1995: 38–39). The closed growth model procures processes of substitution that raises the specter of belief that human conceptions of reality can be unified and social progress obtained without the moral law. Dewey was a master of the substitute. He says, we must take man as we find him, on the basis of experience, without "'finding' Man made of stubble blown together on a quicksand" (2008: 214). For Dewey, the substitution of Nature for extra-Nature was key to progress:

> Naturalism rests upon the conviction that, negatively, humanism is a survival of the geocentric medieval philosophy, with its false conception of the place of the earth and of man in the universal scheme, and with its exaggerated teleological interpretation of things; positively, that man and his affairs are a subordinate part of nature, seen in their true place only when nature is made the chief and primary object of study. Incidentally, naturalism almost always has as one of its implications that language and literature are too artificial, factious, and as it were, ornamental, to be a sound basis for education. Science, it is urged, presents mankind with truths concerning realities of existence; language and literature with man's accidental and fanciful reactions to these realities. (1979: 214–215)

It is a line of thought, on the basis of an untamed faith, that all things can be rationally compatible. That with enough science, imagination, and mental work the institution or an individual organization, such as a school or a university, does not need to divide between independence (freedom) and a modern, technical system of production. However, in order to reach this belief there must be some miseducation that results in either a denial of scarcity, including information scarcities innate to production, or a narrower definition of the term "independence." In this line of thought there is often a refusal to see or understand that a trade-off is being made as institutional scale builds up pressure for universal information. But a buildup of universal information causes the depletion of particular information. Once scale becomes a factor, there is little ability to avoid the division of information. While these two types of information are necessary for the production of a complex good, and require some plausible symmetry, growth in the technical framework requires one type of information at the expense of the other. Social choice problems between the individual and the collective are thought inherently resolvable through discovery or creation of the right set of rules, a process of synthesis, when in reality the aggregation process over time does violence to individual and local production preferences (particular information). To reduce the moral law to a mere natural product is a step of this kind (Lewis 2001a: 80); it is designed to elevate the cost of moral knowledge that might interfere with technical progress.

Sidebar: The Principle of Reality Substitution

One of the fundamental questions in social theory has been that how is a highly differentiated society reintegrated (Mayhew 1997: 82).[7] This is similar to the social choice question: How are individual and collective preferences reconciled within the limits of human cooperation to do so (Arrow 1963; 1974)? On Lewis's account, excessive modern systematization and bureaucratic rationalization, through a smaller bureaucracy than Weber had predicted, places a regime of control in conflict with the character and traditional meaning of education, and in conflict with human development. Education, Lewis said, would evolve into processes of conditioning and enslavement where a class of innovators and conditioners would replace teachers (Lewis 2001a: 68).

Sidebar (Continued)

The trade-offs occurring across important centers of public culture and its institutions are seen in theories and practices that transform beliefs, attitudes, and modes of being and acting (essentially worldviews). New theories and practices consistent with expansion capture agenda and lower the price of information through instrumental and technical logic. As John Dewey (1997: 13) noted, "the new logic outlaws, flanks, dismisses—what you will—one type of problems and substitutes for it another type. Philosophy forswears inquiry after absolute origins and absolute finalities in order to explore specific values and the specific conditions that generate them." In other words, perennial questions (expensive) are replaced with progressive and pragmatic ones (inexpensive); the eternal becomes inferior to the temporal on principles of economic valuation.[8]

Lewis (2001a: 44) recognized by the mid-twentieth century that the lower was rebelling against the higher, and that were it to reach its logical end, this rebellion (i.e., "The rebellion of new ideologies against the Tao is a rebellion of the branches rebelling against the tree") would abolish that which gives human beings their humanity. While the idea of the lower displacing the higher does not occur in actual reality, it occurs in perceptions of reality through various instruments of unification nourished by economic growth and technique, including the powerful instrument propaganda. Not the old, coercive kind of propaganda found in totalitarian states, but a new kind working across all public and private sectors, which subtly requires no dictator[9] and whose incentives are unmistakably material in Nature. Most of all is its ally *libido dominandi* (social domination and political control) (53–81). Propaganda can take many forms but what is common to all forms is the social construction at odds with what it means to be human. Final causes (for the sake of which) are swapped for efficient, instrumental causes (by means of which).

A few of the trade-offs between the open and closed models illustrate the direction of thought. These substitutions range from philosophical to social to moral. Supernatural is substituted for the natural, necessary is traded off for the contingent, infinite for finite, eternal for temporal, true universal for false universal, spirit and matter for mere matter, one over the many exchanged for the many over the one, unity of multiplicity for unity of simplicity, the Tao for the void, final causes for efficient causes, noble for ignoble, incalculable for calculable, open universe for closed universe, subject for object, human for artifact, the I – Thou situation for the I – It condition, cognition for perception, conscience for instinct, free will for determinism, purpose for mere function, convictions for preferences, common sense for method and expertise, reason for rationality, correspondence for coherence, wisdom for technique, ground – consequent for cause – effect, science for scientism, qualitative for quantitative, deduction for induction, a priori for a posteriori, normative for descriptive, value (ought) for fact (is), dynamic for static, individual for collective, community for collectivity, social welfare for economic growth, quality for efficiency, spontaneity for planning, knowledge for information, education for schooling, and teachers for conditioners.

Modern sources of the self, to borrow Taylor's (1989) phrase, shifted to observable entities within Nature. The press of Nature's demands on social structures intensifies the function of roles and role-playing within institutions such that people's central identities are divisible to the roles themselves and not something higher or more significant. As MacIntyre (1999) has noted, over the last sixty years or so, human beings in the West have increasingly divided selves, a consequence of certain social structures and institutional forces. First questions such as the unity and plurality of the world (or universe) are subordinated to temporal and practical questions of pressing utility, and the task to claim or reclaim a genuine self clearly becomes far more difficult (Gunton 1993: 18–19). Technical-epistemic thought of the social and natural sciences had (and has today) no use for cosmology, theology, metaphysics, ethics, let alone the moral force from an invisible (but real) Tao. As Lewis remarks, giving up the claim to truth would mean, "No more theology, no more ontology, no more metaphysics.... But, then, no more Naturalism" (2001b: 33). Even so, to be outside the Tao is to be—in our present state of affairs—inside the framework of an assumed cause-and-effect uniformity of Nature—a set of framework commitments that, apart from certain question-begging problems, cannot allow transcendent Reason or theoretical and practical reason a foot in the door. There is of course a certain crude narcissism and truncation within this line of thought. Lewis

Sidebar (Continued)

was quick to ascribe to the technical impulse a methodological partiality for truncated thought that is due consideration.

[S]ince the sixteenth century, when Science was born, the minds of men have been increasingly turned outward, to know Nature and to master her. They have been increasingly engaged on those specialized inquiries for which truncated thought is the correct method. It is therefore not in the least astonishing that they should have forgotten the evidence for the Supernatural. The deeply ingrained habit of truncated thought—what we call the "scientific" habit of mind—was indeed certain to lead to Naturalism, unless this tendency were continually corrected from some other source. But no other source was at hand, for during the same period men of science were coming to be metaphysically and theologically uneducated. (65–66)

Why, if Lewis is correct, does the substitution principle seem to work? We must keep in view that these substitutions facilitate the expanding domain of Nature by reducing the price of information. In effect, the process is a progressive turnover in the institutional structure of society and culture, lowering the cost of society in one direction (secularism) and raising it another (divinity). It dislodges in the minds of many institutional actors an older ontological order—represented by the moral law—for a newer order: Nature and its "virtual," creative processes of lower selectivity. Lewis's (2007: 220) idea of "cosmic developmentalism" is not only a shift in models and worldviews but also a shift in the ground of power relations among and between people. It is the quest and liberation of that old temptation of man, *libido dominandi*, in which man himself is the final standard of all progressive things; it is the near-immutable attraction of the sweet poison of the false infinite (Meilaender 1998: 8–44).

At the lower level of reality that is Nature, education as an institution becomes a simple matter of conditioning the environment, delivering efficiencies of scale through technique, lowering the relative costs of schooling, and revealing whatever was useful at that particular moment. Lewis's words through Lord Feverstone are indicative of this view: "If Science is really

> given a free hand it can now take over the human race and recondition it: making man a really efficient animal."[10] This sentiment is remarkably similar to the belief held by John Dewey (1932).[11]

Sameness, as Lewis repeatedly observes, predominates among natural men. Sameness is achieved by dividing the measurable from the immeasurable in a manner that standardizes platforms of communication and the environment of exchange in one unmistakable direction. All information in alignment with general principles of the technical framework, supported by naturalism, receives preference across the institution; elites and managers regard information (preferences, convictions) and events (expressions of freedom) situated outside as a costly deviation. One can imagine what this process does to the pursuit of complex human goods like education (for an idea, see Aeschliman 1998; Smith 2003 and Scott 1998). Naturalism secures flat, uniform information platforms that promote expanded production and consumption opportunities as the philosophic ground for economic growth outside of the Tao.

It is an important artifact of Enlightenment thought that an instrumental view of human beings is necessary for social coordination, or at least the modeling of social coordination.[12] The naturalistic framework achieves a level of social unification on secular grounds, as Dewey (1960) said, within a common secular faith. Based upon unification, it requires the institution of education to wed rationality to Nature and its processes such that knowledge lying outside of the governing framework becomes irrational and an enemy of social progress (too divisive). Social progress in the naturalistic sense is thought coextensive with economic growth and, thus, requires a cost-lowering mechanism of information (Rodriguez, Loomis, and Weeres 2007: 15–30). Social friction is resolved when ontic uniformity exists in which nothing stands outside the domain of Nature. After a common commitment to such a general view proceeds among elites, the policy-making class, and the marginally educated, by effect of schooling, a perfectly applied psychology, and economic and social incentives (Olson 1971), new rationality and naturalism become powerful allies "to make our species whatever we wish it to be" (Lewis 2001a: 59). This is developmentalism at its core: improve and progress, not just adaptation.

The attenuation of morality is relatively easy to understand once we delimit the connection between the public sphere and the modern nation-state. The advance of material growth and its effects has extended very far across the public sphere in Western and, now, in Eastern societies (e.g., India, China, Malaysia). The public sphere began to emerge in Europe during the nineteenth century through coffee houses, literary and other societies, voluntary associations, and the growth of media (e.g., professional journalism). In the effort to order the State, parliaments and other agencies and institutions of representative government sought to manage the public sphere. Management of it required the creation of rules, norms, and customs throughout its institutions. As philosopher Ian Hacking suggests, "[T]he idea of human nature was displaced by a model of normal people with laws of dispersion." Hacking shows that the development of statistical laws increased the surveillance capacity of the State over the public sphere, and this information environment, we argue, informed the rule-making functions of nation-states, "developed for purposes of social control."[13]

We can think of a public sphere as composed of society, culture(s), and their institutions. A public sphere is set off against private domains of individuals and groups. It is "made up of private people gathered together as a public and articulating the needs of society with the state" (Habermas 1988: 176). For Jurgen Habermas, the success of the public sphere is justified on rational-critical discourse where everyone has the ability to participate equally, with the supreme communication skill being the power of argument. The problem for Habermas and others is that the belief does not match well to reality. The public sphere has little capacity to secure free, legitimate, and equal participation in cultural discourse across public spaces.

Rutherford (2000: 18) argues the important point that success of the public sphere depends upon

- extent of access (as close to universal as possible);
- degree of autonomy (citizens must be free of coercion);
- rejection of hierarchy (so that each might participate on an equal footing);
- rule of law (particularly the subordination of the State); and
- quality of participation (common commitment to the ways of logic).

However, "success" of this kind is thwarted by the logic of the expanding domain of Nature and the technical model. In the technical growth model each of these elements is redefined. Specifically, all five elements are resolved by the growth of scale, continually pulling the data toward uniformity and tying production to a standardized reference system, thus making a gradual, at times punctuated, unification out of diversity within the public sphere. The expanding SI, in its technical (lower-cost) orientation, labors to eliminate the core questions of morality, freedom, and knowledge by substituting questions of value with questions of material fact. Without antecedent questions regarding freedom, what we call or experience as individual or collective liberty, negative or positive freedom, will not be genuine freedom at all. It will merely be—since man in this framework is merely a natural object—variation inside the inexorable sequence of cause and effect.

The liberty that humanity is losing in an expanding institutional environment is a certain independence from the rigidly interlocked jurisdiction of the chain of spatiotemporal Nature. Lost is freedom of the human mind in the act of knowing from the huge nexus of nonrational causation (see Lewis's *Miracles*). Yet access to the public domain remains near total, due to the private sphere shrinking proportionally to a public–private convergence and the intrusion of rules on negative freedom. Citizens are free of coercion because there is no dictator forcing them to choose; citizens are making rational, voluntary choices in response to institutional incentives set before them. They are using their rationality to assent to the rules. The technical growth model requires only a small inner ring of mandarins and significantly less bureaucracy than one might imagine.

Our integrated theory of institutions, through the light of Lewis's multitiered argument, shows how a number of long-standing and recent questions in political philosophy are answerable. Since the secular State exists on the basis of normative presuppositions that it itself cannot guarantee, it must achieve authority on proceduralist (e.g., Kantian) understandings of the constitutional state. Essentially, this is an autonomous self-justification of political rule through systems of positive law, without antecedent conditions (entities or institutions), whose aim is to garner rational assent from the governed. Societal structures and political institutions achieve solidarity within the demos, not on the basis of moral law, but by shaping cognitive attitudes and normative expectations the State requires of its citizens. The model and attribute of growth in the technical version is how a society with a plurality of worldviews can achieve a normative stabilization with a smaller bureaucracy and yet a larger State. Interestingly, this is one pillar of Lewis's argument in the *Abolition of Man*. At some future age, when the reduction put forward by the technical model reaches zenith effect, a "master generation (itself an infinitesimal minority of the species) [will arise, whose] power will be exercised by a minority smaller still. Man's conquest of Nature, if the dreams of scientific planners are realized, means the rule of a few hundreds of men over billions upon billions of men" (2001a: 58).

Chapter 2

The Ontology of Education as an Institution

The Social Institution and the Model and Attribute of Growth

Human nature is the fundamental problem for institutions. The problem that has united political, economic, and cultural institutions since the dawn of the Industrial Revolution (1830s), if not long before, is the need to understand and control variation in human nature (choice, chance, randomness, freedom, reason). For the expanding social institution (SI), human nature is a center of cost and must be dealt with on the strictest terms by central planners. It possesses variation in expressions of individuality: thoughts, beliefs, values, attitudes, feelings, actions, choices and decisions, gifts and talents, the strivings for who we want to become and how we want to proceed in the complex dimensions of life. Early scholars of the social sciences came up with two practical solutions to control the cost of human nature: the invention of normalcy and, correspondingly, the idea of making up people by inventing categories (Hacking 1990: 1–6, 160–169). " 'Normal' bears the stamp of the nineteenth century and its conception of progress, just as 'human nature' is engraved with the hallmark of the Enlightenment. We no longer ask, in all seriousness, what is human nature? Instead we talk about normal people. We ask, is this behaviour normal?...We have almost forgotten how to take human nature seriously."

The solution to the control of variation is information entropy (division), the creation of a space of abstraction—a probability space where regularity and prediction supervene onto human nature in order to tame chance (Hacking 1990). Antecedent reductions, abstractions, and substitutions lodged against the individual and his social reality trims the information base and empowers the technical and statistical model to invent probability distributions thereby confining reality to absolute uniform experience—that is, to a closed, nonrational, cause-and-effect sequence of material relations (Lewis 2001b). This in essence is the idea of controlling cost under expansion. SIs under the technical growth framework was from the Industrial Revolution onward liberated from connections to human nature, morality, reason, logic, and truth. Social progress depended on it. These concepts became distortions, facsimiles, and rhetorical devices, kept around for expediency but separated from their full meaning in order to lower costs and prevent a divine foot (Reason) in the door. However, as a reductive ontological and epistemological framework, it carries no weight or meaning for explaining the whole field of reality, especially in education.

This chapter will place more scrutiny on the ontology of social institutions with special reference to education *as an institution*. What is of particular concern to us is the expanding domain of technically oriented institutions and how that growth alters the information base underwriting human performance. Analytic philosopher John Searle noted that SIs have a logical structure and consist of representations of those logical structures. Further, "[a]ny adequate theory about [institutional] phenomena must contain a logical analysis of their structures" (2005: 22). The inherent power of the institution of education, acting as a key determinant for the state of the polity and economy, has the capacity to do great good or the power to do great harm, and scholars simply must account for its structure.

It may be a piercing realization that not much in the way of deep ontological work has been done in education for at least the last several decades. Nearly all education theorists have made practice into a descent. To say that there is a separation taking place between theory and practice is a false dichotomy. The descent of practice is simply a reductive or inadequate theoretical movement. What people are calling practice is actually activity within a technical model of production whose theoretical basis does not do justice to the phenomena and doesn't save the appearances. This means it shuts out information that isn't organized around the direction in which the broader institution is heading. It causes distortion by application of the technical model beyond its narrow boundaries; it fails to recognize the subject-matter with which it deals; it distorts what we know of what people are and their relations; it does not correspond with the categories in terms of which we think and act. Practice, as a reductive theoretical movement, will continue to help sustain the current lower cost direction of educational attainment, where years of schooling is supposed to be (but is not) a reliable proxy for the actual possession of knowledge and skill (human capital). But the price we pay for the imposition of this framework is compression of the education good and an inability to see social reality as it is.

It turns out, then, that it is a timely and important tautological statement that ontology exists wherever there is existence, and to take a philosophical and economic account of that ontology is a necessary precondition for evaluating institutional performance, the institutional model, and its philosophy of education. In fact, every angle of being, knowing, and doing whatsoever presupposes, at the very least, a specific ontology called external realism, which makes the world around us intelligible. Understanding how the SI is supposed to accurately relate and legitimately contribute to human reality is necessary to determine its function and purpose. We cannot simply make up a function and purpose and call the result education. Where this has occurred, it has brought devastating consequences.

While we want to understand the concept "institution," the institution is not a mere concept. As we have said in Chapter 1, the SI is a reality: a powerful nospatial, nonphysical mediating social entity that possesses distinct existence and has attributes that impact and are impacted by human reality. Let us consider several of its attributes. Attributes are qualities inherent to things (Loux 1978).[1] The attributes of institutions are, for example, "properties" (e.g., rules, information, incentives, rights, customs), "kinds" (e.g., private, public, legal, divine, educational, political, cultural), and "relations" (e.g., regulating between individuals and collectives, economic growth and social welfare, planning and exchange, order and liberty, teaching and learning). Properties are the sort of characteristics a thing or entity has. They are either universal (had by more than one entity at the same time, in the same way) or particular in nature (had by one entity in a unique way). Kinds are classes of things. In the present case, classes of institutions can be identified by the kinds of goods they are designed or intended to produce. Relations are the formal and informal orderings and connections between things, such as across or between institutions (e.g., the law, media, and schools), between individuals and collectives, and so on.

Institutions cannot simply mean "the rules of the game" for what now might be obvious reasons. Though that meaning helps to constitute another important feature of institutions, SIs are more. While they are both enabling and constraining entities, the neo-institutional economic literature (e.g., North 1990) has for practical reasons tended to focus primarily on their constraining functions, hence the emphasis on rules. We argue that the rules that institutions have are properties, which is to say that rules on their own—as important as they are—are insufficient to what an SI is and the type of complex mediating, enabling, or regulating work that it performs. Properties are not stand-alone things—they are not the sum of the identity of an entity; they are had (possessed) by something more fundamental. Rules are not entities, they are properties of entities. Rules do not exist *ex nihilo*; they imply the existence of another thing (e.g., an intelligent agent or collective of agents.) Yet it is also important to recognize that rules, as properties, are a key part and help to order the information environment of the SI. They are economizers on human action, linking more efficiently with recurring patterns of human action. Rules set up and define offices, specify action, set forth penalties for their breach, signal rational dispositions and thought, etc. If the rules tilt in a certain direction, as in the technical growth model, this direction likewise tilts the overall information base of the institution. And this shift affects what people think, value, and believe. In the context of institutions, the term "rule," then, is to be understood roughly as "a socially transmitted and customary normative injunction or immanently normative disposition, that in circumstance X do Y" (Hodgson 2006: 3).

Even more than rules, philosophical presuppositions, and their effects, reveal the standing or direction of an institution. They will give indication of its basic orientation, that is, its information direction, moral health, and informational logic, and its reality and knowledge commitments. Inside the jurisdiction of the moral law, which attaches to all known human reality, a paradox surfaces that we must work to resolve. On the one hand, institutions are called on to observe normative first principles of Reason, a more humane composite form of man, and more diverse forms of knowledge and information than they do (or can) outside of the law. On the other hand, this normative constraint enables beliefs to match up with the truth conditions of things and states of affairs and attaches a cost to beliefs that do not, culling beliefs that are unwarranted or inaccurate; it makes certain that more and diverse information and knowledge is infused into institutional operations than would otherwise occur when operating outside of the law, where reductive tendencies lurk. Ergo, information-sets tend to be more robust and varying under the supreme and antecedent institution of the moral law.

It is widely thought that when SIs take their queue from the moral law the information base narrows significantly. Some of the more recent atheistic, naturalistic accounts of reality are more harangues than reason and sound argument. These works tend to project an infantile representation of the moral law and Reason as being products of narrow and ignorant information environments. In reality, Reason (God), as the author of the moral law, has a wider information base than does Nature. Lewis (2001b: 37–51) makes this point very clear in his book *Miracles*. In fact, Lewis argues that there is an asymmetrical relationship between Reason and Nature: Nature is contingent to Reason; Reason is not contingent to Nature. There are several good texts that have dealt with Lewis's *Miracles* argument and we will not rehearse those arguments here (e.g., see Reppert 2003). It is sufficient for our argument to stipulate that the domain of Reason has a wider information base than mere Nature, including all information that leads to knowledge, choices, and decisions, including anything within or about Nature.

Another way to project this truth is to say that institutions under the moral law tend to manage open information systems and models. This makes their reform or correction possible because there is an ability to appeal to an objective, mind-independent authority outside of the SI. C.S. Lewis (2001a: 43) says in the *Abolition*, but for that objective law (the Tao), by which claims are adjudicated, the SI is reducible to emotivism, subjectivism, and an ethics of vanity, utility, and power. "This thing which I have called for convenience the *Tao*, and which others may call natural law or traditional morality or the first principles of practical reason or the first platitudes, is not one among a series of possible systems of value. If it is rejected, all value is rejected. If any value is retained, it is retained." The conscious or unconscious act of splitting the two—splitting Nature from Reason—and pairing institutions to mere Nature entails the consequent effect of restricting the information base of institutions. This is one of the most important errors in social theory; there simply can be no legitimate moral reform without an objective criterion outside of man himself.

Outside of the Tao, institutions create constant isomorphic pressure around standardized forms of information, garnered from substitute sources. By switching one kind of information for another, nontechnical for technical, narrower and reductive forms of knowledge result. As a result, the expanding institution is not merely narrower in its information base, but is often at odds with what it means to be fully human. In other words, the SI loses capacity to regard man in one or more of the following four senses (White 1968):

1. man as he was intended,
2. man as he has become,

3. man as he may become, and
4. man as he has yet to be.

While growth under the moral law requires SIs attend to all four senses of man (1)–(4), the institution of education under a technical model of growth tends to emphasize (3) and (4), regards (2) only from a materialist, evolutionary perspective, and altogether ignores (1). This is information entropy; a breakdown and state of disorder in knowledge. There is, on the one hand, a post-Darwin pattern of refusing to acknowledge that man has (must have) an extra-natural purpose or *telos* (1), while, on the other hand, reducing the purpose of man and his development to survival (randomness) and improvement (nonrandomness). We will discuss this contradiction in more detail later in this chapter and in Chapter 3. For now, in its closed and technical form, growth places the institution at odds with historical and philosophical complexities of human reality. By distorting the information environment, e.g., dividing Nature from Reason, splitting the material from the immaterial, rationality from reason, the consequent information loss tends to distort human relations across the environments of education (e.g., across planning and exchange). A reduction of freedom is one product of imbalance in the distribution of information in the social system. The noumenal world of meaning, value, and liberty is traded off for the phenomenal world of the technical model. Lost from view are many of the past successes and time-tested mistakes and lessons of human culture; the values and wisdom of generations developed over centuries; the manner in which good education has always proceeded. Technique substitutes for moral and intellectual virtues. Suffice it here to observe that the path dependence that closed growth sets is "an inner and an outer conformity to the demands of a specific form of organizational life" (Rodriguez, Loomis, and Weeres 2007: 75). It is, quite simply, the philosophical and economic prelude to the abolition of man.

We also want to understand the phenomenon of growth in a deeper way, particularly in light of the vital role that education plays as a cultural institution in the generation of human, social, and moral capital. Growth is both a *model* of thought and a specific *attribute* of expanding institutions, setting a framework for operations. Institutional growth is generally regarded as the expansion of trade (Romer 1990, 1994), the expanding domain of the rules, an increase in the number of participants, and the scaling of market structures. Growth provides both a framework for social reality and a categorical direction to thought and action. Growth creates strong efficiency pressures, which lead to standardization and integration of rules, which in turn mark the direction of communication, production, and exchange. In the school setting, the demand for growth requires an institutional trade-off of information—local control (the particular) for centralization (the universal) (Tyack 1974). This process takes the form of the creation of laws, policy measures, property rights, and norms of conduct that progressively extend the category of the general interest and replace private rule with public rule, liberty for order, uncertainty and risk for renewed confidence. In terms of social choice, growth leads to coordinated preference changes in the information base of SIs; the collective base widens, the individual domain contracts.

Not only is growth a kind of thought that shapes the sustainability of the education enterprise, but its influence also demonstrates that there are tight linkages between education and economics. This point is not widely understood and we would do well to pause and bring to awareness a new understanding. There is an influential school of thought that argues against mixing education and economics, including the old institutional arguments made by Meyer and Rowan (1977) that sees education as a domain apart from markets, including arguments made from within the Public Choice literature.[2] Yet since the existing pathways of information determine what forms of production and interaction are possible, it is now implausible to hold the Public Choice and Meyer and Rowan positions.

In the 1970s many scholars distinguished between social and economic institutions. The argument was that education, unlike markets, grows not on the basis of economic efficiency, but through certainty built around loose coupling, myth and ceremony (Meyer and Rowan 1977). In its extreme version the theory argued that education would lose legitimacy if it focused on the quality of its output and the cost of producing it. That hypothesis, of course, is now being put to empirical test (basically nullified) by the standards and testing movements.

The impetus to separate education from economic institutions may have arisen from the well-established observation that schools and universities tend to minimize or disregard monetary costs: one is reminded here of Howard Bowen's remark that educational organizations spend virtually every dollar they take in. But there is another kind of cost operating that connects education with a broad range of other institutions, including markets, namely the informational cost of making rules to govern production. This cost varies with scale. Growth of institutions or organizations alters the informational base, regardless of whether they operate in the political, economic, or social sphere. The tendency is for scale to set education production on a low-cost information trajectory. Thus, contrary to Public Choice (e.g., Buchanan and Tullock 1962; Chubb and Moe 1990), the differences between public and private education are narrowing (and converging) rather than becoming more distinctive. This is so because both institutional frameworks are subject to similar information constraints; we must not forget that they are united by one overarching technical framework. If we are right, the information content within education necessarily affects the nature of the good being produced. A lower quality, quantity, and diversity of information tends to carry forth a suboptimal good (a poorer education for teachers and for students).

The ontological relation between the economy and education is firm and indisputable. The basis for a new analysis is that the working assumption that politics (public) and markets (private) are autonomous or separate domains is incorrect. Political, economic, and cultural institutions interact across all markets of information and help to determine their efficiency and the range of choice in production and exchange. Educational theorists do well, as a gesture to institutional reality, to assent to this truth in their models.

Now there are two versions of growth under review in this book. The open, transcendent model of growth regards as important boundaries created by the moral law, as represented by C.S. Lewis's Tao (2001a). Here, the nature and function of SIs emphasizes community: it seeks optimal (or as close to optimal as possible) information conditions in the complex development and flourishing of human beings, it accounts for the moral law, it preserves agent sensitivity, it seeks proper function in ends and their means, it has individual learning organizations reaching best possible performance in the distribution of knowledge and skills, and it is a mechanism to achieve correct (just) ends. We will have more to say about the open model in Chapter 5.

Opposite is the closed, non-transcendent model of growth. It seeks a different kind of information base for the production of human, social, and moral capital. It does not account for the moral law, it emphasizes collectivity, it is generally agent insensitive, it divests the idea of "proper" from "function" in the pursuit of means to ends, its learning organizations emphasize educational attainment more than the actual possession of knowledge and skills, and its ends are often insufficient (ontologically) to phenomena in view. There is no hard and fast, no measurable criterion to determine whether a social institution is at any given moment using an open or closed model. We are talking about a dynamic, complex state of affairs. Epistemic humility requires us to limit the reach of our analysis, at this point, and say minimally that there is at time T a general direction of a given social institution SI that can be understood in terms of moving toward or away from an optimal state of affairs (i.e., an open model).

The contrast between these two growth models bears important implications for the objectivity and subjectivity of reality in education. Unlike all previous models of thought, the closed or technical model of growth acts as unifier and economizer of many models and does so as it conceals its own internal architecture, the essential characteristics of its structure, the logic by which its interrelated parts function as an orderly whole. It conceals the means and ends of how it makes abstractions against the individual, as well as obscures (temporarily) the trade-offs, implications, and costs of those abstractions. What it provides to humanity in terms of access to material goods is more obvious to sight than what it takes away from man in terms of his soul, which requires the insight of reason. Lewis (2001a: 74–75) writes in the *Abolition*:

> The true significance of what is going on has been concealed by the use of the abstraction Man. Not that the word Man is necessarily a pure abstraction... [T]he moment we step outside and regard the Tao as a mere subjective product, this possibility has disappeared. What is now common to all men is a mere abstract universal, an H.C.F. [highest common factor], and Man's conquest of himself means simply the rule of the Conditioners over the conditioned human material, the world of posthumanity which, some knowingly and some unknowingly, nearly all men in all nations are at present labouring to produce.

We do well to consider the hidden assumptions and several of the effects of the closed growth model as a worldview. We will then turn and discuss growth as an attribute of the institution. Finally, we will take an initial look at the sustainability of education.

CLOSED GROWTH AS A MODEL OF THOUGHT

The temporal and spatial expanding domain of Nature (Lewis 2001a: 71) is today the environment under which the technical (closed) growth model comes about. Under the expanding domain of Nature, naturalistic abstractions, reductions, and substitutions have been worked out, a priori, as to what counts as reality and what constitutes the human and his domain. In this model, what counts are the material realm and the physical properties of entities; the phenomenal is consistently put before noumenal and numinal.

The philosophy of naturalism[3] has been around for a long time. But not really until the seventeenth and eighteenth centuries, when naturalism bonded to practical production solutions in the economy, did materialist reductions deploy widely across SIs. In the seventeenth and eighteenth centuries, market forces—land, labor, and capital—formally appeared and were predicated on reductions facilitated by naturalism, that is, its scientific spirit and epistemological method. Heilbroner (1999: 27) notes that "[l]and, labor and capital as 'agents' of production, as impersonal, dehumanized economic entities, are as much modern inventions as the calculus. Indeed, they are not much older." Over time, the worldview of naturalism became coterminous with society's progress (Taylor 2007), state interests, and the growth solution. The initial abstractions necessary for economic markets were also necessary for the technical press applied to the growth of nearly every market, and factor prices and proportions adjusted accordingly.

In *The Discarded Image*, Lewis (1964/2007: 220) refers to the shift from medieval to modern models of thought as "cosmic developmentalism," the general evolutionary belief and presupposition that since life evolves from lower to higher (imperfect to perfect), models of thought do too. This is not true, says Lewis.[4] Lewis argues that life evolves from perfect to imperfect and potentially back to perfect again. The change of models does not so much involve the volume of new facts provided by Nature, as it does "when changes in the human mind produce a sufficient disrelish of the old Model and a sufficient hankering for some new one" (p. 221). So far, cosmic developmentalism has proven too powerful an idea to overthrow. Man is the measure of all things; therefore let man measure all things relative to himself. Cosmic developmentalism lowered the price of information on naturalism, and raised information costs against ethical monotheism.

Lewis (1995: 82–93) writes that developmentalism as a Great Myth has unified popular imagination about man. The myth of developmentalism arose prior to 1859 in the poetry of Keats and the music of Wagner. "In making [the myth], imagination runs ahead of scientific evidence" (p. 84). And when the evidence is accounted for, the Great Myth is more likely to be believed not out of reason, empirical standing, or statistical supposition but on ideological ground: it is "the dogma of an amateur metaphysician who finds 'special creation' incredible" (p. 85). The Myth sheds the biological (scientific) hypothesis for the "facts" of developmentalism, that is, that evolution (adaptation) is not about changes but improvements. Progress becomes the rule: things over time everywhere are getting better. Lewis (1995: 86) writes:

[F]or the scientist Evolution is a purely biological theorem. It takes over organic life on this planet as a going concern and tries to explain certain changes within that field. It makes no cosmic statements, no metaphysical statements, no eschatological statements.... But the Myth knows none of these reticences. Having first turned what was a theory of change into a theory of improvement, it then makes this a *cosmic* theory. Not merely terrestrial organisms but *everything* is moving "upwards and onwards." Reason has "evolved" out of instinct, virtue out of complexes, poetry out of erotic howls and grunts, civilization out of savagery, the organic out of inorganic, the solar system out of some sidereal soup or traffic block. And conversely, reason, virtue, art and civilization as we now know them are only the crude or embryonic beginnings of far better things—perhaps Deity itself—in the remote future. For in the Myth, "Evolution" (as the Myth understands it) is the formula of *all* existence. To exist means to be moving from the status of "almost zero" to the status of "almost infinity." To those brought up on the Myth nothing seems more normal, more natural, more plausible, than that chaos should turn into order, death into life, ignorance into knowledge. And with this we reach the full-blown Myth. It is one of the most moving and satisfying world dramas which have ever been imagined.

Man thrives within this Myth for what might be obvious reasons:

He learns to master Nature. Science arises and dissipates the superstitions of his infancy. More and more he becomes the controller of his own fate. Passing hastily over the historical period (in it the upward and onward movement gets in places a little indistinct, but it is a mere nothing by the time-scale we are using) we follow our hero on into the future. See him in the last act, though not the last scene, of this great mystery. A race of demi-gods now rule the planet.... Eugenics have made certain that only demi-gods will now be born: psycho-analysis that none of them shall lose or smirch his divinity: economics that they shall have to hand all that demi-gods require. Man has ascended his throne. Man has become God. All is a blaze of glory. (Lewis 1995: 87–88)

Lewis says there are three reasons why the Myth works. Analyzing these in terms of institutional cost, we believe that Lewis has effectively brought to light the inherently economic reasons for its triumph. First, the Myth demonstrates through the evolutionary size and efficiency of technology that continuous improvement is a reality (p. 90). Indeed, the education field in the United States weds the idea of continuous improvement to reform, while rarely pegging the institution to its fundamental aims. It is harder to hit a moving target, and its managers have every incentive to keep the target moving. Second, change occurs where everything was once something else and everything going forward becomes something else, with latter stages of "becoming" entailing improvement in that thing (p. 91). The Myth sheds old reliance to tradition; the new way is the improved way (p. 92). The Myth enhances technical growth: new models of technology are better and an improvement (they make us believe we have conquered scarcity);

hence, nothing old ought to last (p. 92). And third, the Myth provides political theory with progressive cache: if we can just get the rules right, we can solve the problem of social choice (pp. 92–93).

According to cosmic developmentalism, the substance and order of Reason's authoritative rules, its virtues and ideal modes of being, constrained or disallowed instrumental (manipulable, mutable) views of man and his development. This interfered with human progress. In economic terms, the older order became too costly, too much of an impediment to material growth under the domain of Nature. Nature, growth, and science need reprieve from the moral law. These ideas, for example, are palpable even in Dewey's Depression-era (1930s) writings, where applied science and an instrumental view of things were thought to resolve problems of resource scarcity. Though nuanced in its truth-seeking and truth-revealing activities, the older order represented by the Tao did not allow deviations on clear cases and controversies and no wresting of its power could be had by men. New methods of applied sciences and advanced technical knowledge successfully emptied the world of its qualitative properties and substances—colors, sounds, tastes, souls, minds, feelings, and selves—and condensed and reclassified them as mere products of Nature and experience, mere sensations and the like, in no way real in themselves (Lewis 1986: 81–86). The substitution thus allows a reunification of reality without obvious contingency to a supernatural actor. Colin Gunton (1993: 31) puts the substitution in the following terms: "When God is displaced as the focus of the unity of things, the function he performs does not disappear, but it is exercised by some other source of unity—some other universal. The universal is false because it does not encompass the realities of human relations and of our placing in the world, and so it operates deceptively or oppressively."

Lewis thought that worldview substitution is a web of both intentional and unintentional forces. Free will remains free and is responsible to the moral law even when increasingly powerful agent-insensitive social forces trespass on moral agency. He correctly suggests that there are truer ways of eliciting better, qualitatively more humane models of thought. But these, he suggests, ultimately necessitate the unification of reason and faith. "Reason may win truths; without Faith she will retain them just so long as Satan pleases" (1995: 43). Lewis's ethical model is a tripartite equilibrium strategy derived from his *Mere Christianity* work. The idea is that a morally competent person requires a just relation with himself, with others, and with the divine. Insofar as the social institution assists in the process and administration of justice, the social welfare improves.

Of elemental importance is the type of structure and the kind of theory of reality social theorists choose to build their models. Decisions like these will "determine how much of that total truth will appear and what pattern it will suggest" (Lewis 2007: 223). For his part John Dewey (1997: 8) noted that, "prior to Darwin, the impact of the new scientific method upon life, mind, and politics, had been arrested" by idealism and moral interests. Dewey's argument is roughly that the first principles of reason (for Dewey, it was the first principles of religious faith) interfered with (restricted) technical growth. After Darwin, naturalism took traction as a persuasive, growth-generating social and institutional background model. Darwin's thought had contributed the missing mechanism and sequencing of adaptive selection. Once married to the philosophical view of developmentalism—the idea that everything everywhere is improving—naturalism was endowed with creative properties that reconstituted the purposes of SIs.

If SIs can be said to have a secular purpose, naturalists center it around (1) the background facts of human survival, (2) the adaptive traits and behavior of ancestors, (3) evolution as cause and effect, and (4) natural selection as a theory. Consequently, the SI can be seen as a utility maximizer, and economizer of information, and an instrument promoting survival (for some, anyway). This view is a problem for methodological naturalism, says Lewis (1995: 82–93), because the *content* of evolution as a scientific hypothesis is much different from evolution as popular myth. Inasmuch as evolution as myth superseded evolution as a scientific hypothesis, Lewis (2001a: 70–71) argues that the information trade-offs involved turned costly for scientific objects:

> It is not the greatest of modern scientists who feel most sure that the object, stripped of its qualitative properties and reduced to mere quantity, is wholly real. Little scientists, and little unscientific followers of science, may think so. The great minds know very well that the object, so treated, is an artificial abstraction, that something of its reality has been lost.

The overarching worldview substitution—a closed worldview (naturalism and developmentalism) for an open one (extra-naturalism)—is germane for showing how to think about models and frameworks of institutions on the basis of cost. Information, or, more precisely, knowledge, is the lubricant for the development and exchange of ideas across cultures. Its institutions, and the extent to which abstractions, reductions, and substitutions take place, foster an efficient cost–benefit trade-off. One social reality is chosen for another; one set of conditions is discounted, another counted; one agenda wins, another loses. For the closed growth model, the criterion inducing the trade-off is that thing's (whatever it may be) social utility based on least cost. However, there is another cost not counted in the closed model's calculation: the underdevelopment of the individual, her development, flourishing, and freedom.

It is not terribly difficult to understand why this is the case. Control is the motive. The closed growth model erects standardized information (e.g., rules, curricula), common metrics (e.g., measures and probability distributions), and uniform methods of production (e.g., procedures, so-called best practices), and applies these throughout the trading environment. As James Scott (1998: 183) notes, the production of uniformity in a field is moved along by the activities of counting, manipulating, measuring, and assessing. There are obvious cost advantages to higher decision-making units utilizing specifiable or legible information. In education, uniform assessment procedures are like that. So are uniform curricular preferences. They help to flatten the information platform that allows for the nodes of decision making to centralize. In nearly any large-scale urban school district in the United States it is not uncommon for standardized curricula to be delivered in such a way as to specify what should be covered in every grade-level classroom at every minute of any given day. The cost savings are dramatic when teachers and their students come to be seen as interchangeable units of production. The same holds in higher education with ever wider use of adjunct (contingent) faculty.

Perhaps the most perceptible example of the technical direction of education is within the contemporary ethos of educational assessment. Like their European and Asian counterparts, American schools today operate within a testing culture. Under federal, state, and accrediting agency requirements, authorities test school students annually for their knowledge of curricula and ability to demonstrate certain skills.[5] Testing occurs before students ascend to the next level of educational attainment.[6] Testing—specifically, testing that has been standardized (made uniform)—largely defines educational assessment today. While no one of a serious mind is per se against assessment in education, many people are becoming increasingly concerned that educational assessment has come to mean norm-referenced, standardized testing; testing that becomes "high stakes" in that it is near the *sole* criterion for defining successful education. When the assessment cart is put before the educational horse, causing the horse to push the cart instead of pulling it, students, teachers, principals, and superintendents learn to depend for their professional success on the utility value of these test scores. Even real estate values of local communities and the investment climate of business and commerce of entire regions and states are affected by aggregate student test scores (e.g., they help to signal a schooled labor force). However, the human problem draws our concern here.

> **Sidebar: The Hegemony of the Categories—The Behavioral Objectives Model**
>
> The means of education, in the technical growth model, requires methods, tools, and techniques. As to methods, John Dewey and others provided a pragmatic, technical epistemology that had as its center a social science methodology that could alter (it was believed) the direction of human nature.[7] Dewey sought to replace old certainties rooted within religion with new certainties centered within science, including social science. As for tools, Edward Thorndike and others supplied methods of controlled experimentation and quantitative measurements.[8] I.Q. testing, curricular tracking, and the Scholastic Aptitude Test-exam, which became tightly organized in high schools in the 1950s with the ascension of the comprehensive high school, gave force and direction toward a narrow curricular essentialism, which with time, and help from the U.S. Supreme Court, divorced values from facts. In terms of techniques, Ralph Tyler, a professor of social science at the University of Chicago, and his followers created specific procedures that remain with us today. These techniques and procedures operate on the principles of behaviorism: observable changes in students following the application of precisely applied stimuli. Getting the horse to the trough to drink, whether for his own good or not, requires merely the right technical stimuli reinforced over time. The only trouble is: we are not discussing horses.
>
> The behavioral objectives model may best represent the marriage between behaviorism and new essentialism. The model originated with and was advanced by four primary intellectual works: Ralph Tyler's (1949), *Basic Principles of Curriculum and Instruction*; Benjamin Bloom's (1956), *The Taxonomy of Educational Objectives, Handbook I: The Cognitive Domain*; David Krathwohl et al.'s (1956), *The Taxonomy of Educational Objectives, Handbook II: The Affective Domain*; and James Popham's (1965), *The New Teacher: The Teacher-Empiricist*.
>
> The behavioral objectives model structured learning in a highly technical sense, one that would reduce education and its

Sidebar (Continued)

assessment to an ends-means formula of planning and teaching in order to deliver efficiencies of scale (mass education). It begins with a planning stage by having the teacher identify very specific goals or objectives defined by empirically demonstrable changes in their students. These behavioral goals or objectives necessarily constrain the content of the curriculum and the methods of the instruction. This is so because curriculum and instruction must have as their focus the physically temporal and immediate, whose goals and objectives according to the model must be verified or confirmed within the time frame of the course (usually weeks or months).

Any goals or objectives of either curriculum or instruction that do not align with temporality or immediacy of what the model demands usually cannot reach agenda (certainly not as first-order goods) due to the higher cost and (now) irrelevance of their longitudinal evaluation. The educational payoff under the model must occur by the end of the course period or else administrators will likely deem the course a failure. Contemporary "accountability" rationales and regimes in schools and higher education are affixed to the standards of this model. Teachers, professors, and administrators are all evaluated against this criterion. The table below illustrates the procedures.

Behavior Objectives Model

Stage-1	Stage-2	Stage-3	Stage-4
Objectives (prespecify desired observable changes in student's affective, cognitive, action)	Planning for Instruction (basis of organizational efficiencies)	Instruction (technical proficiency)	Assessment (observable changes)
Objectives-1,2,3 (precise, explicit)	Methods, Activities, Materials (formulaic: may be standardized)	Lessons-1,2,3 (technical efficiency)	Assessments-1,2,3 (observable by anyone)

The model defines educational success relative to the actual achievement of a teacher's initial set of objectives. Achievement of these objectives is determined by techniques and measures of assessment, principles of verification such that a detached observer can "see" evidence that the objectives had been met. The model's simplicity of formula is highly efficient and rational; it locates responsibility for accountability on the teacher and the plan. In a larger sense, it possesses great technical utility for creating an algorithm for mass education. The teacher can use it for formative assessment (e.g., the improvement of teaching methods) and as a summative assessment (e.g., the testing of the objectives). The formula relies on the unsupported objective claim that assessment should be observable by anyone, including those who have no connection with the actual learning situation in question. In short, it is a work of technical genius.[9]

The behavioral objectives model relies on *poiesis*, or the activity of merely producing outcomes, and usually not outcomes arrived at by participants themselves, but by an impersonal bureaucracy. It emphasizes measurable and assessable (empirically demonstrable) outcomes and discounts outputs that are not observable or measurable, or that manifest over the long term (e.g., a well-lived life). In this sense, the model is formulaic and homogeneous, and suggests that its adherents assume an attitude of clinical detachment and methodological noncontingency (objectivity) in order to prespecify educational outcomes. It appears to confuse education as a simple good, say the production of a widget in a factory, with a complex good, as for example the ethical bringing about of an educated human being. The model marries *poiesis* to *techne*, which only requires technical procedure and does not require the intangibles of good human teaching known in Western and Eastern traditions of education for centuries.

All of this is in contrast to the educator's approach using *praxis*, the social realization of excellences that an educator "has come to appreciate in his community as constitutive of a worthwhile way of life."[10] In the educator's life, it is the realization of one's professional self and a student's development in a caring, relational learning community committed to the pursuit of truth, moral understanding, and wisdom, in addition to questions of vocation and gifting, that bring value. *Praxis* occurs in a complex, contingent, heterogeneous, nonpredictable, nonformulaic type of environment, which requires practical knowledge (*phronesis*). Examples of a professional learning environment

> **Sidebar (Continued)**
>
> that values *praxis* look like the finer International Baccalaureate or Classical Education programs, or particular public schools where teachers are regarded in both content and pedagogy as masters and tutors within their classrooms and, therefore, are legitimately responsible and accountable for the learning environment. The institutional implications of a confusion between these two approaches to curriculum and instruction (*poiesis* v. *praxis*) can lead to a profound underdevelopment of human beings, as well as rising levels of social inequality.[11] The systematic and impersonal rules of *techne* facilitate production certainties that may be readily assembled but it does so while losing information vital to the nature and perception of the education good.

The complex dynamics of human learning occurring within a classroom are often traded off for the proxy of the test score and assessment procedure all driven by the process of controlling costs for scarce educational resources. Consequently, the score defines educational success and access to higher levels of educational attainment. However, this trade-off, where it occurs, fails to recognize that the good, which educational organizations do, is *not* reducible to or accounted for in the Adequate Yearly Progress (AYP) score required by the federal No Child Left Behind Act (2002). As the "nation's report card" since 1969, the National Assessment of Educational Progress (NAEP) likewise aggregates test scores in core literacy areas in order to determine levels of student achievement, instructional experiences, and school climate, which typically follow knowledge and skills frameworks set by the National Assessment Governing Board (NAGB).[12]

Meanwhile, the many federal and state processes of planning and statistical aggregation largely ignore the diversity of individual talents, skills, capacities, and desires among schoolchildren and college students. Assessment and its outcomes (test scores) come to influence and characterize the curricula and succeed in simplifying the teacher–student exchange. Teaching to the test becomes standard practice. For example, school districts today will opt to give their students snippets of literature in anthologies instead of requiring students to read whole books written by important authors in order to teach the valuable test-taking skill of time-sensitive comprehension and text analysis.

This cause-and-effect relationship is known as the "law of the instrument" where the test (instrument) is the driver, not the product of human exchange in the learning process. The institution substitutes new ends with measurable utility (lower cost) for traditional ends of education, such as intellectual virtues, wisdom and moral understanding (higher cost).

Lewis (2001a: 67) commented that the conditioning processes by decision-making units rests on more than chance and variation. It rests on uniform information of a specific kind, the kind that tends to shift decision-making control from the individual to the many, as regulated by a few elites (pp. 53–60). Since control over decision making is power, and the span of control of hierarchical units depends on assorted simplifications of reality, including the composite nature of man and the range of his knowledge, authority becomes impersonal in proportion to the division of information.[13] Narrow the range of information available to social choice and fewer people get to be the real decision makers; the inner ring becomes the power base of the SI (Lewis 2001c: 141–157). Further, elites insulate themselves by using impersonal authority (the rules) to socialize risk and by expanding the scope of their decision making; thus hierarchy becomes an economizer on costly knowledge and a protector of entrenched interests.

What is particularly interesting about the technical direction is that bureaucracy shrinks proportionally to the centralization of rules. This is different from how we traditionally think of bureaucracy and places into question the model of Max Weber who believed that liberty in modern societies requires the bureaucratization of the SI. In contrast, Lewis (2001a: 53–81) well knew the Platonic caution, that democracy in the old sense is often threatened internally by oligarchs, but somehow realized that central control, planning, technique, uniform rules, etc., would lessen the need for vast bureaucracies. Universal rules and technique would shift the fulcrum of power from the demos to a "few hundreds of men over billions upon billions of men" (Lewis 2001a: 58). And in the breakdown of bureaucracies the State has to get stronger (gain more decision-making power) because of the need for a stable set of rule systems that they operate under, thus defining the present and future role of the State more clearly.

The abstractions, reductions, and substitutions that thrust and parry against human reality move the economizing process along on principles of efficiency. Efficiency is a complementarity between market expansion and universal information. As growth overvalues universal information, the centripetal impulse feeds the decision-making loop with lower-cost information as decisions escalate increasingly away from a subordinate decision-making unit (e.g., an individual, a family, a school, or a community) to one nested upward within the hierarchy (e.g., a state, national, or international committee of education). As the individual human participant becomes mere noise or variation, production results are reducible "to a few key indicators which are to be institutionally rewarded or penalized" (Sowell 1980: 16). In education this looks like a universal category of production, e.g., an aggregate test score, the I.Q., or an aptitude test. Those key indicators can never, of course, tell the whole story because considerable amounts and kinds of information and knowledge are excluded from production and evaluation, including the particular information embedded in individual human being as well as local forms of culture. And when particular (individual, local) information is depleted from the complex calculus of production, an ensuing social harm is more likely to occur where the good at issue is complex (Scott 1998).[14] The harm lies in the counterfactual opportunities foregone to individuals and society due to a narrowed opportunity set for the pursuit of knowledge, skills, experiences, and the creation of ideas (Cuban 2004). These represent the possible worlds that might have been obtained under a different stock of knowledge and information, under a different set of social conditions, under a different institutional structure.

In another of his brilliant examples, C.S. Lewis illustrated the situation with which we are confronted today: the rapid underdevelopment, under-maximization of human beings by an increasingly uniform educational system indifferent to a student's particular talents and needs. Writing of the Tousle-Headed Poet, a character in *The Great Divorce*, Lewis (1973: 7) pointed out the problem:

> He appeared to be a singularly ill-used man. His parents had never appreciated him and none of the five schools at which he had been educated seemed to have made any provision for a talent and temperament such as his. To make matters worse he had been exactly the sort of boy in whose case the examination system works out with maximum unfairness and absurdity. It was not until he reached the university that he began to recognize that these injustices did not come by chance but were the inevitable results of our economic system.

A key intellectual challenge for the educational theorist or social philosopher is to consider if what expansion prevents from being produced may be more important to society than what it actually produces. There is no limitation that we know of to the volume of information that can go into a production process. However, production processes are limited by the kinds of information that can be effectively utilized in production. When illiberal institutional conditions constrain greater ranges of knowledge and information, undervaluing particular information, actors tend to define decision making on terms of positive assent to the prevailing institutional order; freedom becomes submission to collective aspirations. The group or the collective becomes the true object of social reality, and it alone is real. This can be seen clearly in collectivist societies. Rationality is defined narrowly as the act of projecting or asserting ourselves together in some unified way, in a collective orientation toward the higher principles of progress and power.

We can now understand that cosmic developmentalism, as a worldview, serves as an ideological predicate for closed, technical growth. It entails a rational commitment to perpetual progress and virtual reality without mistakes, without costs. And since educational systems around the world are moving toward a condition of fewer qualitative distinctions, that is, social environments with significantly less diversity and variation, this serves as strong empirical evidence that the closed growth model is (or is becoming) the leading production model around the world. All of which occurs in the dominating context of Nature and the theory of naturalism. In reducing reality to physics, reducing man to physical properties, reducing knowledge to the technocratic attitude of scientism, reducing ethics to emotivism or mere subjective expressions of psychological states, and reducing social institutions such as education to less expensive forms of reality, a social harm is done. The harm lies in the displacement of entire fields of knowledge (e.g., theology, philosophy) from social choice, from which theoretical reason accesses final causes and comprehensive forms of truth.

Perhaps the burliest exemplification of the displacement comes from John Dewey's (1920) *Reconstruction in Philosophy*, who, as the archetypal cosmic developmentalist, directly attacked old philosophical commitments in order to replace them with new ones centered in science:

> As for philosophy, its profession of operating on the basis of the eternal and the immutable is what commits it to a function and a subject matter which, more than anything else, are the source of the growing popular disesteem and distrust of its [*sic*] pretentions; for it operates under cover of what is now repudiated in science [...] To the vested interests, maintenance of belief in the transcendence of space and time, and hence the derogation of what is "merely" human, is an indispensable prerequisite of their retention of an authority which in practice is translated into power to regulate human affairs throughout—from top to bottom. (p. 13)

In contrast, Lewis (2001a: 67) claims that at some late stage in the process of the technical model (the one that Dewey wanted), during the increasingly mechanical processes of reality, a class of conditioners reduces learning to the external control of physical impulse. In a world where only physical properties and their relations exist (naturalism), there is literally no place for truth and knowledge as such, no cardinal aim of learning, no way to escape from conditioning. Such a world cannot accommodate nor account for any claims, ideas, or dispositions about representations of internal or external states (Willard 2000b; Lewis 2001b).

One might suppose that the philosophical contradictions, such as the logical inconsistencies entailed by naturalism and the technical model, would worry and alter the mental framework of key participants within the institution of education; that reason might come to rescue us from living lives of inconsistency. It does not worry the pivotal players because (1) as Conditioners their mental models have already been altered and (2) the "'trousered ape' and the 'urban blockhead' may be precisely the kind of man they really wish to produce" (Lewis 2001a: 11). Ideology may come into play, but the better answer may be that the model and attribute of growth conceals the trade-offs well enough to heighten its many concrete benefits (e.g., increased trade, services, material goods, educational attainment), at the same time keeping human costs opaque (e.g., the loss of individual freedom, the diminution of knowledge and skills). Growth's chameleon-like character creates a sense of human progress by denying to other key attributes of institutions a place for discussion, for example, values, scarcity, risk, time, and the price factors of information. Material gains cover up any suspicion of immaterial cost (e.g., information loss), people making unconscious trade-offs for material success, that is, for the seeming prosperity of Faustus's "gold and guns and girls" (Lewis 2001a: 77). Because trade expands on the confidence of a utility payoff to investment, social costs must be concealed because too much uncertainty tends to inhibit expansion; the prospect of risk can be growth inhibiting and must be attenuated.

An economy growing through time will normally experience a general rise in the cost difference of information. In the present case, the overarching mechanism that helps to remove costly dissent among the masses is naturalism, the underlying basis of cosmic developmentalism. As we have seen, naturalism provides fertile ground for the technical model of growth. It helps expanding institutions to achieve the necessary architecture to surmount modern economic challenges, such as problems of organization and resource scarcities, without interference from ghosts in the human machinery. Debates in biotechnology also show how a reductive view of human persons can resolve traditional ethical dilemmas about scientific experimentation (Elshtain 2008: 85–95). Sterilization, cloning, organ harvesting, destroying embryos for stem cells, and other medical procedures are justified on the cost–benefit premises of progress. When naturalism links to the economic philosophy of developmentalism, the progressive idea that humanity advances on the constant and evolutionary liberation of Nature's material growth, it facilitates a fall in the price of information, perhaps most of all artificially separating fact ("is") from value ("ought").[15]

Ethics as traditionally understood has no place in the activity of technical growth. Sentiment is equated with emotion, not pegged to the first principles of theoretical and practical reason. The technical institution proceeds "to reduce reality to the wishes of men," an observer-dependent situation in which soul is traded off for manipulative power in *anima*, in what Lewis calls the "magician's bargain" (Lewis 2001a: 71, 77). However, the trade-off of soul for power does not liberate, as developmentalism holds. If we are to believe Lewis, and there is compelling reason to do so, the trade-off tends to enslave the human being, not to liberate him (p. 72). The "magician's bargain" shifts the basis of liberty from the individual to the collective (the expanding institution). Over time, individual participants must forego increasing categories of their decision making in order to participate in the collective direction. To "get along," individual human beings give up their own preferences and convictions and receive security and order in return. The institutional participant may initially believe that this is the least cost direction. Reality suggests otherwise. The magician's bargain or trade-off delivers freedom into the rigid, liberty-limiting grip of spatiotemporal Nature. This is an irredeemable cost to both the individual and to society.

The main point of our argument, about which we have tried to be explicit, is that various abstractions, reductions, and substitutions do in fact achieve economic growth, such as more trade and larger market structures. But economic growth occurs without an accompanying progress in the social welfare. In fact, costs rise against the social welfare, against political systems, against the individual, against educational freedom, against local communities where the community is absorbed into mass society (Callahan 1962; Tyack 1974). Proper understanding of the cost of institutions in the social order is assisted not by distinguishing markets from politics, but by distinguishing economic performance from social welfare.

We can also show the problem by asking two simple questions related to freedom. Does freedom inhibit growth? People will agree that it can. But turn the question around and people will instinctively disagree that growth inhibits freedom. Economic growth is thought to unleash freedom. Yet the coordinating and economizing authority of the closed growth model causes the space of individual choice to contract, not expand, perhaps not in real terms but on the basis of a perception of a collapsed zone of decision making, on the basis of an institution-dependent social construction. It is like a return to Plato's Cave, an environment where the perception of reality is constrained and yet it seemingly reduces one's risk (thus appearing to deliver more certainty). Many people prefer the Cave to reality. The trade-off for closed growth (less material risk), then, is the confinement, not the enabling, of individual or local freedom. But it is more than that.

By shaping public liberty, the model of growth sets limits on what qualifies as acceptable (rational) expressions of freedom. The liberty that humanity is losing is a certain independence from the rigidly interlocked jurisdiction of spatiotemporal Nature. Lost in the human mind is the freedom for acts of believing and knowing out of the huge nexus of nonrational causation. This loss indicates a socially constructed perception of a restricted zone of choice (not a real one, but an artificial one). A restricted zone of choice then entails a perceived loss of freedom in the range of actions an individual can take. For example, hidden is the full range of desire-independent reasons to act and believe in ways that promote justice. Substituted are the desire-dependent incentives to act consistent with the expanding social institution. This is a path-dependent behavior that is an effect of standardization.

To avoid a vicious case of determinism in which there is no way out, that is, no counter options outside a kind of slavery, our argument insists that even within this pattern, there is no absolute diminution of moral responsibility to act as one should: the "ought" originating from Lewis's moral law continues to imply "can." No one in institutional reality is off Reality's hook; the moral law is what it is and requires what it requires in spite of expanding technical SIs seeking to conceal it. We agree with MacIntyre (1999) that moral responsibility in the social sphere holds where (1) the acts of moral agents are intentional; (2) the incidental aspects of those actions ought to have been known by the moral agent; and (3) the reasonably predictable effects of actions also ought to have been known by the moral agent.

Yet what few have recognized is that the enlarged domain of spatiotemporal Nature conceals from view the full range of freedom and moral responsibility, particularly when small "r" reason disconnects from large "R" Reason, and when rationality (*ratio*) separates from reason (*intellectus*). The outcome is that individuals are locked into a world like Plato's Cave (into a matrix), and without the immediate, self-sustaining ability to break free from the shadows of a false and suboptimal reality. Indeed, the Cave may provide some psychological, rational comfort in a universe of apparent uncertainty. Like the Cave, institutions under technical growth reduce uncertainty by eliminating possibilities from a range or class of possibilities.

Over time, the costs rising against individuals and society is so significant that a nonlinear social regress occurs. Outside of the moral law, at each technical turn of growth's screw, the social welfare begins to dislodge from old, traditional time-tested forms of culture, not to mention objective morality itself. "The demos depends for its identity on all the truth-bound history of culture, on all the lessons learned from trial and experiment, and on the trial and error observation that leads to behavioral consequences (e.g., war, economic prosperity and depressions, social unrest, or advancement)."[16] Once separated from the old ways, the new ways help the demos, under the authority of Conditioners, to master both the physical and social environment as well as Nature itself. The new ways, propagandists argue, expand the choice of human destiny (Lewis 2001a: 51). In reality just the opposite is true.

Sentimentality for the old ways is of little concern to the institutional Conditioner because control and power is bought to cover risks arising from an impersonal universe. From Hobbes to Weber, social theorists have recognized this idea. The premium for social stability in an impersonal universe is the eventual loss of private identity, knowledge, and freedom. It might help to think of Lewis's (2001a: 72, 76) "magician's bargain," where power is gained (by some) at the price of soul, as a naturalist twist on Pascal's wager: place your bets on Nature (and all it would entail) because it is perceptibly more real and will give you material gains. Never mind the potential loss of humanity.

It is unexceptional that this contest between two metaphysical poles should continue into the twenty-first century. The conflict between naturalism and reason has been prominent in philosophical thought since ancient times. One of the earliest voices to articulate this encounter was Plato's. Plato describes the naturalist position in the *Sophist* (246B):

> What we shall see is something like a battle of gods and giants going on between them over their quarrel about reality. . . . One party is trying to drag

everything down to earth out of heaven and the unseen, literally grasping rocks and trees in their hands, for they lay hold upon every stock and stone and strenuously affirm that real existence belongs only to that which can be handled and offers resistance to the touch. They define reality as the same thing as body, and as soon as one of the opposite party asserts that anything without a body is real, they are utterly contemptuous and will not listen to another word.

Plato's view maintains that the worldview struggle is intentional. Much of it is. Mutiny against Reason has a long history and much of the theoretical contest has been intentional, a product of thoughtful human agency. Works of such men as Protagoras, Lucretius, Bacon, Hume, Saint-Simon, Feurerbach, Comte, Marx, Nietzsche, Dewey, and many others endorse in their respective views the philosophical tenets of interlocking naturalism against which Reason was thought impervious. These works were influential. While many of the views held sway with vital areas of high culture of the day, more recently the uniform impetus for life outside of the moral law began to reach an upward slope at the dawn of the Industrial Revolution and the rise of machines (Lewis 1962: 9–25). After machines were initially adjusted to the efficient industry of men, men would later be adjusted to the efficient industry of the machine.[17] The relationship between the school and its students followed this same shift.

As we have seen, the logic and ascendancy of naturalism provides an accessible and constructive ontology for the technical model of growth. It endows the model with morphogenetic and morphostatic qualities that create and sustain growth. These adaptive qualities represent various reductions, abstractions and substitutions propped up against foundational knowledge of reality and the human. There is a direction whereby generations of people have grown up under the dominant influence of this order, with their beliefs, values, needs, and day-to-day dealings having been conditioned by it. The information preference developed by growth is built up from the economizing actions of individual agents and emerges in the form of rules, policies, norms, and customs. As we know, agents normally respond to perceived changes in prices or institutional constraints by substituting in the direction of lower-cost information. This produces effects that go far beyond intentions of the individual agents themselves. Ultimately, it secures belief that unification is the criterion of rational conduct; that to be rational is not to want things to be other than they are.

Rationality separated from reason expands in the congenial epistemic environment of technical information, making growth appear benign to the common institutional actor. Over time there is diminished capacity to call into question the direction of social institutions and the costs born to the social welfare. The institutional actor becomes so inured to his role, clinging to the path set out before him by the institution, that he loses capacity to put into question the institutional rule structure and socially established standards with logic and confidence. He can no longer adopt MacIntyre's maxim: "Always ask about your social and cultural order what it needs you and others not to know" (1999: 328). And finally, by expanding its rule-making activity, growth acts as a catalyst that transforms culture and society, further separating the demos from their own history, the local culture, and their elites (Lewis 2001a: 53–81). All of this puts into play the open question of human development and educational sustainability.

Growth as an Attribute of Social Institutions

We have thus far examined the nature and effects of models of thought relative to SIs. Our general argument has been that the background philosophies of naturalism, scientism, and developmentalism are helping to underwrite a new model of social reality that radically affects the information environment, and which portends to be the quintessential unifying model going forward. It is a model that delivers vast amounts of goods and services under efficiencies of scale. What by now may be entirely obvious, the depletion of information is a serious problem for the educational enterprise because it depends particularly upon a range of diverse information for its means and ends (production). Over time, education sustainability shifts focus from rich inputs (optimizing costs to production) to efficient outputs (minimizing costs to production), thus changing the nature and perception of the education good. We have seen this change occur before, for example, in the Efficiency and Standards movements where the test score and other assessment schemes become the criteria for successful means and ends (Callahan 1962). Sustainability is redefined in technical terms. In order to talk about this process and its effects on education in a way that avoids category mistakes, we need to accurately wield an understanding of growth as an attribute (or property) of SIs.

It might be most philosophically accurate to say that growth itself is not an entity, a being, or a substance—it does not *have* properties. Rather, it is a property *had* by an entity, e.g., the SI. As a property of an entity, it is also correct to speak about growth as an attribute;

attributes and properties for our purposes will be synonymous for both terms are taken to mean a quality or characteristic of a thing. But what kind of attribute is growth?

Growth's ontological category tends to be organic to the relations and conditions of phenomena. It involves appearances as well as realities of physical entities (e.g., like human beings) and nonphysical entities (e.g., SIs). It is an evolving set of relations within social reality arising from and conditioned by certain types of institutional environments.[18] As a relation, growth manifests within the context of a social entity such as the SI or the State. It becomes a controlling order and links to and collapses all other relations of the SI, making them subordinate to that new order. In the next chapter, we equate technical growth to a body's improper hormonal level creating the conditions of gigantism. Technical growth in the SI does something similar. Only there exists, within the growth attribute's underlying structure of relations, coded reductionistic views about reality, about human beings, knowledge, and goods and society that create an imbalance within the institutional system. It is a kind of DNA activates or actuates emerging properties.

Growth's relationship to conditions of the environment presuppose earlier (logically prior) principles, categories, and questions preceding growth's existence as a relation, but which are necessary conditions for its obtaining. Put differently, growth does not occur *ex nihilo*. Like gigantism in the human body, technical growth spawns from a prior set of ill-coded information conditions, as for example, specific events, movements, worldviews, and the concrete actions of people. It might be best to simply say that growth as an attribute relies on and is activated by growth as a model. The former does the practical work of the latter. This is why we discussed growth as a model prior to discussing growth as an attribute. As an attribute, growth is contingent to these earlier things; it is a signal (an effect) from an even more fundamental state of affairs expressed through ideas of human origins, development, and progress, the advancement of economic and political order, etc. In the technical or closed view, growth as an attribute becomes the means by which to achieve social, cultural, political, and economic goods at least cost. It has the ability to lower production costs on one side of the ledger by dividing the domain of information, by standardizing and aggregating. On the other side of the ledger, it raises costs on the individual and society.

Many economists, philosophers, anthropologists, and social theorists correctly believe that SIs impact human reality in important ways. Some economists have offered a shorthand definition of institutions as the formal and informal "rules of the game" that govern fields or domains of human interaction.[19] Yet SIs represent more than rules; they are also proxies for deeper forces. The fact is that institutions are nonnatural phenomena. It is a useful tautological statement that nonnatural phenomena do not logically occupy a strictly naturalist model of reality. We might ask, for example, where precisely is the institution? This is "where" in the spatiotemporal sense. SIs do not function in the natural sphere. They are not constituted physical entities. Noticeably, naturalism as a philosophy of reality cannot give a coherent account of institutions as entities. Materialists like Searle must reduce them to mere observer-dependent social constructions, ultimately a product of biology and evolutionary dynamism, and leave out any nonnatural or extra-human dimension.

On my view the traditional opposition that we tend to make between biology and culture is as misguided as the traditional opposition between body and mind. Just as mental states are higher-level features of our nervous system, and consequently there is no opposition between the mental and the physical, the mental is simply a set of physical features of the brain at a higher level of description than that of neurons; so there is no opposition between culture and biology; culture is the form that biology takes. There could not be an opposition between culture and biology, because if there were, biology would always win. Different cultures are different forms that an underlying biological substructure can be manifested in. But if that is right, then there ought to be a more or less continuous story that goes from an ontology of biology to an ontology that includes cultural and institutional forms; there should not be any radical break. (Searle 1995: 227)

An institution—any institution—does not occupy physical space, is not a set of physical properties, is not a field of force, and is not the result of or reducible to a particular chemical-electrical event in a brain or collective set of brains. Institutions are nonnatural phenomena in at least two senses. Both of these senses compare favorably to a corporation or firm.[20] First, like a corporation, an institution can have its activities represented in two or more places at once. Second, an entity, the State, recognizes by artifact of law and other communicative acts another abstract entity, a corporation, as a nonphysical person. In the words of Chief Justice John Marshall (1809) a corporation is that "invisible, intangible, and artificial being, that mere legal entity..."[21] As a nonphysical person, a corporation is said to act in that it has certain legal and financial powers of agency. Yet for most SIs the mode of existence entirely depends upon a human substratum (Hodgson 2006: 7), but not on Searle's purely biological (materialist) substratum. His account is insufficient to produce anything, let alone a multifaceted social institution.

Institutions, like corporations, are noncorporeal entities. Unlike corporations, institutions are not regarded as legal persons and do not possess powers of agency. Taken in the widest analysis as social entities, they are conceptual aggregates symbolizing broadly regulated fields of human activity, which extend control and signal informational pathways. An institution represents the climate of social affairs. What weather is to the physical environment, institutions are to the social environment; like weather, an institution can produce treacherous conditions as well as procure safe conditions for social activity. However, concrete humans beings can change the social institution; reform is always possible even if odds do not favor it.

It is of little help to think of institutions merely as rules because we are right back to the question of spatiotemporality, "Where precisely is a rule?" No one has "seen" a rule. A rule is not a physical thing. A rule can be tokened in a speech act or by ink on a page (e.g., a constitution), but the rule itself, being a nonphysical property, is itself nowhere directly perceived by the physical senses. Faculties of the mind (reason and rationality) intuit and understand a rule. Rules, like institutions, are nonnatural phenomena. Neither is a rule some random information. Nature as such cannot provide a rule. Nature may have represented within her certain regularities of physics, chemistry, and biology but that is much different than Nature authoring (originating) a rule *sui generis*. A rule implies intelligence, agency, a rule giver, it conveys reason (mental activity), and it connotes purpose. The interlocked closed system of Nature, on her own, cannot provide a rule because it is not an originator of final causes: it can never be the final cause of intelligence, reason, or teleology. This is a serious philosophical problem for the developmentalist who regards naturalistic philosophy as carrying objective, normative weight. As Plantinga (2008) shows, it is one thing to accept the premises of evolution as a method or means or as the efficient cause of biological change. It is an altogether different question to offer exclusively naturalistic explanations for change, order, and regularity, and then claim that the explanations are sufficient for Nature to produce final causes. To do so begs the question. And in naturalism, our own "cognitive or belief-producing faculties—memory, perception, logical insight, etc.—are *unreliable* and cannot be trusted to produce a preponderance or true beliefs over false" (Plantinga 2008: 37). It is even a problem for the subjectivist. On what ground in mere Nature does she rely? The social function and design of the institution are of vital concern to composite human reality. Function and design are seen even in physical entities: The *purpose of* the heart is to..., The heart is *designed to*...(Chisholm 1996: 131). Now we should briefly note that the purpose and design of something *in* Nature are different from attributing the final cause of purpose and design *to* Nature. Likewise, institutions exhibit purpose, structure, and, some would argue, design. The purpose of an institution is defined in significant part by the good(s) it produces or exchanges. As Arrow (1974: 57) notes, the code of an institution "may be supposed governed most strongly by its primary functions." In other words, the institution's teleology helps to determine (or at least inform) its structure as well as its information base. Its function (what it does) and design (what it was intended to do) should align. Included here is the institution's information economy. If the composite nature of the good is complex, then the function and design of the institution's attributes will account for complexity, including its pathways and patterns of information. As design implies intentionality, it consists of knowing the necessary conditions under which the good is produced, accounting for relevant factors of production. Together, function, design, and structure align planning and exchange so that there is a greater likelihood that the complex human good is achieved.

The human substratum, that permanent and unchanging root of social institutions, gives form to institutions and is given form at the macro levels, on the levels of society and culture, as well as the mediating level of institutions, where individuals and small-scale communities (including organizations) rely on producing and acquiring goods and services and where exchange is consummated. The substratum fundamentally influences the belief-forming practices about the existence, identity, and activity of individual human beings and the value of local communities. Yet when functioning properly, institutions are sensitive to specific and concrete human beings and local communities. The Hippocratic oath could be applied in this context as a good rule of thumb: ideally SIs should do no harm and much good. Social institutions do not have the moral right to dehumanize the human being. Indeed, part of the meaning of proper function involves an institution's capacity to foster individual moral agency in reliable ways, expanding the domain of freedom consistent with the reality of moral law, which together reinforces the SI's particular connection to the Tao. Alasdair MacIntyre's (1999: 314) comments are apposite and deserve to be cited at length:

[F]or recognizing that they have good reason to acknowledge the authority of evaluative and normative standards that are independent of those embodied in the institutions of their own particular social and cultural order, and so share equally in a capacity to be able to transcend in thought the limitations of those established standards.... Disagreements about what these evaluative and normative standards prescribe and what awareness of their authority consists in have not precluded widespread agreement in ascribing to normal adult human beings as such a capacity that makes them responsible as individuals for not putting their established social and cultural order to the question, if and when they have occasion to do so.

As non-spatiotemporal entities, some institutions, then, are not social constructs (e.g., the moral law) while other institutions are social constructs (e.g., the schools). Money as an institution is a good example of an institution that originates as a social construct (Searle 2005: 9). A dollar bill is not just a piece of paper of a certain sort that could be exhaustively described by chemistry and physics. A dollar bill is a piece of paper that people *intend* to use *for the purpose of* engaging in *freely chosen* economic exchanges; it is itself an *institution*, one that conveys certain universal rules of barter and exchange. What makes a piece of paper a dollar bill is the reality behind the italicized words in the previous sentence; which are all mental and not physical notions that make reference to the invisible mental states of individuals that constitute the relevant group. These mental notions are nonnatural features of reality, not reducible to chemical processes of brain states. So it is for all SIs, and this is the vital point to keep in mind: they are nonnatural phenomena whether or not they are observer independent or observer dependent. This is their modal distinction, the logic by which their existence is contingent and agent sensitive. The distinction relies on the fact that SIs are modally dependent on and inseparable from, but not identical to, social reality itself. As nonnatural entities, their function is to help preserve, create, and convey information and knowledge as well as to mediate complex human affairs.

Not all social institutions are observer dependent. They exist and function on the human substratum, one composed of beliefs, feelings, and attitudes (Searle 2005: 4). As Hodgson (2006:7) notes, "institutions depend for their existence on individuals, their interactions, and particular shared patterns of thought. Nevertheless, any single individual is born into a pre-existing institutional world which confronts him or her with its rules and norms." Over time, under the technical attribute of growth, the SI creates a powerful social reality—a set of interdependent social constructions—that conceals important aspects of the human-dependent substratum. These social constructions include institutional facts, rules, status functions, and obligations such that the institution is no longer seen as human dependent, no longer answerable to the human being. Rather, the expanding SI alters the ideal individual–institution relation and arrangement whereby the SI becomes a taken-for-granted notion in the minds of many participants. The institution becomes virtual, immutable, irreversible, and seemingly perpetual. Like the physical forces of Nature, social institutions come to be seen as determiners, not the determined; seen as inevitable expressions of collective will, a place where the individual gives way to the crowd.

This set of affairs is a setback from the ideal ontological situation. Human beings suffer the loss of individual agency and become opaque against the evolving and expanding institutional form. Searle (2005: 11) admits that institutional structures can create desire-independent reasons for action. So they do, but this is not the end of the story. What happens is that the attribute of growth confuses institutional participants where supposedly desire-independent reasons for action produce desire-dependent reasons for action. The problem is that people forget to act the way they should by forgetting to acquire important knowledge from reliably independent sources. The ability to act for reasons that have little or nothing to do with one's own desires (e.g., self-interest) is necessary in order to do what may be required by the moral law (the doctrine of objective value). As Lewis writes, "he who surrenders himself without reservation to the temporal claims of a nation, or a party, or a class is rendering to Caesar that which, of all things, most emphatically belongs to God: himself" (2001c: 53). In the technical system, however, nearly everyone is making adjustments to their choices and decision making in the direction of collectivity. After rationality is divided from reason (making the shift more likely by neutralizing reason), universal information splits from particular information, action aligns on the desire-dependent criterion of rationality. A turnover in the rules formalizes the process. Institutional actors submit their agency to the new rules and incentive structure, a signal that bears the path of rational action.

Conclusion

In essence, we are describing the SI as a framework for human agency where millions of interacting human beings make choices, decisions, and conduct their daily lives in work, learning, and play. It results from the interplay between millions of individuals mutually adjusting their beliefs and activities to the beliefs and activities of others. It is this social environment that most humans occupy. It has terrain to negotiate, climates to which to adapt, structures to construct and deconstruct, and enabling and disabling qualities. It also has ontic and epistemic characteristics, such as background conceptions of reality and knowledge that shape agenda in what range of affairs the institution will allow: what counts as reality, what qualifies as rational, what decisions are allowed, how much agent sensitivity is bestowed. There exists within an institution's framework an underlying structure of relations, shifting patterns and directions of information, and other philosophical and economic commitments that presuppose unifying or unified views about reality, human beings, knowledge goods, and orderings of society. While these underlying views fluctuate over time, under the technical growth model their tendency is to expand along common and more uniform characteristics. The attribute of growth becomes the practical mechanism that moves the process forward. For education systems, the core institutional problem lies in the breakdown of the human substratum which leads to the attenuation of the complex institutional environment required for human development and flourishing.

Chapter 3

The Epistemological Disabilities of Growth: How Expanding Markets Exchange Knowledge for Ignorance

On the subject of growth in the modern age: as far as it is a doctrine of power, we agree. As far as it is a doctrine of knowledge, we disagree. For it can be shown that a critical conflict emerges between the foundational principles of knowledge and the direction of the whole system of development under which we now live.

We are going to maintain that as long as the process of growth in commercial and social life continues on its present course, the world's institutions will endorse as legitimate methods that sustain the view that physical nature is all there is. And as long as some version of this view of reality influences popular thought and increases as a ground of action, subjectivism, as the premise of all logic and judgment, will go deeper and spread wider. And, no less surely, so long as the psychology of subjectivism prevails, the structure of knowledge, understood traditionally, will increasingly be seen as uneconomical, and the trend toward doing some kind of violence to it, even its elimination, will be welcomed as a sign of progress.

Of this trend we know no better example than what we find in the modern institution of education. There are many indications that the education community as a whole, and the university in particular, has bought into the idea that the traditional conception of knowledge, that is, knowledge in the sense that the vast majority of mankind has conceived of it for thousands of years, is no longer valid. It used to be taken for granted, especially prior to the twentieth century, that there is an objective reality to knowledge, that to know something is to represent or apprehend the subject matter as it is, that knowledge is determined by the truth that is known. Plato, Aristotle, Aquinas, Husserl, and others asserted something amounting to this, and it is still a view assumed by several significant philosophers in our own day. However, across university life, in every discipline and field of inquiry, it is now common to deny the credentials of this view. We have reached the stage where to undermine these old necessities of knowledge and knowing is no longer a recognized sign of irrationality. Nowadays in academe, it seems simply natural that the structure of knowledge is a social concept, a subjective sentiment. Knowledge now refers to descriptions of social or technological processes of belief formation; it refers to what people accept as real, to whatever the group or community decides it is. According to Professor Willard (whose thought on these matters casts a clarifying light), "Knowledge becomes what, for the time being, passes for or is accepted as 'knowledge'. It becomes a kind of practice—perhaps the 'best professional practice'. It is belief in a certain social setting" (2000: 2).

What we are experiencing in education is similar in effect to the phenomenon known as gigantism: the perpetual growth of a human being, the cause of which is not health, but disease. Outwardly, the giant is the image of great strength. But this misleads us; for we have come to know that a severe disorder is active deep in his body, and this is the true source of the giant's size. It is the same way with this whole institutional grasp for growth, of which education makes part. This is the type of growth that works not on the basis of balance, but on the basis of distortion. And what it distorts, in this instance, is the essential structure and meaning of knowledge.

At this point, the critic is very apt to say that knowledge is in no danger of loss and only stands to gain. He may challenge us with the claim that progress in knowledge occurs automatically in expanding markets; that knowledge is both growth produced and growth producing—in other words, that the relationship is one of mutual reinforcement. This argument always has fresh evidence to support it: the prodigious advance in technology, the greater mobility in economic life, the increase in luxuries and wealth, indeed all the new powers and practical innovations that have come to the aid of the human race. On such evidence all parties would admit that growth and knowledge are closely related. And certainly a defense can be made that it is difficult, if not impossible, to secure one without the other.

But it is very important to notice that our argument so far supposes no complete separation between knowledge and growth. We are not going to say that there is a total discontinuity between them. It is a fact apparent to common sense that in order for growth and development to occur we must have some knowledge of what we are developing. Our contention is that the content, scope, and meaning of knowledge are being altered to fit the preferred (subjective) categories of the growth model. As we will see, under the efficiency pressures of expansion, the institutional order proceeds on a course of putting into place a lower-cost materialistic premise for all knowledge and knowing. With the rise of scale, the constant tendency is to detach the structure of knowledge from its independent, objective status, that is, from its connection to truth and reason. This way of growth, as we now see it, urges us in the direction of providing a more cooperative account of knowledge, toward passionate belief, relative entities, and opinion. But we contend that every step made in this direction, lower in cost though it appears, really means a breaking down of those conditions that make knowledge possible. Knowledge detached from truth grows into high-cost ignorance.

If we want to explain in more detail how the forces of growth create a social framework within which knowledge cannot prevail, we must then turn to C.S. Lewis. In a single sentence of *The Abolition of Man*, Lewis captures the essence of the problem. "Every conquest of Nature," he said, "increases her domain" (2001a: 71). Here, and throughout much of his writing, Lewis makes us aware of a disturbing paradox. As man conquers Nature, man becomes the possessor of decreasing power over Nature. He tells us that all our efforts to grasp and retain, to immerse ourselves in new and better things, to eliminate the obstacles to pleasure, and to grow without assignable limits, indeed "every sort of becoming," involves the conquest and control of Nature. The danger that Lewis detected was that as we unlock the secrets of the external world and master our environment, we spread the view that the vast machine of material Nature is all there is. This means that we tend to see and explain things more and more in naturalistic terms. This is the road to inhumanity. As Lewis said, "We reduce things to mere nature in order that we may 'conquer' them" (2001a: 71). The logical outcome of this process is to take the final step of reducing man to a natural object. What we find in Lewis is the insight that "The demand for a developing world" leads to an unprotesting submission to Nature (2007: 221). Once more, according to Lewis, "it is the magician's bargain: give up our soul, get power in return. But once our souls, that is, ourselves, have been given up, the power thus conferred will not belong to us" (2001a: 72).

Here we want to show how the phenomenon just described by Lewis plays a considerable role in altering the epistemic orientation of the social order. To do this we need to go into the operation of growth more fully. Our starting point is the proposition that political, economic, and cultural markets expand on similarity, not difference. This may be put in the form that growth (in its manifold varieties) chooses the information path of least cost. Or we may say that growth gears the prevailing system of institutions to measurable forms of information. Expanding markets prefer this kind of information because it is comparatively easy to acquire, process, reproduce, and transmit; and because it is compatible with a capacity for bringing interchangeability, consistency, mobility, prediction, efficiency, and control into all areas of life. When lived out, this preference will be experienced as the pursuit of uniform standards, commonality, and fairness in the creation of rules, regulations, rights, language, methods, and norms of conduct; those events that conform to and extend the category of the broader interest and are conducive to production and control on a large scale. Thus, going on inside all of this institutional activity, at a level hard to observe, is a trade-off of information, a system-wide substitution in the least-cost (universal) direction (Rodriguez, Loomis, and Weeres 2007: 3).

The good economist will immediately see what this means. He will see that market expansion is a movement to societal disequilibrium. This view is both heretical and important. For while he was right in assuming that institutions reduce information costs by mitigating the uncertainty of individual decisions, he now sees that under the forces of scale they tend to do so in a definite direction. With that in mind, he will see that in reality the system of institutions introduces a distortion or a bias into the information base of markets, which of course means that they generate information costs. If this is true, he will be compelled to admit that there are preferences, rights, values, and relations that absorb these costs in the world economy, which means, for example, that the price of holding a certain view or engaging in a certain activity goes up. And so he will find clear reason to believe that socioeconomic growth is the very trend that may lead to a higher balance of costs in the social order.

This recognition shows that where we tend to go wrong is in assuming that progress is automatic in growth. It comes naturally to the modern to suppose that expansion always is a sign of improvement; that it means a change from lower to higher, from worse to better, from error to truth, a motion of markets to optimal states. Reason of course allows for this possibility. Yet there are no adequate grounds for affirming the view that expanding markets tend to move the social sphere toward a situation in which equilibrium prevails. It simply is error to assume that growth's production always is greater than its counter-production, that growth discards no irreplaceable wealth or value, and that what it can bring to the world is vastly superior to that which it may take away. If our argument has been sound, then we must reject at once the idea in the mind of the modern that the investment program of growth necessarily leads to an increase in total welfare. Our point is that growth's apparent progress toward balance, zero costs, and perfection is illusory. The growth process is everywhere laboring to produce an abstract universal, a simplified, thinned-out reality. Its true love is abstraction, not reality.

THE QUEST FOR UNIFORMITY IN THE MASS PRODUCING AGE

Opportunities for expansion increase by moving things in the direction of uniformity. This is true of all markets and the institutions through which they function. To move in this direction requires the formation of categories and common reference points in measures, methods, laws, rules, language, preferences, and values, all of which together tend to create a system of reliable expectations—the very formula we need to keep the world prosperous. These ideas are, of course, not exactly new. For instance, the main outlines of this process were known and working back in the eighteenth century. That was a period in which the growth of populations, cities, states, commerce, and the development of new and better machines intensified the need to stabilize society. As these systems extended in size, relations and energies had to be redirected. The aim then, as it is now, was to construct spaces of commonality and comparability, to find better methods for counting and controlling territories, people, and trade.[1] Measurement and the recording of accurate data were essential to governing the expansion.

The emergence of the centralized nation-state and the rise of the scientific and industrial revolutions increased the need to accurately measure and classify more things: births, deaths, marriages, poverty, crime, disease, tax revenues, lands, crops, animals, and so on. In essence, the drive to expand raised the demand to appraise and quantify the health and wealth of countries.[2] And this in turn increased the need to deal with the variation in those measures. At this point we shall not be surprised to hear that the main problem for growth, the thing that has always blocked its way, is the inherent variability of Nature. No part of Nature seems to be free of irregularity and unlikeness. Sharp dissimilarities tend to turn up in everything we see and do, as in our measures of the motion of planets and in our normal ways of life, in how we think, feel, and act. The trouble with variation is that it grows conditions in which there is less capacity for calculation, communication, and cooperative outcomes; it makes things less comparable, which means that it lowers the level of prediction and control. The basic point is that variation can generate enormous costs (assessed in money or other terms), which explains why it is intolerable to expanding systems. Hence, the key to sustained expansion lies in finding the means by which to liberate the social order from the grip of variation (cost). That is, growth needs a method by which to minimize the effect of variation on measurement, neutralize the problems of independence and bring highly variegated phenomena together and under control. This was something made possible by statistics.

Statistics began as a mathematical method in service of the State. In its initial stages, statistics was a science that analyzed and described populations and regions by means of averages and relative frequencies. Historian Theodore Porter noted that before the nineteenth century, statistics "...was an ill-defined science of states and conditions" (1986: 11). Alain Desrosières likewise found that "Statistics in its oldest, eighteenth century sense was a description of the state, by and for itself" (1998: 147). Statistics at that time was a political solution to the problem of distributional conflicts, personal politics, and unruly independence. In practical terms, it was a way of working toward greater uniformity, a way to discipline decisions and make the personal lives of citizens more visible and intelligible to authority. It developed early on as a new and relatively low-cost means of summarizing facts about the world and managing the ordinary details of daily experience. It was a way to record prices and production, to quantify and describe movements of goods, money, and people. Mainly it was, and still is, a numerical tool for extending territory and power.

The early theoretical work on probability and the estimation of error, circa the eighteenth century, by Bernoulli, De Moivre, Bayes, Laplace, and others helped lay the mathematical groundwork for a major shift in statistical thought that took place in the first half of the nineteenth century. The important change occurred in the 1830s when the Belgian astronomer Adolphe Quetelet provided a new scientific approach to society. By combining social statistics and the probability calculus (astronomical law of error) used in science, he sought to extract general laws and create a social physics from the available data on crime, suicides, and marriage (Desrosières 1998: 10). In essence, Quetelet transferred the expectation of discovering regularity from the field of physical science to the field of human affairs. With this new approach, the basis of which was the logic of large numbers, he showed that it was possible to fit the flow of variable human experience into the scientific grid. What he showed, in other words, was that even in the case of highly variable social life the distribution of the averages of a large set of numbers would follow the shape of the "error curve" or "possibility curve" (known today as the normal distribution, Gaussian distribution, or the Bell curve).[3] This conformity to the curve seemed to indicate that people were subject to universal laws of the same status as the physical laws of nature. It seemed to suggest a structure and unity beneath the diversity of individual cases, a common cause to diverse, particular events.

The strength of the new statistical method was that it gave man the ability to discover regularity in collective life without having to take account of the causes of the variation of individual events. As Porter (1986: 6) stated, "... it seemed to be possible to uncover general truths about mass phenomena even though the causes of each individual action were unknown and might be wholly inaccessible." Quetelet's technique gave substance to the belief that all the errors and confusions at the individual or local level would average out to yield a stable system at the macro level. Yet he saw something more. From his study of the physical characteristics of the human body, Quetelet became convinced that the mean value of the normal distribution denoted a new reality. He saw the mean as representing the ideal type, "the average man," and the variation from this ideal as representing error.[4] For him, the essence of the phenomena lay in the average. Porter further explained, "Quetelet allowed his average man a temporal dimension as well as physical and moral ones, thus giving him a mean rate of growth and moral development over his average life" (1986: 53).

What filtered down to the general view from all this was the belief that the social body had a will and reality of its own; that the average (the representation) was a true value above the level of individual diversity; that the general entity was logically superior and autonomous in relation to its elements of origin; and that the human intellect could create reality through the abstraction called statistics. These beliefs were destined to persist. By the end of the nineteenth century, they had integrated into everyday discourse. By the end of the twentieth century, they had, in manifold ways, transformed the development of modern society.

It would be accurate to speak of the new beliefs and methods assembled under the name of statistics as being in full compatibility with the logic and demands of growth and thus, as being part of a wider, one might say revolutionary, movement of unifying reforms of social institutions (SIs). For nearly two centuries the rise of the statistical method has been at the center of the effort to bring unity and control to the human experience. This effort was in full view across the decades of the twentieth century when use of the statistical method succeeded in pulling the proliferation of data toward uniformity. By tying the individual to the social whole, by connecting man's life with the conditions of Nature, and by creating a simpler, more efficient productive process, the statistical model helped to level the social terrain, to generate impersonal (lower-cost) information, and to advance an ethic of averages—all things which proved highly beneficial to governments and economies. H.G. Wells was reported to have once said, "Statistical thinking will one day be as necessary for efficient citizenship as the ability to read and write" (quoted in Howie 2002: 197, n 87). Well, today we see that reasoning in probabilistic terms dominates popular thought and prevails in many, if not most, areas of life. It is the preferred means by which to mediate nearly every public relationship and outcome and to settle nearly every issue imaginable.[5]

We cannot fail to notice that modern man has taken refuge in the concept of statistical probability. We use it today in business, medicine, agriculture, education, entertainment, politics, and nearly everywhere else as a method by which to judge the comparative advantages of different uses of resources. It is our main tool and base for making decisions about the introduction of products, research and development, investing, assessing risk, legal strategies, medical procedures, financial forecasting, public policy, etc.. Its use as an instrument of proof has become routine in nearly all fields and academic disciplines, extending the range of technical explanation and giving us the greater capacity to adapt Nature to our needs. The practical influence of the tools of mathematical statistics has extended far and has come to be associated with the scientific mentality—that is, with neutrality, objectivity, and rationality. "Nowadays, the theory of probabilistic induction is often held up as a formalization of scientific method, the way a scientist ought to think" (Howie 2002: 21). This has added to the sum of its reputation as a unifying framework within which every event can be explicable in terms of general laws. The use of statistical probability, we can be quite sure, has become the directing method of humanity. It has increased our taste for the abstract; and it has led more and more often, in today's world, to a social system that operates in the rationality of the collective rather than in that of the individual.[6]

The modern acquiescence in the statistical model shows that the way we go about measuring things is not insignificant. Our means of quantification has altered our assumptions and predictions of events, the form of our empirical questions, our moral language, and our attitudes toward each other. It has changed our fundamental concepts and categories, our thoughts and actions, how we convey information, how we perceive time and space, and our identity as human beings. Today, it has become part of our overall approach to life to quantify from probabilities, and to believe that the statistical method is an ideal source from which to draw reliable knowledge of reality. The thinking in the contemporary world is that a statistical description or a judgment of probability yields genuine knowledge and provides us with unshakable rational truth.

We do not doubt that the statistical method has broadened our options of belief and investigation. It is quite clear that it has opened new lines of speculation and extended the range of possible inference. But the more we look into the matter the more we realize that a formidable argument can be raised against the idea that it is an adequate means of reaching certainty and truth. This speaks to questions of knowledge. These we must now consider.

THE TECHNICAL IMAGE OF PHILOSOPHICAL NATURALISM

About 100 years ago, with the advent of quantum theory, scientists discovered that things in the atomic world have the potential to behave either as particles or as waves. What caused this result, they did not know; they only knew that in calculations it produced uncertainty. The more precisely they chose to measure the momentum of a fundamental particle, the less precisely they could measure its position, and vice versa (the Heisenberg uncertainty principle). This discovery was of sufficient importance to change the conceptual base of science. "Gone was the luxury of supposing that a single reality existed, that the human mind had reasonably clear access to it, and that the scientist could explain it" (Gleick 1992: 243). All descriptions of known phenomena would henceforth be in terms of probability. Science began pointing in the direction of subjectivity.

As Pearcey and Thaxton explained, "Classical physics assumed that there is an objective world which we can observe and measure without essentially changing it. But on the quantum level, it seems impossible to observe reality without changing it. Depending on which experiment the researcher selects, he can make atomic entities exhibit either wavelike or particlelike characteristics" (1994: 193). Many scientists found in this reason to conclude that we can never completely separate the subject from the object, the observer from the observed. In other words, they saw in quantum results grounds for believing that human observation (measurement) could influence physical events. The far-reaching effects of this view were not fully grasped. No one quite saw how deeply it would affect all branches of science. Who could foresee that it would bring forth and strengthen doubting practices, that it would be followed by claims that man's thoughts have causal power over nature, and that it would support the inclination to regard all knowledge as approximate and provisional. No one (apart from a few accurate thinkers like Orwell and Lewis and Hayek) could foresee the extent to which such views would take firm root and reach their full absurdity in the social sciences and extend down into the thoughts of the masses.

Now we may fail to see how anyone, cultured or not, could draw the conclusion that ultimate reality is something dependent on man's mind. It seems to go against all our common sense and intuition. But let us not linger here to dispute about the question of observer-dependent reality. Different opinions can be honestly held. It is more important to realize that with the rise of quantum theory the ordinary acceptance of knowledge in its relation to things was changed. No more absolutes, first principles, or undeniable laws of logic; no more realism, exact values, or complete descriptions of physical states. From the point of view of modern physics, knowledge had passed into the realm of the subjective. It was now a flexible concept. It was now a matter of psychology. Thus we have seen arise the belief that there may be as many logics, truths, and universes as there are perceiving people, which is so characteristic of our modern age. The new physics, and the ideology that grew with it, made it possible to speak of intrinsic uncertainty, of events that have no causes, and of being dead and alive at the same time and in the same relationship; it made it possible to speak of a world in which man had at last attained the power not only to control nature but also to create it. We are makers of reality. We determine our ends. The laws of Nature are up to us.[7]

Today in the most highly educated circles it seems quite natural to take these beliefs with full seriousness and to respect them as common scientific wisdom. But acting on these concepts is another matter. A moment's thought shows us that the forms of our perceptions, our language, and all our daily experience and instincts seem to demand a certain commitment to an objective order. It is always necessary to remember that science is at no liberty to depart from the doctrine of objective reality, that is, from the idea that there is an external world in which things exist independent of our observations and consciousness. It must continue to act on the older principles of absolute value, necessary truth, and a knowable, external universe. The methods of science must presuppose that the course of Nature is uniform—that it always goes on the same way—and that every contingent event (observed or unobserved) has an antecedent cause.[8] Be it noted, in passing, that an effect is by definition something created by an antecedent cause. The point is that a scientist may bring his disbelief in a causal, orderly universe to his scientific work. But where then is the ground for his opinion? Where is the basis for his system of values and for understanding the world as it is? His logic and judgments will be subjective, mere sentiments. In practice, it will not be science at all; it will be merely a caricature of real science, highly speculative, and quite useless as an instrument capable of analysis and prediction. "As a result," to quote Pearcey and Thaxton, "most physicists continue to work within a basically Newtonian [classical] worldview in practice, even if they reject it in theory. They rely on common sense realism, speaking of electrons in the same way they speak of billiard balls and inclined planes" (1994: 208). In this sense, at least, the scientist becomes an unwilling witness to absolute truth.

This being the case, we do not for a moment wish to deny the benefits of the statistical approach. We already know that quantum probabilities have been essential for explaining the structure and behavior of entities at the very smallest scale. By all accounts, and in the opinion of almost every practicing scientist, this approach provides reliable experimental predictions and is by far the most successful technique we have for describing the properties of the physical world. Yet, it is not always remembered that once we represent a phenomenon statistically, we place that phenomenon under the assumption of the uniformity of Nature; which, in our era, is presumed to mean the total interlocking sequence of material events, the closed, impersonal, nonrational chain of cause and effect. In other words, and this is our real concern, the statistical probability model pertains only to a sense-perceptible type of reality; it admits only the physical or physically derived dimension of existence. Thus anything put in that framework, and this includes people and their thoughts, can be no more than a product of blind natural forces, a mere event with physical or material causes.

It is with respect to these assumptions of scientific method that C.S. Lewis offered some of his most illuminating insights. In *Miracles*, Lewis explicitly recognized that the whole idea of probability depends on the principle of the uniformity of Nature. He made it very clear that we could not sever this connection to absolute uniform experience without making the laws of probability groundless. As he said, "The expectations based on the law of averages will work only for undoctored Nature" (2001b: 90). For Lewis, it was this idea of uniformity that led to trouble. Thus, he raised to a high level of importance the implications of the uniformity issue or, as he also called it, the question of the openness of the universe.

Lewis addressed both sides of the argument. On the one hand, he said: "If the movements of the individual units are events 'on their own', events which do not interlock with all other events, then these movements are no part of Nature" (2001b: 19). It follows from this that if the individual units are no part of Nature, then the principle of total uniformity does not hold. And if uniformity does not hold, then the probability construct is at once suspended. As Lewis was careful to point out, "Can we say that Uniformity is at any rate very probable? Unfortunately not. We have just seen that all probabilities depend on it. Unless Nature is uniform, nothing is either probable or improbable. And clearly the assumption which you have to make before there is any such thing as probability cannot itself be probable" (p. 163).

On the other hand, concerning Nature as a closed order, Lewis claimed that if the behavior of the individual unit were inside the interlocking laws of Nature (i.e., if Nature is a closed order of material relations only), then every event would, in principle, be explicable without remainder as a by-product of that total process. Here Lewis describes the irrational prospects of such an order: "If all that exists is Nature, the great mindless interlocking event, if our own deepest convictions are merely the by-products of an irrational process, then clearly there is not the slightest ground for supposing that our sense of fitness and our consequent faith in uniformity tell us anything about a reality external to ourselves. Our convictions are simply a fact about us—like the colour of our hair" (pp. 167–168). It is all too apparent what this implies: knowledge would cease to occur. For all our thoughts and reasoning would be meaningless impulses. They would simply be sensations, a part of the whole mass of nonrational events. What we often fail to realize is that, "Unless human reasoning is valid no science can be true" (p. 21).

Though it was not the main target of his analysis, C.S. Lewis proved that the probability construct is a theory dependent on the nonrational, that it rests on a foundation of subjectivity, and that it leaves us with no sufficient base by which to know and be certain of the external world. To put the matter as simply as possible, he showed that probability works only inside the frame of total uniformity. But then once inside that frame, where nothing can exceed the limits of physical Nature, there is no logical ground for supposing that probability, like all our thoughts, has any meaning.

What has grown more and more evident since Lewis's time is the danger of minds that have been trained to assume the primacy of matter, to place every event within the order of physical Nature, and to accept as true the idea that there is no factual character to the nonnatural realm. We are often deceived. And the whole world pays the price. For in starting from these kinds of assumptions, we have built up an education that is not just skeptical about reason but is clearly at odds with it; that is, an education that rests on the validity of thought but advances a model that involves a denial of the validity of thought. Again, what Lewis has to say is worth attending to:

After studying his environment man has begun to study himself. Up to that point, he had assumed his own reason and through it seen all other things. Now, his own reason has become the object: it is as if we took out our eyes to look at them. Thus studied, his own reason appears to him as the epiphenomenon which accompanies chemical or electrical events in a cortex which is itself the by-product of a blind evolutionary process. His own logic, hitherto the king whom events in all possible worlds must obey, becomes merely subjective. There is no reason for supposing that it yields truth. (2000: 249)

We hardly need add that this is a difficult thing to accept. The implications are unsettling to be sure. And since this is by no means a minor problem, one would expect it to produce major discomfort, especially in the world of academe. But that is not the case. In fact, one would be hard pressed to find anywhere, most of all on any campus, even the slightest awareness that something is wrong. It seems our modern technical ways have convinced us that we have found a universally valid system, one that in principle we can apply to everything, one that can reach the right conclusions, a process that at long last can be trusted to put an end to confusion and solve the fundamental questions of life. We take it for granted that this method of science is in harmony with the flow of human experience, that it leaves out no important factors, and that it leads to no deficiencies of thought about our surrounding environment. The view today is that the use of this model increases the general ability to grasp things as they are, and that it is trustworthy as a vehicle of knowledge.[9]

It is of some importance to remember that all through history various models and frameworks (i.e., the conceptual systems we use to describe and explain experience) have arisen and vied for dominance in society. The trend from ancient times to today has been for a certain model to gain prominence in a culture and then eventually to fall out of favor and lose its privileged status, often to be held in extreme contempt. No doubt there are a whole host of reasons for why this happens. But the main reason, perhaps, is that people come to believe that the old model no longer accords with their recognizable view of life; that is, the culture rejects it largely because it seems to distort the facts of reality.

No one understood this better than the eminent historian of ideas, Isaiah Berlin. In his analysis of the emergence and decline of the great currents of thought, those transforming ideas that gripped the world in their vision, Berlin raised issues that should be at the forefront of attention today.[10] He found that time and again man attempts to apply a method that works well in one area to another, where the range of its application is not adequate to perform the task. In other words, a common error in history is the misapplication of a model to the observed reality. According to Berlin, "...the attempt to apply models which work in one region to another (where a very different method is required) is ultimately a form of irrationalism—of what some have called rationalist obscurantism—the insistence, without evidence, without looking to see, that there is a universal key, that what applies here must necessarily apply there, that what represents progress, knowledge, light in one region must necessarily do so in all others" (2000: 141). And so, as Berlin showed, these ruling models were ultimately rejected for exceeding their proper bounds, for distorting reality, for omitting too much of human life, for destroying too much of the total texture of experience, for dissolving man into abstraction.

It is a step forward to realize that in the modern era the main method we use to explain the world suffers from these same deficiencies. The technical (statistical/probabilistic) model and ultimate reality clearly are not so harmonious as might be supposed. It is enough to say that a wide gap tends to open between fact and the way this model represents fact. And yet, oddly enough, none of this seems to matter; these deficiencies have not led the public mind to reject it. In fact, rather than losing influence, this analytical method is a rising force. All over the world there is growing assent to it. And there is no sign that our allegiance to it is wavering. At first glance, and from any sober point of view, this trend seems tremendously strange.

However, as we look a little deeper the incongruity ceases to be confusion and becomes perfectly clear when we realize that it is in step with the general pattern of development, when we realize that the forces of expansion and the technical model have the closest possible affinity. To that situation we now turn.

THE IRRESISTIBLE TECHNIQUE

C.S. Lewis recognized by mid-twentieth century that the lower was rebelling against the higher and that were it to reach its logical end, this rebellion (i.e., "The rebellion of new ideologies against the Tao is a rebellion of the branches rebelling against the Tree") would abolish that which makes man human (2001a: 44). It would do so by way of bloodless (irredeemably technocratic and inhuman) social, political, and cultural institutions, including what Lewis suggested would be an "omni-competent state [armed] with an irresistible scientific technique" (p. 60). There is of course a strong element of social control that accompanies this technical apparatus: the modern State gains leverage and expands when social entities such as SIs function through controllable (universal) forms of information (Neylan 2005: 23–40).

At this point it bears repeating that markets committed to expansion are anxious to unify and harmonize conflicting interests. The constant tendency is to integrate, to compress everything into a uniform mold. Hence, they undertake to direct the distribution of resources away from (higher-cost) particular information toward (lower-cost) universal information. As we have shown before, "Expanding institutions prefer universal information because it has the characteristic and function of lowering the cost of production; it is mostly measurable, predictable, consistent, and order generating—all attributes that tend to make communication easier, that facilitate calculation, and enable trade to move forward toward impersonal exchange" (Rodriguez, Loomis, and Weeres. 2007: 17). Highly significant should seem the fact that in an expanding environment the technical (statistical) model serves as a primary divider of information. It represents the information path of least cost, supporting the system-wide substitution in the direction of universal information. This is a system that rests upon a deficiency of information; it deals with the class, with chosen samples, with instances of the type. The natural unit is the whole, not the individual. Indeed the very strength of the technical model is because of its exclusion of all but a very narrow set of recurrent similarities and of noting only the common characteristics of experience. That this method increases the institutional environment's capacity to control variation, that it creates a distortion in the market information system, that it is liable to perversion, makes it a major part of the rules of continuous growth, a unifying framework, an effective force for integration that is able to cut across all loyalties and transcend economic zones and markets. The basic principle to grasp is that social aggregation takes place not through a broadening of information, but through a narrowing of it.

Sidebar: The Culture of Educational Assessment

Several prominent examples mark the turn toward the technical model. One obvious place to start is noting the rise of the testing and measurement industry in the early twentieth century. Its chief aim sought to lower the economic costs (in time, etc.) of human assessment. During World War I, a professor at Harvard University, Robert Yerkes, was granted permission by the U.S. Army to administer 2 million I.Q. tests to recruits. Its administration helped military leaders quickly route recruits to jobs compatible with their mental ability. It is not difficult to imagine that those who scored a lower I.Q. went to the front-lines of battle.

Likewise, during World War II, the Army General Classification Test, another standardized mental test, was administered to 10 million servicemen in order to quickly classify their utility to army-related tasks. During this same period, testing for intelligence aptitude was also established in the civilian world. Since 1900, the College Board essay exams had tested what a student learned during their time in high school. That changed in the 1940s when the College Board essay exams, which had been hand-scored by evaluators (a costly procedure), were substituted by the Educational Testing Service's (ETS) Scholastic Aptitude Test (SAT), a machine-scored exam that assessed (predicted) aptitude for success in higher education.

With looming college enrollments on the horizon, following the rapid expansion of secondary education and post-World War II opportunities, for example, spawned by the various GI Bills, the need to control the costs of expanded access created the immediate need to assess human beings differently than before.[11] The SAT and other aptitude tests served as screening proxies for regulating who could attend higher education and where. The change from achievement-based exams like those of the College Board essays, to aptitude exams, such as the SAT, also spawned a new, very lucrative secondary educational market. Test-taking preparation became another educational skill that needed development and firms were quick to fill that void. Today, test preparation is a multibillion dollar industry. And test preparation in schools today occupies a month or more time from the curriculum; they too are responding to the incentives and directions set by the technical model of education.

The founder of the ETS, Henry Chauncey, joined Dewey and others in believing that the methods of social science would reform human nature and deliver a better, more efficient social pact. Social science would finally supersede old religious dogmas by applying technical rationality to pressing social problems. For example, on October 5 and November 22, 1948, Chauncey penned two diary entries that are entirely consistent with the elite thought of that day: (1) "the social sciences are at last freeing themselves from the bondage in which they have been held by ethics, religion, prejudices, [and] value judgments"; (2) "Our mores should not be derived from ethical principles which stem from religion but from a [naturalistic] study of man and society."[12] Two years later, Chauncey outlined his "hierarchy of values" which gave social science first position in determining a new humanistic social order.[13]

These ideas also appeared in the new leadership of higher education, including in Clark Kerr, the chancellor of the University of California (UC), the largest and most prestigious public university system in the world, during the late 1950s and 1960s. Kerr, a labor economist by discipline, sought to recreate social structures including a new labor force through education and built on principles of social science. In this regard, Kerr noted "Manpower development is a uniting theme; cultural transmission a divisive one in the world of higher education."[14] Needing to fulfill its role under California's master plan for higher education, the University of California became ETS's largest client. ETS assured the UC that the SAT test would help sort only the (statistically probable) highest performers into their student body.

Some might be tempted to dismiss these dispositions as peculiar to a time and place, where positivist tendencies captured

Sidebar (Continued)

agenda. However, they remain in full force today as ETS and its leadership attempts to corral what remains of differentiated higher education into a set of uniform metrics and college exit exams. From an economic and institutional point of view, ETS in a recent proposal (2006), *A Culture of Evidence: Postsecondary Assessment and Learning Outcomes*, is attempting to secure further gains from expanded trade by creating a new market based upon the "accountability" movement.[15] Under the supposed moral warrant of accountability, ETS proposes to test students before college entry and then again test these same students upon their exit (perhaps if they are really clever, at various points in between), attempting to measure the value added by colleges and universities. If ETS is successful in pairing its proposal to recent policy recommendations by the Commission on the Future of Higher Education (2006), calling for public universities to measure learning with standardized tests, this becomes a rather lucrative enterprise (given 4000 higher education institutions in the United States where some 1.3 million students exit each year with a bachelor's degree).[16] More importantly, students must be shaped in order to be assessable by these tests, which will further condition (narrow) the information environment of higher education, just as it has for the schools. What this means in the clearest possible terms is that the umbrella of homogenization will slowly descend over faculty work in higher education, the way it has over teachers' work.[17] This phenomenon in effect raises costs against academic freedom.

The effects of the technical model of schooling in the application of business principles to its management are an effect of social science writ large. "If it can be managed, it can be measured." Jurgen Habermas, a neo-Kantian philosophical force behind the construction of the European Union, reveals the critical purpose behind uniform measures. "Methodologically speaking, measurements fulfill two functions. Data that have been measured have the advantage of making possible a reliable simplification of controversies about the accuracy of existence claims; measurement operations that can in principle be repeated guarantee the intersubjectivity of experience. Measurements are also of interest in the construction of categories. Data that have been measured have the advantage of being precisely defined through operations; the measurement standards permit subtle distinctions and thus more precise descriptions than are possible in everyday language, even though the operational definitions themselves remain dependent on ordinary-language explanations."[18]

Business models such as total quality management (TQM), used widely in the efficient manufacturing of simple goods, focus on the visible, measurable, and repeatable processes of production designed to enhance employee output and capture customer satisfaction.[19] Likewise, the balanced scorecard, originating from Harvard University's business school, emphasizes metrics for evaluation of all production processes, including purposes, strategic goals and initiatives, and communication.[20] Under such models human valuation takes on a new focus: performance is tightly coupled to measurement; if something, say some human area of concern cannot be measured, then it either does not exist or is not considered important. Oblivious to its adherents was the obvious fact that this principle itself cannot be measured and, so, by its own standards, either does not exist or is not important. Nevertheless, these systems of managing business largely govern the management of education, schools, and higher education.

Educational managers use business models in order to deal with the problem of scarce resources and their allocation (e.g., who gets what within public schooling). Principles and techniques of social science provide the administrator with relevant tools to allocate and manage these resources efficiently. Efficiency becomes *the* criterion of management success, including what takes place in the school classroom. And the field of psychology makes available thousands of metrics ("instruments") for the educational manager which school could assess faculty, staff, and students for employment competency, for student learning, and for indicators of cognitive, emotional, and even moral growth. Much of this work reinforced the technical framework, which itself is an ally of philosophical behaviorism.[21]

In all essentials, this distorting (reductive) process is a movement of ruling out the Tao (i.e., self-evident principles of theoretical and practical reason) and instituting in its place subjectivism as the premise of all value, logic, and judgment. It is a process, therefore, that goes far to explain the degradation of knowledge from its proper, that is, its classical, status.

Let us give greater specificity to this claim by describing, in very simple terms, the established approach of the technical (statistical probability) method. The technical method involves the construction of equivalences. All data modeled within it begin from equal status and are equally dependent on the total system. It is an inductive approach that involves an arguing to, not from; which means that it does not view matters from above, from transcendent, objective forms. In other words, its data descend from no absolute principles. In this framework, the world is emptied of values and meaning. There are no irresistible claims of truth. There are no final purposes or causes.[22] There is no reference point by which to criticize or judge existing beliefs. There is no higher or lower, good or bad, right or wrong; all are meaningless words.

The natural appeal of this method is very great. For use of the statistical construct tends to maximize the illusion that we no longer have to accept some arrangement that reality gives us, we no longer have to accept truth and logic as binding upon us. With no necessary connection to truth and reason, with no ultimate authority or standards to settle matters, one is now free to be inconsistent. It is important to understand that the rules of statistical probability can be satisfied in conjunction with representations that are false. By this we mean that a specific statistical statement may be internally consistent without bearing any relation to reality.[23] We are mistaken, therefore, if we suppose that a statistical result or statement necessarily represents the objective state of affairs. We are wrong if we believe that the numbers it generates automatically correspond to real things.[24] Make no mistake about it. The structure of the technical model can accommodate contradictory positions in a single formula. Bear in mind, for instance, that while this model must proceed on the assumption of uniformity, it can hold together and provide a space of validity for both the data of nonindependence and the data of independent action (nonuniformity). We are of course aware that the scientific method, by the very nature of its content, cannot prove or disprove the question of an open or a closed universe. Yet the virtue of calculating in probabilities is that we can have it both ways: it provides a malleable space for man to construe ultimate reality as either lawless and provisional or orderly and fixed. It may equally validate and confirm both poles of a contradiction.

Sidebar: 729 Times Closer to God: An Open Letter

Dear Colleague,

We may have discovered a solution to the dilemma of spiritual outcomes and their assessment. New brain research has been able to identify specific regions of the brain that activate when a person is willfully attending to spiritual (numinous or noumenal) matters and concerns. MRIs, CAT scans, etc., produce empirically verifiable evidence that when a person is praying, or is thinking about Jesus, or is reading Holy Writ, or is worshipping in song, or working on a new economic theory with Christocentric lenses, or is loving a neighbor in the proper way, this particular region of the brain "lights up." Let's call it the "God spot" in the limbic system.

Technology may soon exist whereby electrodes can be planted within these specific regions of the brain such that they reliably signal to an external device whether these regions are being used (developed) by that person. The device could record how often and under what circumstances the "spiritual" regions of the brain are used and perhaps even the degree of intensity of the use. As you will immediately see, this solves the social science problem of error in self-reporting, diagnostic surveys, pre–post testing, pastor reports, mentor narratives, etc.

At first, the device could be worn by students on their clothes or embedded within a special baseball cap and will signal by color the level of spiritual activity occurring at any given moment during discipleship. Red or scarlet would represent sainthood with incremental levels all the way down to black—the dead soul, a hedonist of the worst kind.

Later, as our assessment technology ramps up, we could use new-generation spiritometers. Instead of denoting and recording a color, which after all only loosely represents a "zone" of spirituality, the new-generation spiritometers will scale spirituality to 100. "Ah good. Sarah moved from 63 to 68 today." "Oh hell, Paul's gone off the deep end, again." In some cases, 100–90 will represent an "A" for spirituality relative to the spiritual outcomes identified in a course or mentoring initiative, and so forth. We'll have machines in our offices or even attached as plug-in devices to our electronic handheld devices like Blackberries that make calculations (e.g., mean, mode, range, standard deviations) that can locate a student's

Sidebar (Continued)

spirituality relative to his or her own history or to any group we want. As mentors, we can also become monitors of spirituality, heightening the efficiency of the discipleship process. In fact, the properly calibrated spiritometer could possess an add-on feature that serves as an alarm. When Johnny takes a dip in his spirituality, Johnny's mentor could be notified in order to, either in person or through a lower-cost proxy (say, a residence life official), find Johnny and, as the saying goes, "buck him up" spiritually. Interventions are no longer left to chance. A faculty member may even get his mentee to an instant state of spiritual nirvana by pressing a special button remotely activating the electrode in the mentee's brain. Never mind the cries of, "don't tase me bro." Calmly reply, "I ain't your 'bro; I'm your spiritual mentor, now let's get better, shall we? We've got spiritual objectives to meet." Of course, we'll have to wait for the lawyers and risk management professionals to approve that. We may first have to socialize the risk.

Besides using the spiritometer as a valuable assessment tool, the device will enable us to understand better how as mentors we can more effectively use stimulus (mentoring) as a correlation to desired response (spiritual growth). Admittedly, this does not resolve the nearly intractable philosophical problem of causation—God, his Spirit, angels might be intervening variables yet to be conquered by human initiative, therefore difficult to control for—but at least we've got the spiritometer to align and measure planned spiritual outcomes.

This is certainly, from one point of view, an improvement in the way discipleship was done in the past. In the old days, it was a messy and uncertain business. Mentors had to devote themselves to the Lord, act in faith, and ultimately leave the work of spiritual growth to God (1 Cor. 3). We can now dispense with all of that higher-cost activity; all of the uncertainty and mystery (even some of the cost-bearing misery and suffering) around spiritual growth is resolved. All we have to do is leave it to the production function (the plan, the formula, the method) of spiritual growth. At first, spiritual growth production plans will be several, each striving for prediction and control. Ultimately, however, they will unify around one technical model of production. The student will no longer be responsible; the

> plan and its implementation of spiritual growth will be held to account. Higher-education accreditors will admire what we've done to make the trade-off; bending God's model to the world's model will win deviance points at the next accreditation. In fact, once we've turned the technological page to get there, Christian higher education will finally be able to (empirically) prove—to itself and to the secular academy—that spiritual growth is a legitimate concern in the development of students. It exists (it's in the brain, after all), and because it exists, as one wag put, it can be measured. Religious scholars can finally take one step closer to the formal legitimation of God to the world.[25]

All this helps us to see that operating strictly within this framework, we are rationally free to claim autonomy from self-evident principles, free to create our own ideology; free to choose for ourselves the reality we wish to adopt. What we have is a method that furnishes the opportunity to argue, explain, and transact without the constraints of reason: a method that allows us to alter the properly basic starting point for human knowing, that is, to maintain a conception of knowledge that has been detached from truth, logical relations, and noetic unity, which are the necessary elements in any condition of knowledge (Willard 2006: 6). Indeed what we have is a framework that permits us to create a structure of knowledge that is socially useful to expansion, that responds effectively to society's material wants and needs—a framework that allows us to demote knowledge to the rank of belief, which at last leaves us free to "believe in anyone and anything."

These points should leave no doubt as to why the technical system appeals to the acquisitive nature of modern thought. Such a method has proven effective in generating and sustaining expansions; it has worked well to enlarge the circle of wealth and relations of exchange. The long list of tangible pleasures derived from the use of this technique has lured us into believing that it is a system of liberation, an emancipator of human will and power. Indeed the public has come to identify the technical method with the common good, with the path to human happiness and unlimited opportunity. People see it as the rational means to expansionist ends. Here we need to stress by way of Berlin that: "What the scientific method can achieve it must, of course, be used to achieve" (1969: xxvi). Yet it is necessary to recognize this worldwide method for what it is. One must remember that the technical framework imprisons, in the sense that it confines man and his acts of knowing to the determinism that reigns in Nature, to the cause-and-effect necessity of the material world. This system is telling us to interpret human thought and representation in naturalistic terms. It is telling us that knowledge is something other than objective truth: a mere by-product of sensation, a behavioral or psychological response to stimuli. Thus, as more social and physical phenomena are analyzed and situated in this framework, the tendency is to view knowledge as being determined not by the truth known, but by material relations in the formal (inductive) processes of the law of averages. We are heading, via the technical model, for the view that the only valid source of knowledge is a controllable, formalized process that lies within the vast nonrational system of Nature. Already some 60 years ago C.S. Lewis was warning the public about the dire effects of attempting to explain all of reality in this naturalistic way: "It goes on claiming territory after territory: first the inorganic, then the lower organisms, then man's body, then his emotions. But when it takes the final step and we attempt a naturalistic account of thought itself, suddenly the whole thing unravels. The last fatal step has invalidated all the preceding ones: for they were all reasonings and reason itself has been discredited. We must, therefore, either give up thinking altogether or else begin over again from the ground floor" (Lewis 1970: 138).

It is obvious to us that reliance on the technical model has released tendencies to experience and regard the first principles of knowledge as rival to expansion. Dr. Willard gave similar expression to this point when he linked the maximizing mind-set with the general effort to move the constraining influence of truth to the periphery of human thought and life. He said: "Human desire is of course not bad in itself. It is good. But unchecked by reason and reality it always opposes truth as 'Real Truth' that puts us in touch with reality; for desire unchecked always demands more than reality can give. Therefore there is a deep human desire toward setting truth aside, and what better way to do this than by just denying its reality altogether—or at least its accessibility" (Willard 1998: 12).

This is the pattern that society's institutional structure is bound to follow since separating the tradition of ultimate principles from the logic of growth is one of the chief ways that modern markets expand. We remind the reader that the direction is not toward truth, but always toward the most we can get—toward more "gold and guns and girls," as Lewis once put it (2001a: 77). But the price we pay for all this is to bring forth an inadequate information base for communicating the necessary laws of knowledge. What this comes down to is that the trade-offs decided upon within the expanding system create an order in which the traditional meaning of knowledge does not merit preservation.

That education as an institution would roll along in this direction is entirely understandable and quite logical. At the lower level of reality that is Nature, the system of education becomes a matter of conditioning the environment, delivering efficiencies of scale through technique, lowering the relative costs of schooling, and spreading the disease of intellectual and moral relativism. Such a system emerges readily from a social order in which erasing the essential distinctions between man and Nature, between ought and is, and between reality and appearance are leading features. It has thus come about that education is trying to shape itself while blurring distinctions and seriously misemploying productive factors; that is to say, it is trying to shape itself while compressing all relations and subject matter into the framework of science. In such conditions, it is almost inevitable that education would foster an environment of uncertainty and confusion, where it advances skepticism about the standards of knowledge even as it must in practice accept those standards as valid. It must be very clearly understood that if, following the view suggested by education, we look upon knowledge as mere coherence of beliefs, as socially created and sustained, as probable and subjective, then this leaves us with no certainty about axioms or inferences on which our knowledge depends. Most critical, perhaps, and less commonly realized, is that such a conception of knowledge leaves us without the basis to place limits on state compulsion; it leaves us with no standing ground against the encroachments of an omni-competent power.

Expansion, however brought about, always interjects optimism and a sense of power and upward movement into the institutional setting. Therefore it is tempting, but it would be a great error, to think of our modern era as a period in which the analytical abstractions of development are advancing the necessary conditions to guide thought into conformity with reality. Growth in its present manner and direction cannot fulfill the epistemic category. As a little inquiry will show, expanding education does not save it.

Chapter 4

Educational Sustainability and the Obsolete Man

Man and the expanding domain of Nature

With this sketch of the fundamental problems of social thought nearly behind us, let us press on and apply our theory more fully to the question of educational sustainability. What has become obvious to this point is that man as human cannot survive the modern liberation of material growth, the expanding domain of Nature. The reason for this becomes obvious after working out the institutional logic of the technical model of education and its productive activities. The technical model of production simply denies to human beings the necessary qualities, attributes, and purposes that make men and women human. If man per chance physically survives the institutional environment under technical growth, it will be in material form, it will not be surviving as man *qua* human. He will continue to exist by becoming something else, something less than human—a shadow of what he was intended to be, an obsolete figure in the drone of numbers percolating among central planners. Yet the institution of education diminishes the human in ways that are not always obvious. It is not like Solzhenitsyn's description of Stalin's Gulags, where becoming opaque and undifferentiated against the crowd of enslaved humanity became a survival skill. It is more subtle, a diminishment in degree, a progressive and incremental sacrifice, not yet so total as to become conspicuous, but consistently attenuating human qualities, properties, and virtues.

In the *Abolition of Man* argument, C.S. Lewis observes that two categories of reality are in tension. On the one hand, he argues, there exists as "reality" a set of observer-dependent institutional facts (social constructions) generated by the modern institution of education that engages in both enabling and constraining activity. It enables a new, socially constructed approach toward reality (subjectivism) and, at the same time, levies a destructive constraint on the information base to the individual – collective problem of social choice, advantaging a collective and disadvantaging the individual. It is a modern reality whose principles, in the growth environment, are drawn from some combination of subjectivism, scientific positivism, cosmic developmentalism, but most of all, naturalism. On the other hand, says Lewis, this new reality screens from view observer-independent teleological facts about what human development and flourishing should plausibly look like. It seeks to prevent a change of the rules when those rules would originate from within the Tao. Reform of men's public affairs from an externality like the moral law is prohibited; purely secular reasons are what count in public discourse (see Audi and Wolterstorff 1996; Audi 2000). The third chapter of the *Abolition* describes the powerful social construction that acts as a propagandist, where power and persuasion lower costs in one direction but raise them in another, where man's history and teleology mean very little and break from tradition and reality. Man as human becomes less able to exercise the intellectual and moral virtues because final causes have been traded off for efficient causes, and ends for means.

In the new reality any reliable reference to the brute facts of the moral law, any legitimate appeal to the objective mind-independent sphere escapes us: "We make men without chests and expect of them virtue and enterprise. We laugh at honor and are shocked to find traitors in our midst. We castrate and bid the geldings be fruitful" (Lewis 2001a: 26). The "is" and the "ought" have been formally separated, though the "ought" creeps back in under the argument: "When all that says 'it is good' has been debunked, what says 'I want' remains. It cannot be exploded or 'seen through' because it never had any pretentions. The Conditioners, therefore, must come to be motivated simply by their own pleasure.... My point is that those who stand outside all judgments of value cannot have any ground for preferring one of their own impulses to another except the emotional strength of that impulse" (pp. 65–66). Instinct, technique, convention, and power are the new virtues. Rationality survives without reason as its guide. The modern institution of education asks its participants to stipulate to these new terms of production and the education of valueless facts ensues.[1]

It should surprise us then that there is no final or ultimate agreement on the two interrelated questions: what man *is* and what his education ought to be.[2] It should surprise us because social institutions like education function as though the question has been settled, though the questions in the naturalist outlook are ultimately meaningless. Look clearly at nearly any Western nation-state; its education system will reveal an instrumental view, a powerful naturalistically driven view directing its educational discourse, its economy of information in public policy, its curricular preferences, its patterns of practice, and its assessment emphases. These systems make bold claims about educational progress while compressing the human being into a technical system. The nature of the individual person, which is the subject matter or good of education, resists the compression effectuated by this technical method. But in an expanding environment, as the local gives way to the global, the institutional rules work to eliminate such resistance. We have seen this pattern before. The cult of efficiency movement from 1900 to 1930 is but one example (Callahan 1962).[3] Another is the "one best system" of schooling (Tyack 1974). The adjusting of men to machines movement in the 1930s and 1940s is another (Bell 1947). For reasons of cost, measured by efficiencies within the technical framework, where "the final answer to every educational question...must be left to the educational measurer" (McCall 1922: 9),[4] the old model of education and its knowledge base, its emphasis on moral and intellectual virtues, does not enlighten or constrain SIs in the manner it once had (George 2001, 2001a).

Lewis's approach to the perennial question of man's identity and his education pares the complex field of possibilities to two general categories. The first is an open view of the universe that includes spirit and matter, characterized by complexities of inquiry which birth wide realms of knowledge, including the fields of theology, metaphysics, and ethics. The open view allows for qualitative, substance – property distinctions vital to human identity. These permit the drawing of accurate distinctions between and within substances, or basic entities in themselves, and properties, which are the attributes and quality distinctions possessed by substances (Loux 2006). This view also emphasizes the quality of relations between individuals and collectives, between people and their SIs. The open view assigns suitable weight to the condition and direction of the social welfare. The Italian economist Vilfredo Pareto (1906: 13) once wrote, "Political economy does not have to take morality into account. But one who extols some practical measure ought to take into account not only the economic consequences, but also the moral, religious, political, etc., consequences." It is not that economic expansion and material wealth are unimportant. Rather, according to the open view, economic growth and material wealth ought not come at a significant expense to the individual, the demos, or the polity. In other words, the social welfare situation that so concerned Lewis and others operates as a key restraint on Nature and its material level of reality. Much of education has lost sight of these first principles.

The alternative is a view that the universe is a closed system. Methodological commitments ultimately bind answers to biology, chemistry, and physics. The closed view tends to emphasize economic and material expansion over normative questions and conditions rendering individual life and the social welfare to the technical solution. Human beings come to be defined as role-players in a game, chess pieces sacrificed here and there during a match. In this regard, Alasdair MacIntyre (1999: 313) comments on the understanding that human beings constitute much more in their relationships:

My awareness of and understanding of myself as an individual is exhibited in and partly constituted by the various acknowledgements of that individuality by others and my ability to respond to those others as individuals and not just role players. This mutual acknowledgement of our individuality characterizes some of our social relationships rather than others and some of our social relationships more markedly than others. And central among such acknowledgements are those judgments in which we evaluate individuals as individuals, in respect of their virtues and the goodness of their lives.

The institution of education *outside* of the Tao faces a minimum of three problems: (1) the transcendent nature of human beings, (2) human virtues and purposes, and (3) individual personality and expression of freedom.[5] How does social thought account for these human attributes within a strictly naturalistic framework? It doesn't and it can't. The modern institution of education cannot afford to recognize human nature as it is. To keep expanding, it must ignore, deny, or redefine (1)–(3). The institution in the technical growth state of affairs simply redefines the good on new terms; categories are invented, an aggregation procedure is set, interventions are identified, a range of individual actions narrowed, and social welfare functions imposed. "The crucial link between individual and social action is the presence of what may be termed a *social mechanism*. This can be described by specifying two types of elements: (1) a range of actions available to individuals; and (2) a social outcome defined for each possible choice of actions by all individuals... The interests of classical political philosophers and modern social choice theorists alike have been concentrated on the design of social mechanisms. Any design problem involves an idea of the good" (Arrow 1981:1376, 1379). When the good is obfuscated by the technical mechanism the obsolescence of the individual expands.

In the open view an important part of recognizing the individual person is realizing that he or she is a spiritual (immaterial) being as much as a physical one, recognizing that a key to the good is located as much with the immaterial heart as the plasticity of the brain. Lewis gives great attention to the chest or heart of man. In the *Abolition*, he writes:

The head rules the belly through the chest—the seat, as Alanus tells us, of Magnanimity, of emotions organized by trained habit into stable sentiments. The Chest-Magnanimity-Sentiment—these are the indispensable liaison officers between cerebral man and visceral man. It may even be said that it is by this middle element that man is man: for by his intellect he is mere spirit and by his appetite mere animal. (2001a: 24, 25)

The loss of the middle element is the loss of a key part of being human. On this basic level alone, when various institutions (e.g., the family, the schools) leave the heart underdeveloped by not inculcating just sentiments into the student, society is prone to becoming heartless and bloodless.

In this chapter we examine the human and the modern institution of education by exploring distinctions between choices and decisions, the division of rationality from reason, and how the institution sustains itself. These subjects will bring us to a clearer understanding of Lewis's question that on what basis does education function outside of the Tao.

THE CHOICE – DECISION DISTINCTION

Education is in a significant way concerned with the development of beliefs and belief-forming practices. Beliefs are the rails upon which human beings act. The nature of beliefs and their truth relation are of paramount concern because beliefs that are in error about something can in certain circumstances produce actions that do harm, either by omission or by commission. A society or community bears a significant cost when these kinds of errors occur (e.g., injustice, incivility, genocide).

As we saw in previous chapters, SIs impact and are impacted by the belief systems of human beings comprising them. Beliefs are in significant part a product of two faculties of the mind: reason and rationality. We will not here give an account of the disembodied status of these mental faculties, though there are good reasons for supposing that mental faculties are not reducible to embodied brain activity (McGinn 2000; Moreland 2008).[6] The brain is important for cognitive function, but so is the performance of the immaterial mind; we note briefly that in the disembodied state the brain is not a necessary condition for mental activity. In other words, some realist form of metaphysical dualism is likely true and is a commonsense position (Moreland and Craig 2003). For our purposes, we will presuppose this warranted view for the remainder of the chapter.

As mental faculties, reason and rationality can be unified, and are unified at age appropriate levels when education works properly. A properly educated person in time comes to be both rational and reasonable. In our daily lives, we learn to adjust the means to ends in order to reach internal coherence, the aim of rationality, and we learn how to identify the right ends, the aim of reason. These two faculties are interdependent with the will, which is that specific executive element that directs reason and rationality to attend to something, such as the acquisition of information and knowledge for choices and decisions. Within the context of attending to beliefs, including the reality to which beliefs are purported to correspond, as well as the manner in which beliefs are formed, stand choices and decisions. We briefly discuss the differences between choices and decisions before turning to a discussion about reason and rationality and the sustainability of education as an institution.

The economic literature makes an important distinction between choices and decisions, one that might help us to understand more completely how the technical apparatuses of SIs work to delimit individual agency. Arrow (1984: 56) writes that choices may be viewed as unreflective and even unconscious activity, implying that decisions are reflective and conscious. Economist Richard Thaler and legal scholar Cass Sunstein (2007: 19–22) more recently suggested that the cognitive structure is one divided between an automatic, unreflective system and a willful, reflective system. The former enables an effortless response to environmental stimuli; the latter enables a slow and effortful deliberative process. Thaler and Sunstein argue that a "choice architecture" can be constructed by "choice architects" (society's mandarins) in order to manipulate environmental conditions and various SIs that will "nudge" participants toward an ideal, mutually beneficial social choice response. What Thaler and Sunstein do not appear to realize is that it is the institutional mechanism for the division of information, activated within the model of growth, that secures "direction in production without appealing to a sense of obligation beyond consent," keeping coercion to a minimum (Rodriguez, Loomis, and Weeres 2007: 77).

Such a force draws on time and its stages of growth and on the accumulation of precedents to eliminate the motives for the pursuit of ends that may not conform to what seems to constitute the productive forms of education. Its pattern of expansion offers unity, security, and sufficient strength to divert demand into the direction of attainment while preserving the impression of free choice. Indeed, it does not call for the abdication of choice or liberty; rather it demands rationality and sublimation of choices and options to the exigencies of its productive process.

Our own view contrasts the nature and tendency of choices and decisions in the following way:

Choices	Decisions
Economic	Philosophical
Unreflective	Reflective
Rationality	Reason
Data	Logic
Belief coherence	Truth correspondence
Behavior	Motives
Defaulting to habit	Willful action
Preference orderings	Virtue balancing
Utility maximization	Community interdependence
Agent-dependent knowledge	Agent-independent knowledge
Narrower information base	Wider information base
Initially less costly	Initially more costly

The technical model of education is sustained when emphasizing in students the development of a choice architecture, centered on rationality. Even the new Essentialist (standards-based) curriculum, where values are separated from facts, emphasizes the choice architecture. Yet we are not arguing that the development of choices, in the economic sense, is by itself a bad thing. We are insisting that proper human development includes the development of economic *and* philosophical man, enlarging the developmental capacity to make reliable choices and trustworthy decisions, the ability to economize on information where appropriate, and to maximize the costs where necessary. In this sense, we acknowledge Hayek's (1945: 528) caution:

> The problem which we meet here is by no means peculiar to economics but arises in connection with nearly all truly social phenomena, with language and most of our cultural inheritance, and constitutes really the central theoretical problem of all social science. As Alfred Whitehead has said in another connection, "It is a profoundly erroneous truism, repeated by all copy-books and by eminent people when they are making speeches, that we should cultivate the habit of thinking what we are doing. The precise opposite is the case. Civilization advances by extending the number of important operations which we can perform without thinking about them." This is of profound significance in the social field.

Hayek's caution notwithstanding (Lewis made a similar caution a few years earlier, 2001c: 67), the problem today is that the institution of education under a technical framework relies on the cost-lowering logistics of aggregation: formulas, symbols, statistics, procedural rules, social welfare functions, and other data that displace the full range of human development, including the use of reason. SIs like education (or health care and justice systems) circumscribe the individual's philosophical approach to decision making into the economic approach of making choices. Decision making is a more expensive process; it takes more time, taps a wider set of information, handles exigencies of the particular and universal, and is less dependent to the technical situation.[7]

Choices and orderings depend on the utility-maximization criterion. In neoclassical economics this means maximizing the relative satisfaction or pleasure of consuming goods, services, and the performing of various types of work. As Samuelson (1955: 91) notes, behavior is reductively and circularly explained "in terms of preferences, which are in turn defined only by behavior." Arrow raises an interesting issue for the theory of rational choice, commenting that the distinction between choices and decisions on reductive variables "may be defective" for two central reasons: "the effect of one part on the individual's ordering with respect to another, which may be termed the *interdependence of values*, and the limitations imposed by reality on the simultaneous achievement of values in several areas, which may be termed *jointness of resource limitations*" (1983: 57). In either instance, reality gets in the way of tight economic modeling. The economic modeling of human behavior while abstracting the person from the complexities of human nature and his or her environment is a loss of information and is a challenge for the social theorist (see Beinhocker 2007).

Those things that could not be eased into a mathematical formula—such as camaraderie, pride, morale—were left out of the analysis, even though they might be added as an appendix in case a tiebreaker was needed to decide between otherwise equal solutions. By extension, if a subject could not be measured, ranged, and classified, it was of little consequence in systems analysis, for it was not rational. Numbers were all—the human factor was a mere adjunct to the empirical. (Abella 2008: 59)

But the larger point that we want the reader to take is that the SI in the technical model will tend to stress choices, not decisions. This is not different from the standard rational choice presentation, one that relies on a narrow methodological individualism (Becker 1976). Choices respond narrowly on the level of instinct, that is, to a simple and reductive information environment (Satz and Ferejohn 1994). Choices are narrowly serviceable and pragmatic; the scope of their concern is an agent's utility maximization. Decisions, being a product of insight, reflection, and reason, access regions of reality that choices typically do not. Decisions tap a wider information base prior to action. It is not too difficult to see how the use of reason and reflection in decision making can inhibit or obstruct the asymmetric process of "nudging" an individual toward a predesigned social "choice architecture" (Thaler and Sunstein 2007: 81–102). However, the individual cannot completely be abstracted from his nature or physical and social environments without a cost.

Sidebar: The Insufficiency of Rational Choice Theory

As the closed model of growth steers the social institution to move firmly outside of the Tao, it calls on its participants to function on viciously reductionistic principles. The closed growth model trims the composite nature of man, conferring on him the status of a purely natural organism, a species of the nonrational universal cause and effect (Lewis 2001b). This is ironic given that rational choice theory—a view originating from social science concerning persons and their making choices—posits heightened rationality in consequence of the reduction (Richter 1971). Yet Nature *by itself* is neither rational nor irrational, and it cannot be a source of rationality. It is nonrational and so are its causes and effects. This proves to be an irresolvable dilemma for naturalism. The dilemma is resolved by linking rationality to certain evolutionary processes of human choices (Skyrms 1996).[8]

Sidebar (Continued)

After detaching from Reason rationality is reasserted on new ground and in a new form on the belief that Nature (the natural) and Nature's material goods provide the principal impetus for choices within a social contract. "[N]atural selection is bound to preserve and increase useful behaviour" (Lewis 2001b: 32). This new rationality, where desire dependency pursues fitness (Simon 1990), is lurking in background to theories of choice. Amartya Sen (1977: 323) summarizes the process view of rational choice theory:

> A person's choices are considered "rational" in this approach if and only if these choices can *all* be explained in terms of some preference relation consistent with the revealed preference definition, that is, if all his choices can be explained as the choosing of "most preferred" alternatives with respect to a postulated preference relation. The rationale of this approach seems to be based on the idea that the only way of understanding a person's real preference is to examine his actual choices, and there is no choice-independent way of understanding someone's attitude toward alternatives.... [O]nce we eschew the curious definitions of preference and welfare, this approach presumes both too little and too much: too little because there are non-choice sources of information on preference and welfare as these terms are usually understood, and too much because choice may reflect a compromise among a variety of considerations of which personal welfare may be just one.

This relatively new view of rationality allows the principles and processes of naturalism and developmentalism to alter the content of and standard for rationality. It places rationality as a concept in an equivocal, desire-dependent position, threatening its legitimacy as a reliable criterion for belief and action (Trigg 1993: 225). The instrumental view of rationality survives through the ontic descent of man and the widespread division of market information under scale, each affecting (and being effected by) substitution favoring the use of naturalism, which liberates institutional conditions that trigger significant material (economic) gains from trade. While growth delivers many goods and services that serve as important internal verification for the use of rationality for public policy, growth wrongly acts as the criterion of social progress. The human condition is much more complex than the reductive measures of economic output.

One of the most striking characteristics of the contemporary world is that rationality and individual liberty may now be seen as incompatible. Rationality is found today co-opted by "virtues" arising from expanding markets and politics, in the code and measures of globalization, and in the collective ordering of social goods, such as efficiency, social cooperation, reduction of risk, greater certainty of information and its direction, less friction (cost) in trade, standardization of rules, flattened communication, and more secure property rights. This is all seemingly fitting: it is rational to be on the side of institutional expansion (economic growth); work and development on behalf of nation-states, cosmopolitan political bodies, and trading organizations proceed on this assumption.

An important argument in the *Abolition* is that a well functioning education system will help the student to inculcate through habit an ability to make reliable choices in a given set of circumstances. In situation A, say seeing an attractive or sublime waterfall (the example Lewis uses), the student has a duty to accord to reality what is properly due and choose, among several options, option B, that is, to recognize and appreciate the objective beauty of the waterfall in a manner that occurs in harmony with reason, "so that when Reason at length comes to him, then, bred as he has been, he will hold out his hands in welcome and recognize her because of the affinity he bears to her" (p. 17). Educating students how to objectively and reliably order preferences, convictions, and sentiments before the age of life-changing choices and decisions implies at least two things: (1) that a reliable doctrine of objective value exists that all persons, and especially educators, should hold fast and (2) that the institution of education will accurately recognize that the moral law is a product of Reason and is the overriding social institution. Lewis feared that both (1) and (2) were being replaced by subjectivism. Lewis said that the modern education system will teach its students *how* to choose, that is, how to use rationality for choices, as well as *what* to choose, but not on the basis of doctrines like objective value or mind-independent institutions like the moral law. So, there is nudging with reason and the moral law, and nudging without reason and the moral law. A prominent sociologist puts the problem in these Lewis-like terms:

We say we want a renewal of character in our day but we don't really know what we ask for. To have a renewal of character is to have a renewal of a creedal order that constrains, limits, binds, obligates and compels. *This price is too high for us to pay*. We want character but without conviction; we want strong morality but without particular moral justifications that invariably offend; we want good without having to name evil; we want decency without the authority to insist upon it; we want moral community without any limitations to personal freedom. In short, we want what we cannot possibly have on the terms that we want it.[9]

THE DIVISION OF RATIONALITY FROM REASON

Our own analysis, like Lewis's, does not make the familiar mistake of thinking that when all is cut away the metaphysical contest is between two complete *systems* of thought. It is not. It is indeed a contest, but one between, on the one side, a genuine mind-independent reality, represented in part by Lewis's references to the doctrine of objective value and the institution of moral law and, on the other side, certain human conceptions and models of reality that are radically incomplete or that have made fatal errors. We must remember that naturalism is a philosophical position, not a scientific one. Lewis (2001b: 39–40) observes in *Miracles* that "the relation between Reason and Nature is what some people call an Unsymmetrical Relation. Brotherhood is a symmetrical relation because if A is the brother of B, B is the brother of A. Father-and-son is an unsymmetrical relation because if A is the father of B, B is *not* the father of A. The relation between Reason and Nature is of this kind. Reason is not related to Nature as Nature is related to Reason." The present error would only be compounded by trying to forge some form of neutrality to mediate between the two. Error of any kind is made possible only by there being a mind-independent reality to begin with.

Reason is different from rationality in important and irreducible ways, though the two terms are often used in social science literature interchangeably. For example, when Nobel economist Herbert Simon (1983: 7–8) claims, "Reason is wholly instrumental. It cannot tell us where to go; at best it can tell us how to get there. It is a gun for hire that can be employed in the service of any goals that we have, good or bad," he conflates the term (and the specific faculty) "reason" with the subordinate role and instrumental function of rationality. This may or may not be intentional. It may be an accident of equivocation, a product of miseducation, or even an artifact of hope, though it is difficult to know. What it signals is a clear failure to understand the nature of reason as a human faculty.

The fruit of reason's privilege—the principal warrant for reason's importance for human life and for good education—is that it enlarges human capacity for self-correction along the path created by moral law (Lewis 2001a: 74–75). Treating oneself and others with respect and justice is the work of reason. Reason grants access to first questions and principles that reveal antecedent conditions to human flourishing and proper function. Rationality tends to focus on second and tertiary things. Reason sends a person to the correct authority concerning first questions; rationality sends him on a path that coheres with prevailing institutional direction. Without reason to direct and guide, rationality *qua ratio* is prepared to serve any authority.

In the *De Futilitate*, an early 1940s lecture given at Magdalen College, Lewis (1995: 57–71) makes certain distinctions on the subject of reason that are important to cite in full:

> As I have said, there is no such thing (strictly speaking) as *human* reason: but there is emphatically such a thing as human thought—in other words, the various specifically human conceptions of Reason, failures of complete rationality, which arise in a wishful and lazy human mind utilizing a tired human brain. The difference between acknowledging this and being skeptical about Reason itself, is enormous. For in the one case we should be saying that reality contradicts Reason, whereas now we are only saying that total Reason—cosmic or super-cosmic Reason—corrects human imperfections of Reason. Now correction is not the same as mere contradiction. When your false reasoning is corrected you "see the mistakes": the true reasoning thus takes up into itself whatever was already rational in your original thought. You are not moved into a totally new world; you are given *more* and *purer* of what you already had in a small quantity and badly mixed with foreign elements. To say that Reason is objective is to say that all our false reasonings could in principle be corrected by more Reason. I have to add "in principle" because, of course, the reasoning necessary to give us absolute truth about the whole universe might be (indeed, certainly would be) too complicated for any human mind to hold it all together or even to keep on attending. But that, again, would be a defect in the human instrument, not in Reason.... It seems to me that the relation between our sense of values and the values acknowledged by the cosmic or super-cosmic Reason is likely to be the same as the relation between our attempts at logic and Logic itself. (p. 68)

Now, let us examine the concept of rationality in more detail. Philosopher Alvin Plantinga (1993) identifies five meanings of the term rationality:

(1) Aristotelian rationality: "man is a rational animal"
(2) Rationality as proper function
(3) Rationality as within or conforming to the deliverances of reason

(4) Means – ends rationality, where the question is whether a particular means someone chooses is, in fact, a good means to her ends
(5) Deontological rationality, the giving of assent only to that for which one has good reasons, good evidence

For the moment, let us stipulate to (1). For if we cannot stipulate to (1) there is no use reading on, or reading at all. That leaves (2)–(5). Given what we have initially said about the division of reason from rationality, the technical model of growth prevents rationality as proper function (2) as well as rationality within or conforming to the deliverances of reason (3). In both (2) and (3), rationality as a lower cognitive faculty requires the higher cognitive faculty of reason to keep it within the overarching framework of reality. But reason itself has already been divided (split) from rationality by the technical growth model. For the purpose of cost, it would be difficult for the technical model of growth to proceed on instrumental terms if an institution maintained human capacity for (2) and (3). Both would make it more probable that the proverbial whistle would be blown on the concealed trade-offs taking place under unrestricted growth on its technical terms. The abstractions, reductions, and substitutions necessary for the technical growth model would receive challenge, causing friction and conflict that might threaten growth. That leaves (4) and (5). Herein lays the power of the social structure and our general concerns.

Education as an institution can condition environment E such that person P will construct and develop some large number of his social beliefs, SB (and belief-forming practices), in line with E. Therefore, $P(SB) = E$. The construction and development of belief formation occurs in some combination of personal experience, intuition, reason, and authority, facilitated by SIs (e.g., the schools and the media), which together act to influence E. On this conception, socially constructed beliefs are largely experience and framework dependent, which underscores the need for SIs to function properly. Mean – ends rationality (4) functions to align $P(SB) = E$. That is its utility. If the institution is out of proper function, as under the technical model of growth, and means – ends rationality is all that we have to work with, that is, for knowledge acquisition, the potential moral problem is made obvious to most of us. At some point in the process of belief formation total subjectivism looms large as a viable alternative model for education. Under Nature there is no power to prevent this state of affairs from realization. This is precisely what Lewis was getting at in the *Abolition*. Rationality as a human faculty becomes a gun for hire; it becomes a dependable responder to innovations of virtue—a device ensconced to the virtual reality created by Lewis's Conditioner. Through reductionist forms of rationality, whoever controls E will likely control $P(SB)$. The key instrument in the control of E is the SI, the logic and structure of its information economy, its rules, agenda, etc. So, deontological rationality (5) really is a function of the environment, that is, environment E. If that environment does not reflect reality as fully as possible, then there is an increased probability that "good reasons" and "good evidence" are more likely to be understood simply in terms of the closed information network of the technical institution. Lewis (2001a: 63) anticipated the reduction of the old idea of duty (deontological rationality) to this newer version:

[Conditioners] recognize the concept of duty as the result of certain processes which they can now control. Their victory has consisted precisely in emerging from the state in which they were acted upon by those processes to the state in which they use them as tools. One of the things they now have to decide is whether they will, or will not, so condition the rest of us that we can go on having the old idea of duty and the old reactions to it. How can duty help them to decide that? Duty itself is up for trial: it cannot also be the judge.

Indeed, it is for this very reason that the definition of educational problem depends in large measure on the constraints entailed by E. Lewis (2001a: 20–21) himself suggests this: "Hence the educational problem is wholly different according as you stand within or without the *Tao*." There is E *with* the Tao and E *without* the Tao. Lewis's axiom holds true for all complex SIs, including law, medicine, and political systems.

A central premise of the *Abolition* argument is that the loss of access to first principles of theoretical and practical Reason does not bode well for the environment of education. At best, propagation and initiation are subverted in favor of propaganda and conditioning. Similarly the central message of Lewis's fictional work, *That Hideous Strength* (2003), a complementary argument to that of the *Abolition of Man*, is that a period of dehumanization follows the effective elimination of reason and the instrumental turn of rationality (we have in mind Lewis's repeated reference to "extreme rationalism"). The notion of "proper function" requires the development of and interplay between reason and rationality (Plantinga 1993). The traditional good of education has been to pursue the ethical development of these faculties. An improperly functioning education system trades off reason (higher cost) for rationality (lower cost).

Notice the significant shift in how people relate to reality. Rationality as the cognitive faculty *ratio* no longer means the aim of getting in the right relation to truth, employing the correct means to access the truth of things. It means instead getting into the pragmatic relation to the SI, with little ability to evaluate that institution's informational direction. The means and ends of rationality are seduced away from the pursuit of truth in its full density.

The division of rationality from reason, followed by a progressive attenuation of rationality, is a key move in the information patterns set by expanding SIs. Conscience is little help here because it too falls sway to downward causal pressures from the institution and its significant influence on the environment. When working properly, conscience brings to one's awareness the internal and external forces pressing upon one's will to act on what is correct. If conscience interplays with the faculties of reason and rationality, then the division of rationality from reason necessarily affects the use of conscience.

We need to remember that an aim of a good education system is the suitable alignment of the faculties of knowing to the proper distribution of justification for knowing. Sense-perceptible experience is one important way of knowing and is a basis for the scientific method. It has earned significant justification for knowing about the natural and social worlds. Still, knowing in the scientific and social worlds requires something more: it requires reason and rationality to work jointly. Reason gives us our ends and rationality the means to achieve them. Yet the technical institution has little use for reason and every use for attenuated rationality. To see this clearly a deeper review of the term "reason" in Lewis's thought is required.

Reason in one sense means the mental power or faculty of intellect (*intellectus*) employed in adapting thought or action to an end.[10] Reason, as Lewis suggests, is the criterion for objective order; it provides an end consistent with the moral law (Lewis 2001a: 19). Reason as a term once referred to "rational soul" where two immaterial compartments of soul worked together: the lower *ratio* (rationality) discovers truths inductively, that is, a systematic process of investigation, and it is distinguished from the higher *intellectus* (reason), that is, the faculty of intellect seeing self-evident truths (Lewis 2007: 156–161). For centuries, humankind used the faculty of intellect to recognize self-evident truths and the faculty of rationality to acquire knowledge when truths were not self-evident.[11] Before the eighteenth century, nearly all moralists "believed the fundamental moral aims were intellectually grasped . . . they would have made morality an affair not of *ratio* but of *intellectus*" (p. 158). The "linguistic result of [the reductive process] was to narrow the meaning of the word *reason*. From meaning (in all but the most philosophical contexts) the whole Rational Soul, both *intellectus* and *ratio*, it shrank to meaning merely 'the power by which man deduces one proposition from another' " (pp. 159–160). The widespread advance of the scientific (inductive) method coalesced with the attenuated framework of rationality, not reason. It is not that the scientific method is anti-reason. Rather, it is non-reason.

All possible knowledge, then, depends on the validity of reasoning. If the feeling of certainty which we express by words like *must be* and *therefore* and *since* is a real perception of how things outside our own minds really "must" be, well and good. But if this certainty is merely a feeling *in* our own minds and not a genuine insight into realities beyond them—if it merely represents the way our minds happen to work—then we can have no knowledge. Unless human reasoning is valid no science can be true. (Lewis 2001b: 21)

What's more, under the technical model of growth, rationality as a term loses nearly all of its connection to reason. A simple example points to this truth. In learned societies, it is rare to hear the question, "Is that reasonable?" One is far more likely to hear the question, "Is that rational?" This is especially the case where the field of activity is touched by a social science and the influence of Hume, Weber, and others. Once the term connected formally to the social sciences, it took on instrumental qualities quite separate from objective and normative senses of reason and logic. The idea behind *homo economicus* is that human beings are rational to the extent they seek with self-interest individual desires at least cost. The idea follows Bentham's philosophy of utilitarianism (or utility analysis); it is an outgrowth from naturalistic assumptions. Self-evident truths give way to empirical probabilities and utility functions. In addressing the broader idea, Sen (1977: 336) even goes so far as to say that the "*purely* economic man is indeed close to being a social moron."

In contrast to pistol-slinging utilitarian rationality, reason signals a more stable teleology; it points out that higher reason is built into the fabric of individual consciousness and social life. Reason signifies objective purpose; it gives a person capacity for duty-oriented agency beyond mere adaptation for survival, that is, to act for human development and against injustices and abuses of persons and the environment when harm threatens and ensues.[12] The noetic effects of sin of course make it imperfect by itself. Lewis (1995: 43) attests to the limits of human reason:

[Though] Reason is divine, human reasoners are not. When once passion takes part in the game, the human reason, unassisted by Grace, has about as much chance of retaining its hold on truths already gained as a snowflake has of retaining its consistency in the mouth of a blast furnace. The sort of arguments against Christianity which our reason can be persuaded to accept at the moment of yielding to temptation are often preposterous. Reason may win truths; without Faith she will retain them just so long as Satan pleases. There is nothing we cannot be made to believe and disbelieve. If we wish to be rational, not now and then, but constantly, we must pray for the gift of Faith, for the power to go on believing not in the teeth of reason but in the teeth of lust and terror and jealousy and boredom and indifference that which reason, authority, or experience, or all three, have once delivered to us for truth.

The presence of reason as an epistemic faculty presupposes the ability to transcend the persuasive effects of SIs when they threaten moral agency. The absence or corruption of reason lowers the moral guard on which the cost-intensive effects of material growth remain concealed. This view took hold of one of Lewis's (2003: 40) fictional characters, Lord Feverstone, in *That Hideous Strength*:

The third problem is Man himself. ... Man has got to take charge of Man ... obvious things, at first—sterilization of the unfit, liquidation of backward races (we don't want any dead weights), selective breeding. Then real education, including pre-natal education. By real education I mean one that has no "take-it-or-leave-it" nonsense. A real education makes the patient what it wants infallibly: whatever he or his parents try to do about it. Of course, it'll have to be mainly psychological at first. But we'll get on to biochemical conditioning in the end and direct manipulation of the brain [...]. It's the real thing at last. A new type of man.

The institution acts as a hidden source of habituation where rationality and belief-forming practices are influenced by exogenous "mechanisms of imitation, conformism and constraint" (Hodgson 2003: 171). Outside, the *faculty* of reason resides in the mind where reason *as an activity* targets truth (or the truth relation) as the aim of its activity (Warnock 1967).[13] In this sense, reason possesses a normative quality. "All possible knowledge, then, depends on the validity of reasoning" (Lewis 2001b: 21). By itself rationality is not truth dependent, it is agent dependent; rationality is multiply ambiguous. Cohen

(1993: 416) examines nine separate meanings of the term "rationality." The seventh is the one that concerns us here; it is the one that the model of growth relies on for its success. Rationality "is exhibited by actions that further the purposes or interests of the agent. Thus, if a model of economic behaviour is said to assume the rationality of those operating [in market conditions], what is implied is that each agent conducts his transactions in the way that will maximize his [interests]. And, where the agent cannot be certain about what will promote his purposes or interests, rationality is often assumed to require him to prefer that course of action which will maximize the arithmetical product of the probability and utility."

Many, of course, will find it distasteful to have us rain on the growth framework's parade, but our responsibility as scholars is to argue that coherentism is an unsuccessful way to proceed in life because it sees warrant (belief justification) as involving *only* the relation between beliefs and desires. What if the beliefs of a mad man link to desire? Without reason as its guide, rationality is a faculty that functions in the category of instinct (Lewis 2001a: 79). An institutional actor (say, an educational leader) may be entirely *rational* (coherent) in believing or doing X when the reality and truth of the issue calls the actor's *reason* to believe or do Y. Reason is independent of desire and preference; rationality is desire and preference dependent. Reason accesses self-evident truths and first questions; rationality depends upon inferential ground. The old social problem for education was how to conform the soul to reality. The development of the proper function of reason *and* rationality was the answer. The new educational problem is how to constrain reality to rational people and their systems (Lewis 2001a: 77). This is the commonly accepted problem but not at all the problem we (or Lewis) are concerned with. Institutional emphasis on rationality is the answer; it divides otherwise unified and compatible faculties in order to secure a lower-cost pathway for institutional participants. This is how the social choice problem is settled.

In the growth scheme, all information that coheres with a technical order (e.g., tenets of naturalism and developmentalism) is given first preference. The logic and cost differential of this information lines up well the criterion of rationality. Reducing the human to natural characteristics works as both cause and effect of material expansion, seen by participants as an active condition for economic growth. Matching the instrumental view of persons to information patterns and exchange conditions of a technical model of production significantly pressures the decision sets of individuals, setting them along a path of least cost. It does this by trimming the information base from which to make decisions and allocate resources, removing vital (higher-cost) information from the calculus of human existence and exchange. The model regulates what type of information is allowed to reach productive agenda. As one might imagine, such patterns and conditions tend to depreciate certain aspects of human experience, e.g., the exercise of reason, making experience largely fungible to technical efficiencies, reducing learning to schooling.

Consequently, we should look at the faculty of reason as a cost generator: it is an inhibitor to technical forms of expansion. SIs functioning outside of the Tao cannot afford the price of its activation. While activation of its native and extra-natural powers does not guarantee force of opposition to what is going on, it does make opposition to injustices more probable. Reason left dormant ensures that human experience, such as an individual life or social welfare, comes to be seen not as something that possesses deeper origins, meaning, and relations; beliefs and actions no longer echo in heaven. Quite the contrary, experience suffers a qualitative loss of the beauty and complexity to be found in personal, affective relationships between self and others, self and God, self and Nature. These aspects of human life may not altogether disappear. Yet each of these relations is separated from first questions and principles of human reality; they become deviations from the norm, allowed to exist but never permitted to be normative and public.

The effect fosters what is called, following existentialist Martin Buber, a pragmatic I – It social situation (Lewis 2001a: 79).[14] The state of affairs produces less costly, perhaps more useful, and, importantly, quantifiable forms of education while enlarging predictability and control within the institution. Contrast the instrumental view of persons with the opposite view within the Lewis's Tao: "Next to the Blessed Sacrament itself, your neighbor [the individual] is the holiest object presented to your senses" (Lewis 2001c: 46). It takes reason to assent to this human valuation. Within the Tao, reason demands that the human person be regarded as having individual identity and a dignity unique to him or her, each person representing an irreducible unit of value, an individual of inherent, even infinite worth. The higher, reason-bound view of human persons is absent in the technical framework. Institutional scale and resource scarcity unite to foil this costly view of persons.

Gilbert Meilaender (1998: 59) cites Lewis's "reality principle." "Persons truly stand in need of one another; they need to give to one another; and they need to be joined with God in harmonious union. Human life is dependent life because it is created life." Lewis of course sees human life in context of the constitution of persons for eternity (Kilby 1964: 183; Lewis 2001c: 25–46). Each individual human being who will live for eternity has greater value (or worth, or significance, etc.) than any given social institution, which may exist for only 1000 years. Though identity of this kind is philosophically foreign to the natural mind and the naturalistic institution, Lewis argued that this high view of human persons ought to be a settled terrain of knowledge. He was correct.

THE SUSTAINABILITY OF EDUCATION AS AN INSTITUTION

We can now proceed to the penultimate question: Is the institution of education sustainable in the long run? Answers depend upon meanings of the terms "education" and "sustainable" outside of the Tao.

There are two ways to wield the term sustainability. Sustainability of education occurs, in the traditional way, in the initiation and propagation of knowledge, skills and experiences (human capital). It is achieved when the means and ends of the institution join to create individual human development and flourishing (a proper sense of being and function and so forth). Under Lewis's *Abolition* argument, education as an institution minimally requires the following for proper function and sustainability: (1) have no significant information malfunction, distortion or imbalance; (2) offer a congenial epistemic environment constrained by the truth about human beings; and (3) achieve the complex good(s) in view.

The second meaning of sustainability lies in the developmentalist sense of the term. Sustainability links to utility, that is, to the serving of the institution itself, the perpetual enlargement of its market structure. When connected to the expanding State, utility becomes a reification of the growth of the market. James Scott (1998: 183) puts this theme to a helpful analysis:

Legibility is a condition of manipulation. Any substantial state intervention in society—to vaccinate a population, produce goods, mobilize labor, tax people and their property, conduct literacy campaigns, conscript soldiers, enforce sanitation standards, catch criminals, start universal schooling—requires the invention of units that are visible. The units in question might be citizens, villages, trees, fields, houses, or people grouped according to age, depending on the type of intervention. Whatever the units being manipulated, they must be organized in a manner that permits them to be identified, observed, recorded, counted, aggregated, and monitored. The degree of knowledge required would have to be roughly commensurate with the depth of the intervention. In other words, one might say that the greater the manipulation envisaged, the greater the legibility required to effect it.

On this line of thinking, the essential unit in which the education good is fully realized is no longer the individual, but the collective, identified as the institution. Outside of the moral law, abstractions, reductions, and substitutions tend to (1~) create a significant information distortion and imbalance; (2~) put an end to a congenial epistemic environment; and (3~) do not achieve the complex good. Sustainability on this meaning cannot produce a rich information and knowledge environment; it requires a simplification, not a complexification of the information base for production.

The mass production of education, on the technical view, leads to (1~) through (3~) due to the mutual problems of scale and scarcity. Isomorphism (or similitudes) is a constraining process that incentivizes, and in some cases coerces, all units in a population to resemble other units that face the same (or a similar) set of environmental conditions (see Dimaggio and Powell 1983). Naturalistic isomorphic assumptions command that no supernatural sphere exists where Reason would give its queue and where the Tao as an institution would help to guide social conditions. Instead, each actor or organization in a relevant field or sector of education scans the field and makes choices that synthesize and homogenize the field. Each organization comes to look the same; each locks into a herd mentality, like frightened sheep on the English countryside. Natural selection involves risk reduction: institutions under this framework reduce uncertainty by eliminating possibilities from a range or class of possibilities. This becomes the dominant view of impersonal institutional change. Lewis observed that there is power behind the Great Myth (evolution as a philosophical position). All other views are subsidiary to the Great Myth as information costs rise against alternatives; it serves as an eliminative enterprise. Rosenberg (2005:7) notes that the "mechanism of natural selection is the only game in town when it comes to the production of adaptive traits, behaviors, institutions, and so on." If this is the only game in town, then playing other games bears a cost. The overarching reduction to Nature clears up some uncertainty about exchange and production in an environment of material scarcity (Alchian 1950). Reductionism enhances predictability by extending premises of naturalism out to views about human beings, to social frameworks, to institutional structures and information sets (Wilson 2004: 1–13).

Given all that we have said, there are two general ways to talk about education as a production activity. The traditional way is to link the term "education" to the development of knowledge, skills, and experiences (human capital) *and* commensurate levels of attainment. On this account, attainment is in fact a reliable proxy for the actual possession of human capital. The second sense of education tends to emphasize attainment as a reliable, taken-for-granted proxy. It means primarily the quantitative aspects of schooling (e.g., number of years) over the more difficult to measure knowledge and skills. The appeal is to the common experience of consumption. The aim is to increase the propensity to consume, to prop up and forward the interests of attainment, for formal consumption schemes, and the rhetoric of lifelong learning. It bears repeating that education inside of the Tao emphasizes learning and is predicated on the first sense of education, where educational attainment accurately conveys the level of knowledge, skills, and experiences. The crucial issue for sustainability is that a gap between attainment and human capital is occurring for reasons we have discussed elsewhere (see Rodriguez, Loomis, and Weeres 2007: 61–78).[15]

Douglass North (1990: 74) emphasized the need to examine the institutional context to determine the nature of the demand that exists for different kinds of knowledge. He said, "The demand for knowledge and skills will in turn create a demand for increases in the stock and distribution of knowledge, and the nature of that demand will reflect current perceptions about the payoffs to acquiring different kinds of knowledge." It seems undeniable in principle that the incentives embedded within the institutional framework influence the direction and acquisition of knowledge. The specific kind of education received affects the outlook of individuals, alters individual perceptions about the world, and generally determines whether life chances are enhanced or diminished. And yet Martin Trow (1970: 25) warned that the progressive expansion of education, while beneficial in various ways, began to show signs of negative side effects. "As more and more college-age youngsters go on to college, not to be or to have been a college student becomes a lasting stigma, a mark of some special failing of mind or character and a grave handicap in all the activities and pursuits of adult life. The net effect of these forces and conditions is to make college attendance for many students nearly involuntary, a result of external pressures and constraints some of which do not even have legitimacy of parental authority behind them." These concerns have become much more pronounced today, as radical changes in the economic environment, coupled with the popular perception that more schooling promises career success, have significantly increased the pressure on people to "stay in school."

Now it will probably be objected that the individual is free to pursue his or her personal ends and desires, and that no one is prevented either by compulsion or restraint from choosing an alternate course of upward mobility. However, we must understand that the mere existence of alternatives is not necessarily enough to make individual actions free, although they may be voluntary. Things being as they are, many individuals cannot resist the strong currents of social pressure on the criterion of mere rationality. There may be, as many have discovered, significant costs to resisting the acquisition of more schooling—such as the restriction of job opportunities and the psychic cost of being labeled a dropout. Under such pressurized conditions, as Thurow (1975: 185) explained, "defensive necessity forces them to make the investment" in more education.

It is important to understand that the way had already been prepared for these sustainability developments by the educational trends of the preceding century. During the nineteenth century the combination of capitalist expansion, the growth of cities, the breakup of the rural economy, and the ideals of democracy gave rise to conditions that required a vast expansion of the educational enterprise. Each passing decade registered new scientific discoveries and technological progress that, with the introduction of new tools and machinery, had a transforming effect on the manufacturing process of the workplace. Industrialization led to a division of labor and multiplied occupations by the thousands; it also led to the development of organizational hierarchies and job ladders that placed a much higher value on education as preparation for work. It was the Industrial Revolution that gave the country its first steps toward mass social differentiation through the system of education. Analysts Martin Carnoy and Henry Levin (1976: 118) found that the new industrialized society "required a varied school system and a sophisticated selection process to determine who was going to fit where in the production process." As Americans continued to gear educational expansion to industrial needs, the school played an increasingly more important role in allocating workers to jobs in the economy. As the nineteenth century progressed, it became the function of the schools in America to educate the masses, to make social mobility possible, and to ensure the welfare and stability of the State. According to Loveless (1998: 1), "Schools won this remarkable position in society through an alliance with the state: They became public schools."

At the beginning of the twentieth century, educators promised that increasing access to education would lead to greater social and economic equality. The promise appeared to be attainable during much of the first half of the century. The new order of bureaucracy and industrial efficiency operating within the economy was producing middle-class jobs for ever larger numbers of students coming out of the system. The bureaucratic paradigm of work and schooling accelerated standardization of the rules and procedures to get ahead and provided a hospitable environment in which the system of education could effectively expand. The idea of making education universal had been an established goal since the time of Horace Mann in the nineteenth century. However, in that era, and for much of the twentieth century, the goal of expanding education had been enclosed within the larger principles of equality, unity, and socialization. As a guide to practice, the policy of expanding education neither dominated nor took precedence over the organizing principles and goals upon which the schools had been founded and maintained. By contrast, however, in the second half of the twentieth century, the notion of expanding the system of education—that is, getting more people into higher levels of schooling—became the dominant ideological expression that would best produce the common good. The expansion of education has been accepted as an overriding principle governing all particular acts of legislation. The public demand for more education has become a full realization in policy and has surpassed all considerations of establishing the appropriate institutional form for organizing education. While the mass of people agrees on the beneficence of education and on its expansion, no such agreement (other than a technical one) currently exists on the institutional structure of education.

People are well aware that advancement to higher levels of schooling depends on suppressing any tendencies that may not conform to that which seems to constitute the productive forms of education. In this context, the preservation of individual options gives way to the imposition of the preferred options of the formal hierarchy. The diversity of individual preferences is traded off to the preferences of educational priorities. As an efficiency instrument, it is perfectly rational for the institution to narrow the scale of values to facilitate the arrangement of centralized priorities. However, the result is that all possible alternatives to the approved categories and habits of education tend to be conceived as diversions of energy toward less variable and valuable interests and occupations.

We can envision, now, why educational attainment (and its furtherance) achieves a prominent position in the production of education today. The uncertainty of exchange generated by the growing disunity between educational attainment and the acquisition of knowledge, skills, and experiences represents institutional risk. Risk is attenuated through the division of information. The progressive separation of information—the division of universal from particular information—has raised the rate of return on attainment and enhanced the role of rational calculation in the production and consumption of education.

This has led to more individually held values being appraised on the basis of their costs to attainment; to more matters of policy being decided without reference to competing conceptions of the good (e.g., curricula, aims, pedagogy); to more questions of value being detached from their moral, ethical, and philosophical foundations. Whether consciously or not, decision makers act systematically to omit whatever information is not applicable to the production of attainment, including information from the objective moral sphere and the means to know it. As the institution expands, it increasingly engages the values people bring to education in accordance with this ideal. Thus, the gap between attainment and knowledge, skills, and experiences represents the area of omitted information, the sacrificed alternatives, or trade-offs in production.[16] It is an indicator of the myriad transactions that do not take place within the systems, those thousands of nonexistent exchanges and complex interactions between persons in schools and in higher education.

The core problem of human capital theory, as it relates to the sustainability of education, is that information is being pushed into the production of attainment, which is the consequence of growth outside of the Tao. As the institution outside of the Tao embraces the material, it leaves important features of the phenomenal and noumenal world of value and meaning behind. The substance of this approach shows up most plainly in human capital theory's devotion to the cause of expanding the system of education. To attach the greatest possible importance to the expansion of formal education and to affirm its abilities to add to the quality of the human agent is the hallmark of theories based on the advance of human capital. The assumption here is that schooling is the most pertinent factor in improving the distribution of individual skills and knowledge in the market, and that it enhances productive efficiency through the general upgrading of skills needed in jobs. From this comes the view that as access to education expands there will be more opportunities for individuals to develop their distinct needs and talents. As the growth model sees it, such an expansion does not in any way offend (or do violence) against the good. The belief is that it offers a stable growth path for the stock of human assets, promising to satisfy the wide set of preference orderings and improve the ability of the population to produce (Mincer 1958; Schultz 1961; Denison 1962; Becker 1964).

On the face of it this view seems plausible enough, but it can be carefully rejected on the grounds that the growth model has a *precisely opposite* influence on the production of education. With the rise of scale, education's rules of production become less able to satisfy the broad information requirements of complex reality. They become an ineffective source of individualized information and are less able, therefore, to meet the diverse needs and interests of the public at large. So too, and for the same reasons, the logic that supports expansion constrains ways of thinking within the institution. It alters the meaning and perception of the education good—the notions of progress, failure, growth of the human being, and freedom. It sets in motion a process in which the starting point for education continually shifts away from the interests, instincts, and abilities of the individual person to the aims and interests of the institution, to the undifferentiated social whole or collective. The greater the scale involved, the clearer this pattern becomes. This is what makes education in the long run unsustainable in the Lewis sense of education.

Because the institution of education today operates on the often-unrecognized or long taken-for-granted philosophical presuppositions of naturalism, the key steps already taken within its information economy are embedded within the rule structure of the institution. A reexamination of those dominant presuppositions would prove costly. The potential cost to a turnover of institutional worldview, which could threaten to brake material (institutional) expansion, acts as an inhibitor against revisiting certain fundamental questions. As North (1990: 83) says, "Stability is accomplished by a complex set of constraints that include formal rules nested in a hierarchy, where each level is more costly to change than the previous one." In this case, the nesting of naturalistic presuppositions about reality and knowledge—their sources and grounds—affects the long-term performance of the institution.

We simply must recognize, if we can bear it, that institutional sustainability in means and ends is derivative of ontological views about human beings. Expanding modern social institutions such as education has not had to work very hard to suppress the richer knowledge regarding persons while presupposing a material, monistic view of reality. Since at least the nineteenth century (C.S. Lewis approximated the main shift as occurring in the 1830s), economic and technological advances began to increase very rapidly and a broad naturalism provided a philosophical outlook for many institutions. Reasons for why this has been the case entail complexities of history we have covered in earlier chapters. However, one significant cause is the linkage of the information and progress. Progress as that term is understood outside of the Tao means something different in character than progress sought from within the Tao.

What we know with certainty is that the cost of information is significantly less in an environment that presupposes naturalism. The material, naturalistic view of human beings fosters an alternative order of rational utility. This is a new order that consciously and unconsciously sets aside Lewis's Tao and creates new meanings around human beings and their social world. In applied social sciences today, it is common and implicitly assumed that the loss of information occurs without loss of value. It shields or settles complex questions about human identity before they can be asked or revisited. This is done by asserting at the outset an overarching materialist vision of reality and then orienting all knowledge and casting all questions around that view of reality. In general the information structure is chosen with a view to cost minimization: all questions and processes of education are thereby located under the technical framework. Add to this the very real resource scarcities and scalar forces and a cost ensues that divides collective forms of schooling (mass attainment) from individual education (acquired virtues, skills, knowledge, and wisdom). In other words, the nature and perception of the education good shifts radically.

Accordingly, information patterns in education today are regulated by quantitative uniformity, not qualitative distinctions; they tend to narrow the information base of a complex good; they collapse the individual into the aggregate, providing comparative stability; education as a term evolves to mean mere attainment (levels of schooling), lowering costs to deliberate adjustments in planning. Hayek (1945) notes that in the technical framework, a "reason why economists are increasingly apt to forget about the constant small changes which make up the whole economic picture is probably their growing preoccupation with statistical aggregates, which show a very much greater stability than the movements of the detail. The comparative stability of the aggregates cannot, however, be accounted for—as the statisticians occasionally seem to be inclined to do—by the 'law of large numbers' or the mutual compensation of random changes" (523–524). This is akin to an actuarial process whereby an information industry develops around forecasting and delivering educational attainment.[17] Yet order and prediction for what purpose? The progressive expansion of the institution is the central aim. Size matters: it brings efficiencies of scale, it shifts control, and the power of decision making from local units to ever more central ones; it brings a turnover in property rights where an older set of rules is reconstituted by the new governing unit that issues them. Even more to the point, expansion of the institution is thought to advance social progress. The progression of social planning advances under the expansion of the institution, which itself requires new rules, order, and prediction. It also requires less costly information. In order to achieve order and prediction, reductive moves against man and his nature are thereby necessary to bring legibility. From the modern economic or sociological point of view, this is the rational approach. Advantages of social utility brought forth by a reduction of man to the natural sphere (the sphere of measurement and positive law) have rapidly increased trade and growth, which has led to a vast expansion of schooling. However, this growth occurs outside of the Tao.

Conclusion: With or without the Tao

What is too rarely recognized is that there has been a simultaneous trade-off in the reduction of man to mere Nature. It entails, on the one hand, achieving tight unification between economic growth and the social welfare (they are seen as the same thing), while on the other hand, lodging an irredeemable cost against individual human beings and their development and flourishing. A miscalculation is made about the nature of the education good. The health of the education good depends upon its complexity and an accurate ontology of human persons. If there is a loss of complexity, or an ontic or epistemic error that loss will usually involve the sacrifice of self-expression and the liberty to achieve personal ends that accord with reason. This gradually leads to incompleteness—it prohibits the full realization of human potentialities; it leads to a diminishment of capability in terms of initiative, creativity, versatility, emotion, depth of insight—many of the skills, experiences, and relations of daily life.

A philosophy of education that fails to account for a full-bodied ontology of human persons and institutions will more easily slip into this reduction at the outset of production. This is where C.S. Lewis's remarkable argument in the *Abolition* comes back in full force on the question of sustainability. The human being – social institution relationship implies that the structure of the institution, as a mediating element between the individual and society or culture, somehow should reflect or mirror man *qua* human being. If man is X, Y, and Z then the institution should reflect that reality. Consequently, the SI's set of attributes ought to perform in means and ends as an extension of this reality. This is the principle of ontological correspondence.

The differences in the approach to education are stark. Education *within* the Tao retains a view of the soul that calls for its care and development, including cognitive and emotional changes in character toward the good (knowledge, skills, experiences, virtues, wisdom). Outside of it, human education is often regarded as "nothing but" conditioning the brain and its functions. Just as "in order that" language will suggest an instrumental view of being, "nothing but" language signals a reduction of organisms to physical systems, essentially resulting in a form of monism. If human beings are purely physical systems, no "ghost in the machine" as Ryle famously put it (1949/2000), then there is no soul, no character, no free will, and no final purpose on which education may direct its attention and activities. Every view of life becomes an impulse instrumental to a context invented in the moment. But naturalism cannot take us where we were intended to go. Indeed, consider the dilemma for naturalism in these terms:

(1) If naturalism is true, there is no irreducible teleology.
(2) Reason (rational deliberation) exhibits irreducible teleology.
(3) Therefore, naturalism is false.

Because the naturalist temper and its technical model cannot allow for qualitative distinctions (Taylor 1989: 3–24), education takes on one or another form of conditioning (Lewis 2001a: 53–81) and straightening (Lewis 1970: 313). In other words, means and ends align on terms of expanding its own domain (e.g., increasing aggregate levels of attainment) without capacity to address individual particularity, individual and moral virtues, needs, and aims. Objects and entities in Nature are not only defined by their material parts but become defined merely in terms of their functions, related to usefulness (means), and not in terms of design or purpose (ends): if useful then true (Lewis 2001b: 33). Purpose and aims are thereby reducible to utility functions or roles, and functions or roles change with whimsical tempo during institutional expansion, never pegged to a formal and final cause, always avoiding the glare of first questions. Defining entities in terms of their material properties and utility functions conflates what man *does* with what and who man *is*, the idea being that whatever man *does* prescriptively tells us what and who man *is*. Backward though this view may be, the idea holds true for the form and purpose of SIs: if education becomes mere attainment (credentialism), then education is defined around means, not ends.

The institution of education inside the Tao looks markedly different. The Tao nudges the institution along a common path of human initiation that advances social progress in terms of legitimate, ethical human flourishing. Education operates from what and who human beings are, including their purposes. As Lewis argues, the Tao is a mind-independent component of reality common to Western and Eastern thought, and has for its target all things properly human. It helps to guide the acquisition of moral wisdom, being, and acting. Lewis's conception and use of the Tao is not a mere literary device.[18] Rather, he recognizes clear historical, cross-cultural evidence for the Tao (2001a: 84–101):

- The Law of General Beneficence
- The Law of Special Beneficence
- Duties to Parents, Elders, Ancestors
- Duties to Children and Posterity
- The Law of Justice
- The Law of Good Faith and Veracity
- The Law of Mercy
- The Law of Magnanimity

Education outside of the Tao offers a common path of conditioning which functions to define social progress on principles of economic (material) growth, giving clear preference to *techne* over *arête*, *metis*, and *sophia*. The domain of Reason's Tao, on the other hand, helps to define man as man as well as to orient his SIs. "In the Tao itself, as long as we remain within it, we find the concrete reality in which to participate is to be truly human" (Lewis 2001a: 74–75). The Tao is a necessary, yet contingent institution to which the Analects of Confucius (1979) and other sacred texts declare man should not depart. It is necessary in the sense of emerging from the nature of divine Reason. It is contingent to the First Cause. Answering a critic on this point about the source of the Tao, Lewis wrote to Clyde Kilby (Kilby 1964: 190; Lewis 2007a: 1227):

If I had any hesitation in saying that God "made" the Tao, it would only be because that might suggest it was an arbitrary creation [*sic volo sic jubeo*; this I will, this I command], whereas I believe it to be the necessary expression, in terms of temporal existence, of what God by His own righteous nature necessarily is. One could indeed say of it *genitum, non factum* [begotten, not created], for is not the Tao the Word himself, considered from a particular point of view?

What we want to recognize at present is that the Tao—the objective moral sphere—exists, whether or not anyone attends to that state of affairs or not. One does not argue against or argue to it; one argues from it (Lewis 2001a: 27–51); it is part and parcel of objective reality—it is in fact a fact;[19] it is a necessary institution under which education can harmonize means and ends. It is an extra-natural moral sphere given to the human domain, an institution that shows the general direction for maximal human flourishing.

The Tao and its laws are both imperative and indicative attributes of reality, and its institutional purpose is to guide human beings along a right path. It helps to provide answers to questions like, "What is the ontic status of human beings?" "What *is* man?" "What is he made *for*?" "*Why* is he educated?" Because these questions are divisive, because they do not conform to methodological naturalism, they are often settled from an institutional point of view outside of the Tao. Doing so avoids interference with the advance of material growth, which the reader will recall is equated in the minds of naturalists with social progress. The Tao must be avoided at all costs because it tends to obstruct the imposition of personal and impersonal constraints on the exercise of instrumental forms of human agency. Lewis writes in the *Weight of Glory*: "Almost our whole education has been directed to silencing this shy, persistent, inner voice; almost all our modern philosophies have been devised to convince us that the good of man is to be found on this earth" (2001c: 31).

Chapter 5

Reason before Nature: The Possibility of Education

Nature, education, and freedom

Perhaps the most overlooked fact about the modern drive for growth is that it involves the elimination of markets. That such a remarkable thing would go unnoticed or be ignored is not at all surprising when we realize that the modern ear has been trained to hear and accept only the contrary—namely, that growth is always the way of progress and a sign that markets are getting bigger and stronger. But the truth is that we are dealing with an expansion that seeks to depersonalize (de-particularize) market activity through the institutional structure and create a macro order minus a real, spontaneous micro order. At this writing, the political economy is everywhere working to set up the rules of production on a wider collective base, in which the starting point for all calculation and explanation is the distribution (think of the statistical curve), not the individual unit.

From the time of Adam Smith on, the view of most economists has been that markets are people engaging in economic transactions among themselves on mutually agreeable terms. Markets are not simply impersonal mechanisms; rather, they are highly personal and informationally particular. It was F.A. Hayek who, in "Socialism, an elaboration of Mises's pioneering article from two years before, argued that economic calculation requires a market for the means of production; without such a market there is no way to establish the values of those means and, consequently, no way to find their proper uses in production."[1]

We argued earlier that this process of market elimination takes place through a systemic method that allows for scale transformation, that is, for indiscriminate redefinition of the conceptual building blocks of free society. What we have at our disposal is a quantitative technique that allows us to obscure the lines of distinction between the ideas of freedom and necessity, reality and appearance, knowledge and belief, man and nature, mercy and justice, markets and command, democracy and statism, and on and on. What this technique supplies is an abstract space of validity to convey information in summary form, to extend the category of the general interest, and to create a structure of knowledge that cannot stand on its own. The world is now authorized, through this inductive method, to speak of truth as a product of human creation, a property of language, as subject to pragmatic adaptation and schemes of rhetoric and power; it is an open question, a potential that can be described in terms of existence relative to other contingent objects and values. The costs to public welfare continue to rise as the homogenizing rules of the expanding institutional order iron out the "lawlessness" of the personal and particular. Wherever this is done there is less ground to prevent the political system from separating the individual person from natural rights, from rights to property, and from the ideas of efficiency, risk, and freedom; once this is done there is insufficient vitality to restrain government from separating the individual's knowledge from decision-making power, disconnecting political liberty from the economy, and removing the constraints of ultimate values and unleashing subjectivism throughout the institutional order. Indeed there is less ground to evaluate or condemn anything at all.

The crucial thing from our perspective is that all of this stands opposed to the prevailing belief that expanding the size of markets leads automatically to an increase in the sum of individual freedom. To think that the world's productive forces are increasing real freedom in this way is a sign of confusion. For whoever believes this fails to apprehend that modern culture, in all its institutions, has reached this stage of growth mainly through a specialized method that rests on the de-liberalizing doctrine of naturalism (otherwise known as materialism or physicalism). The central error of this view, which C.S. Lewis once called "a philosophy for boys,"[2] is that physical Nature is all there is; it is the whole of reality. Here the assumption is that the universe is only an experience of the sense-perceptible, that is, of material things; and thus every event, including "the rational and moral elements of each human mind," is a product of mindless natural forces, of the vast, interlocking chain of cause and effect. Within this closed framework, as many scholars have noted before, man is unable to preserve even a minimum area of personal freedom. Isaiah Berlin drew attention to this point and was correct when he said: "Where there is no antecedent freedom—and no possibility of it—it cannot be increased" (Berlin 1999: 184).

To the best of our knowledge, no influential thinker of the twentieth century anticipated that this constricting conceptual system would be a dominant force in society today. Everyone seemed to suppose that with the emerging theories of modern science the days of the naturalistic account of reality were numbered. Most of the philosophical community thought that it would collapse by the weight of its internal inconsistencies. But what people failed to recognize were the logical connections between science (its materialistic basis), subjectivism, and expansionist policies. In other words, what they did not seem to see was the extent to which the operational ideas of naturalism, in its various technical and inductive guises, would stimulate and sustain the spread of subjectivism as the premise of all logic and judgment, and that this way of looking at life would converge with appeals for unrestrained growth in commercial, social, and moral life. This was rational progress, part of the great creative process of widening the realm of possibility and ushering in a new world of liberty. Options and choices did and do indeed abound in this system. But no one imagined the deeper institutional reality: that this growth was, and still is, at its intellectual core, an extension of the closed doctrine of necessity and a forfeiture of freedom.

For education, in particular, this point cannot be emphasized too strongly, or too often. It is worth repeating, the education that the expanding environment wants to preserve is in substantial agreement with the naturalistic position. Education in the main has grown far too comfortable with the idea that nothing can legitimately claim independence from the natural order. This education finds it natural to detach itself from brute facts, the supernatural, and the eternal. It is now common to regard belief in these things, especially belief in a reality that lies beyond the physical, as misdirected emotions, as myth and fantasy, as regressive, irrational feelings and behavior. This view is all part of the ordinary process of liberated academic life: a world that regularly reminds us that man is a mere material substance, knowledge is a brain-chemistry process of belief formation, and moral judgment is nothing more than an ethic of sociological averages. No serious thinker can study education without becoming aware of the nature of the crises: that the progress of modern education has meant submission to an intellectual current that seeks to place every event within the order of physical Nature. This has meant a turning away from traditional and transcendent values, the rise of empirical and pragmatic affections, an increase in the degree of abstraction and rationality, and a reduction in the dignity and status of the human individual; it has meant proceeding on a course toward a less-complex, less-personal order, in which the whole endeavor to expand, with its inducements to remove particular information, has cleared the ground for the reconstruction of the basic beliefs and values that have traditionally governed the development of the complex human good. This, in general, is the direction of education in the modern era. Education, so formed, is incapable of real freedom and human progress.

There seems reasonable ground for thinking that the present generation is not entirely satisfied with these conditions and desires to renew the social order and organization of education. That there is no shortage of specific plans and calls for practical interventions to remedy the troubles of education seems to verify this claim. But the solution is never to draw policies that originate from and are consistent with the very system of thought that is at the root of the problem and is the real reason for needing to recommend reform in the first place. We ought always to know that any attempted remedy through the technical (naturalistic) model will only further aggravate the crises in education since, as we have shown, this truncated vision will be unable to induce sufficient investment (in information, values, money, etc.) for the right and full development of higher human qualities and abilities. Lewis summed up well what the brain trust of modern culture has repeatedly sought to do. "And all the time—such is the tragi-comedy of our situation—we continue to clamour for those very qualities we are rendering impossible.... We castrate and bid the geldings be fruitful" (Lewis 2001a: 26).

What, then, must we do to forestall this movement and change the direction of effort in education? There is only one place to begin: what we need is extensive change in the modern frame of mind, in the overarching world and life view. No reform is likely to succeed without such a fundamental change in perspective, without a new model of thought to shape and guide us, one that offers a truer account of the facts of reality, one that accords with our recognizable view of life and with our true nature as human beings. We are under no illusions as to the difficulty of this task. Nothing is easy about overturning entrenched beliefs and procedures that have long influenced the direction of society and its institutions. No one has yet devised an exact, non-manipulative or non-compulsory method for modifying the mentality of a culture. Indeed a change in the general outlook only appears when people begin to have doubts as to the adequacy of the basic models of reality that dominate their thoughts and actions. Then they must provide more adequate (less distorting) ones in their place. Any program of reform that is not based upon this knowledge will be an attempt to put second things first and has little hope of success.

In the pages that follow it will occur to everyone, we hope, that C.S. Lewis has provided the general lines upon which the culture, and specifically education, should proceed to solution. Lewis's program of reform reduces to one step: to observe the normative first principles of Reason. We contend, with Lewis, that the order of Reason's authoritative rules, virtues, and modes of being can be brought to bear on practical issues, indicating a specific counter-direction for higher and lower forms of education that includes the ontological, epistemological, and moral conditions for the proper functioning of the institution; that is, for bringing man into a just relation with himself, with others, and with the Divine.

Knowledge is supernatural

The villain of our story, as you have witnessed, is institutional growth out of relation with Reason (and the Tao). This kind of growth, guided and sustained by a certain technical outlook and technical model of inquiry, has led to a disbelief in all reality beyond physical Nature, or, to put it differently, a belief that material nature is the prime reality. It follows, on this view, that when we reason we are not operating beyond the nonrational events of the natural order. Hence, reason comes from non-reason; it is nothing more than "cerebral biochemistry" (Lewis 2001b: 63). In 1948, some 5 years after the publication of the *Abolition* and 3 years after atomic weaponry was used in warfare, Lewis published an essay entitled, "On Living in an Atomic Age" (1986: 73–80). Here he reinforces his line of argument against reducibility to the natural order:

All Naturalism leads us to this in the end—to a quite final and hopeless discord between what our minds claim to be and what they must be if Naturalism is true. They claim to be spirit; that is, to be reason, perceiving universal intellectual principles and universal moral laws and possessing free will. But if Naturalism is true they must in reality be merely arrangements of atoms in skulls, coming about by irrational causation. We never think a thought because it is true, only because blind Nature forces us to think it. We never do an act because it is right, only because blind Nature forces us to do it. It is when one has faced this preposterous conclusion that one is at last ready to listen to the voice that whispers: "But suppose we really are spirits? Suppose we are not the offspring of Nature...?" For, really, the naturalistic conclusion is unbelievable. (p. 78)

Lewis then moves in for the logical pin: "For one thing, it is only through trusting our own minds that we have come to know Nature herself. If Nature when fully known seems to teach us (that is, if the sciences teach us) that our own minds are chance arrangements of atoms, then there must have been some mistake; for if that were so, then the sciences themselves would be chance arrangements of atoms and we should have no reason for believing in them" (p. 78).

The acceptance of this evolutionary picture is what lies behind education's thoroughgoing reconstruction of knowledge in the modern age. Indeed, the education that we must reform is firmly committed to the idea of a nonrational source for rational thought and regards the act of knowing as merely an exhibition of nonrational nature. By treating thought in this way, as merely a caused natural event, education functions to bring forth an inadequate base of information for communicating the real structure and meaning of knowledge. The constant tendency is to part with the ancient tradition of knowledge, that is, to remove absolute truth and reason from our conception of it, and put into place a reductive (materialistic) premise for all knowledge and knowing. Suffice it here to reemphasize the point made earlier in this book: that we may draw comfort from the fact that man cannot completely cut the cord that binds to the substance of Reason and its first principles. Yet the trend of education has for some decades been toward eliminating these principles as a governing force of knowledge and university culture. Knowledge, we are told, is merely sense perception, probable and subjective, coherence of beliefs or statements, and dependent on transient social or group conventions. With this lower account of knowledge in place, education has gained the capacity to respond effectively to the demands and daily impulses of growth; but it has lost the capacity to encompass the fullness of reality and to guide human conduct and dispositions into the moral and intellectual virtues.

At this point we have gone very far to make clear the nature of the problem of knowledge in an expanding system. And now our task is to set a course to restore the proper meaning and status of knowledge and establish a new (actually an old) line of communication and program of reform for education to proceed in the twenty-first century. We should find this a great deal easier if we once again turn our minds to the wisdom of Lewis who offered an integrative principle to help recall us to reality, order priorities, and guide education toward a larger purpose and unity of human meaning and value. What Lewis did was shift the epistemic focus to ultimate, self-existent Reason, that which is beyond the ordinary processes of nature and which "saturates the universe," as the true source of all knowledge and understanding of the world. He said: "The validity of rational thought, accepted in an utterly non-naturalistic, transcendental (if you will), supernatural sense, is the necessary presupposition of all other theorizing. There is simply no sense in beginning with a view of the universe and trying to fit the claim of thought in at a later stage. By thinking at all we have claimed that our thoughts are more than mere natural events. All other propositions must be fitted in as best they can round that primary claim" (Lewis 1970: 138).

Lewis realized and demonstrated decisively that rational thought is part of the Supernatural element in man, and that all knowledge meets in the Supernatural—in God. In making this case, Lewis granted no concession to the presuppositions of scientific naturalism, which he held to be self-defeating and entirely false. His critique is, as usual, on the mark:

Every particular thought (whether it is a judgment of fact or a judgment of value) is always and by all men discounted the moment they believe that it can be explained, without remainder, as the result of irrational causes. Whenever you know what the other man is saying is wholly due to his complexes or to a bit of bone pressing on his brain, you cease to attach any importance to it. But if naturalism were true then all thoughts whatever would be wholly the result of irrational causes. Therefore, all thoughts would be equally worthless. Therefore, naturalism is worthless. If it is true, then we can know no truths. It cuts its own throat. (Lewis 1970: 137)

Sidebar: The Synonymizers

How do we solve all the problems of the world? The modern view is that the way we can do it is by following these three steps: (1) start with the physical imperative, that is, assume that all properties of reality, including human nature, emerge from physical properties; (2) create a formal method of investigation and measurement that operates on the basis of that material assumption (this is the hardest part); (3) then apply this method, with the best of intentions, to every area of life.

You may recognize this formula as the technical (scientific) model. That the nations of the world and all the academic fields

Sidebar (Continued)

and disciplines currently use and rely almost exclusively on this model means, if the top scholars are right, that we should expect very soon, perhaps even within our lifetimes, to see an end to all the serious problems that have ever afflicted the human race.

As a case in point, consider how the fields of neuroscience, psychology, biology, and economics are now working together with industry using new imaging technology to solve the problem of measuring the human brain. The idea behind it is something to this effect: if we can measure the brain (i.e., the neural locus or specific circuitry and structures that give rise to conscious experience, reasoning, and emotions), then we can predict how a human being is going to think and act, and if we can predict human thought and behavior, we can fine-tune and control human decision making. This is thrilling work. It has clear implications for productive systems across all markets, given that there is now a great demand to reduce the costs of psychological errors and the wide variation in human beings. This research promises to increase our understanding of the neural foundations of cognitive errors and mistaken beliefs, of the motivation for working hard, intellectual curiosity, will power, concern for and trust of other people, calculating ability, and how all this influences how and why people make decisions. Opening "the black box of the human mind"[3] will allow us to improve human - machine interfaces; it will give us the ability to reshape and control human perceptions and the emotional component of decision making.[4] Knowing the probability of a person's ability to react in a specific way to a specific stimulus is conducive to controlling variation. And if we can obtain full control over human variation, we can produce more and more of the things we need and want at lower cost. This is a key to unlimited increase and prosperity. In our day, the human mind has become the "building block" of productive systems.[5]

But all this brings up a few questions: Isn't the human mind supposed to be innately immeasurable? Isn't it true that the attributes of the human mind (i.e., consciousness, intuition, rational thought) do not possess a quantitative structure? Aren't the mind and the brain two separate worlds? Have scientists in fact discovered that the origin of the mind is physical? Now these seem to us like fairly good questions. But apparently we are way off for even asking them. The word we get from reputable scientists is that there's no problem at all. They say these kinds of questions have all been resolved through the technical approach. A little reflection reveals how the technical method does this. It's quite simple really. Let us remember step number one from above—the physical imperative. This is the belief that everything is part of the vast, nonrational system of physical Nature and interlocked in its mechanistic chain of cause and effect. This assumption of total physical reality means that the mind cannot be a thing in itself; it is what the physical brain produces. In other words, the mind is dependent, derived, and contingent on nonrational matter. All things mental (including rational thought) are physical (nonrational) in their origin. And as we know, physical existence is quantitative and is therefore measurable in principle.

This is one of the outstanding features of the technical model: it allows us to hypothesize any relevant phenomenon as measurable. Once inside this framework, there is no need to first establish whether the attributes of a phenomenon are quantitative. Rather than discovering real numerical relations (facts), we may simply assign numerals to events according to (statistical) rules, which, as you know, have no necessary relation to reality. The point is to yield numerical data that are consistent with the laws of the technical process.[6] This becomes the definition of measurement. The thing to keep in mind is that the technical model concedes nothing to the immaterial realm. This means it has no essential commitment to absolutes or self-evident principles. Good and evil, truth and falsehood, reality and appearance—these are all out. They become meaningless terms in a purely material context. In fact, all definitions and distinctions are negotiable in this framework.

Is the mind capable of sustaining ratios? Do the assigned numbers connect properly to ratios? Can matter be the very foundation of rational thought? In the technical model we are free to ignore these fundamental questions. Indeed, from the point of view of modern science, such questions are completely irrelevant and devoid of validity. By the logic of their naturalistic position, in which physical Nature is the author of all there is, the categories of the mind and brain are synonymous.

A wise man once said, "What Naturalism cannot accept is the idea of a God who stands outside Nature and made it."[7]

Lewis argues forcefully that rational thought cannot be explained in terms of the total system of Nature. Naturalism in fact discredits the validity of our processes of reasoning by accounting for our thoughts entirely in terms of the cause-and-effect sequence in Nature. As Lewis puts it: "The Naturalists have been engaged in thinking about Nature. They have not attended to the fact that they were thinking. The moment one attends to this it is obvious that one's own thinking cannot be merely a natural event, and that therefore something other than Nature exists" (Lewis 2001b: 65). Also to the point, he said, "It is only when you are asked to believe in Reason coming from non-reason that you must cry Halt, for, if you don't, all thought is discredited. It is therefore obvious that sooner or later you must admit a Reason which exists absolutely on its own" (Lewis 2001b: 42).

The point that Lewis wanted to establish was that by putting Nature before Reason, that is, by substituting a partial system within reality for the whole, our modern culture (and our system of education above all) has got the whole thing upside down. To think clearly about knowledge what we need to understand is that this positioning makes it certain in advance that the relationship between subject and object has no meaning at all. It makes it certain that all thoughts are worthless. We must realize that the motion of material Nature alone does not explain how we could be saying something true as opposed to saying something about our feelings; it excludes the very possibility of truth. In other words, it leaves out all that is specifically knowledge. What Lewis is driving at is the logical necessity of Reason before Nature. This is the essence of the matter. For, "...unless Reason is an absolute, all is in vain" (Lewis 2001c: 135). "Neither Will nor Reason is the product of Nature," said Lewis. "Therefore either I am self-existent (a belief which no one can accept) or I am a colony of some Thought and Will that are self-existent. Such reason and goodness as we can attain must be derived from a self-existent Reason and Goodness outside ourselves, in fact, a Supernatural" (1970: 276). He added: "Will and Reason cannot depend on anything but themselves, but Nature can depend on Will and Reason, or, in other words, God created Nature. The relation between Nature and Supernature, which is not a relation in space and time, becomes intelligible if the Supernatural made the Natural" (p. 276).

We defend this foundation (Reason before Nature) as the only practical means of avoiding the destruction of the culture and as the prior condition for the successful functioning of the education initiative. The thing we want to bring out here is that this approach holds important possibilities for a restoration of the central concepts and meaning of knowledge. Indeed, if there is any hope of restoring the experience of knowledge and knowing, it lies in the affirmation of these initial propositions: (1) that there exists a normal stability or uniformity to the processes of Nature, which means, as Lewis explained, "we must recognize that the data offered by our senses recur in regular patterns" (Lewis 1970: 27); (2) that no knowledge is merely naturally (i.e., sense-perceptually) acquired; and (3) that the light of knowledge is from outside or beyond Nature, that is, that all possible knowledge and knowing rests upon a Supernatural act of human thought.

The consequences of neglecting this are serious. We need merely to point to the wide chasm that separates science from religion in the modern culture and university as one example. Throughout the twentieth century, with the rise of American universities, academic work and life increasingly became committed to naturalistic premises for all explanation and knowledge. In the new intellectual climate, the role of religious faith as an intellectual force continued to decline. Science, with its materialistic method and worldview, became the new orthodoxy and model for what constitutes knowledge and justified belief. As the twentieth century progressed, the builders of the new university were willing to tolerate religious faith as an object of scientific study and for its supporting services, but they drew the line when it came to accepting it as a valid source of knowledge. Their view, in general, was that the progress of humanity meant putting all knowledge claims under the authority of naturalistic and materialistic science. As George Marsden (1997: 14) put it, "The science which would be the model for most of the disciplines would have to be free from appeals to supernaturally based authority. In effect, science would have to be defined purely naturalistically". As Marsden (1994: 131) elsewhere stated, "Standards for science that a priori excluded considerations of faith would become the norm." John Dewey in particular epitomized the emerging materialist ethos. In his effort to free all fields of inquiry from God, Dewey called for a turning away from religion of the past to a future of science, arguing that "because science represents a method of truth to which so far as we can discover, no limits whatsoever can be put, ... it is necessary for the church to reconstruct its doctrines of revelation and inspiration, and for the individual to reconstruct, within his own religious life, his conception of what spiritual truth is and the nature of its authority over him."[8]

In his book *Faith & Knowledge: Mainline Protestantism and American Higher Education,* Douglass Sloan describes the efforts by prominent theologians of the twentieth century to reestablish a legitimate place and voice for the Christian religion within higher education. In response to the growing dominance of science and to the trend of excluding the Christian worldview and its ways of knowing from the academic mainstream, theological reformers created what some have called a "two-realm or twofold theory of truth." According to Sloan:

> This is the view that on the one side there are the truths of knowledge as these are given predominantly by science and discursive, empirical reason. On the other side are the truths of faith, religious experience, morality, meaning, and value. The latter are seen as grounded not in knowledge but variously in feeling, ethical action, communal convention, folk tradition, or unfathomable mystical experience.... The twofold theory of truth, however, has always had an abiding twofold weakness. While it represents resistance against the modern mind-set, it justifies and perpetuates the basic dualism that is a chief hallmark of the modern world: the split between subject and object, fact and value, theory and practice, self and other, science and the humanities, and so on, including, of course, the deep abyss between faith and knowledge. (Sloan 1994: ix)

The twofold theory of truth was an attempt to build a bridge between religious faith and science. As Sloan noted, "The new theologians were convinced that they could combine modern science and scholarship with the fundamental affirmations of the Christian faith" (1994: x). But far from bridging the gulf between science and religion, the way they dealt with the knowledge issue drove the camps further apart. By splitting the single event of knowing into two halves, the Protestant leaders had, in effect, affirmed the validity of science's view of a strictly material reality and source for all possible knowledge. Their position, which we may also call a dual source view of knowledge, anchored knowledge to nonrational Nature and thus precluded from the outset any possibility of unifying knowledge and connecting it to its true Supernatural source. But this raises at least a few questions. Why would the theologians endorse a system that excluded real supernaturalism and that ruled God out as a reality? Why would they further the cause and help establish a doctrine that was so clearly hostile to their own view? Huston Smith gives an answer: "The University's assault on religion placed theologians in a difficult position. They needed to counter it to make a place for their concerns; at the same time, however, they did not want to withdraw from the intellectual life of culture, and higher education had firmly established itself as the primary institutional center for developing the knowledge on which a modern scientific-technological society depends. More important, theologians were themselves products of the university and to an appreciable extent had taken on its coloration" (2001: 99).

It is reasonable to think, in retrospect, that beneath all the rhetoric the leading theologians of the twentieth century were loath to lose their place in the intellectual community and dominant university culture; and so, to that end, they did not seriously challenge the adequacy of scientific naturalism in providing a basis for a genuine account of knowledge. The theological defenders, the presumed guardians of the Christian faith, had backed away from any full-scale confrontation with science and bracketed their belief in the Supernatural in order to be part of modern science and scholarship. In arguing for a separation of truth, they merely established a worse epistemology. They were following, not leading a movement. Sloan brings this out explicitly: "In the end the theologians pulled back from affirming unambiguously the real possibility of knowledge of God and of the spiritual world.... The result was a split that forced the theological reformers back onto faith presuppositions whenever they spoke about religion and onto an increasing reliance on naturalistic approaches to the sensible world whenever they wanted to speak about ethics, science, or knowledge in general" (Sloan 1994: 120).

The complaint we make against the theologians is that the way they framed the knowledge issue amounted to an uncritical embrace of naturalism. Rather than discredit it, they legitimated it. Their strategy had the effect of increasing the materialistic view of reality and its sphere of influence over the public conception of knowledge, which has led, now current in the university, to widespread skepticism against the ability of religious faith to reach any truth. The repeated attempts by the theologians to respond to the social pressure and justify the knowledge claims of the Christian faith worked as a convenient cover for a science that was mired in contradiction and was itself in need of reconciliation to the real structure and source of knowledge. Their project laid the groundwork for modern science to shift the focus away from its own epistemological problem and onto religion; and religion, growing more defensive and compliant, accepted entirely the secular world's claim of a separation between faith and knowledge. Sloan (1994:144) spelled out the situation as follows:

The mainstream Protestant theologians had come to embrace totally the conventions about knowing and the knowable world dominant in the university and modern culture. Neither the neo-orthodox nor those theologians, like the Niebuhrs and Tillich, who often went far beyond a strictly neo-orthodox position, were able to bridge the two realms of truth. The consequent adoption by the secular theologians of only one realm, that of modern scientific and technological truth, effectively eliminated the theological basis for the church's engagement with higher education. The theological collapse was complete by the mid-1960s. It would take only a short time, given a shove by the forces of social upheaval, for the rest of the church's efforts in higher education to tumble in on themselves as well.

The theologians' "can't we all just get along" sort of response to the pressures from science and the university culture stands in sharp contrast to that of C.S. Lewis who, perhaps more than any individual, confronted straight on the basic assumptions of modern science. Arguing and offending consistently from first principles, Lewis called into question the stock assumption that all thought is only a derivative of matter. He challenged the scientist to explain how exactly nonrational matter passes into rational thought (inference that reaches truth). In Lewis's view, it was logically absurd to speak of our reasoning and apprehensions of objective truth as deriving originally from nonrational mental behavior. If our thoughts are merely accidental by-products of the random collision of atoms why should we believe them to be true? Looking at this question Lewis wrote:

> Yet those who ask me to believe this world picture also ask me to believe that Reason is simply the unforeseen and unintended by-product of mindless matter at one stage of its endless and aimless becoming. Here is flat contradiction. They ask me at the same moment to accept a conclusion and to discredit the only testimony on which that conclusion can be based. The difficulty is to me a fatal one; and the fact that when you put it to many scientists, far from having an answer, they seem not even to understand what the difficulty is, assures me that I have not found a mare's nest but detected a radical disease in their whole mode of thought from the very beginning. (2001c: 135)

In that same vein, he argued, "If minds are wholly dependent on brains, and brains on biochemistry, and biochemistry (in the long run) on the meaningless flux of atoms, I cannot understand how the thought of those minds should have any more significance than the sound of the wind in the trees" (Lewis 2001c: 139).

The main thing to grasp is that science, operating out of a materialistic framework, is incapable of admitting or sustaining the essential, self-evident structure of knowledge. It can tell us nothing either for or against truth. It must borrow all of its meaning and all of its ability to make valid inference from beyond material Nature. It is a valueless, single-story world of non-absolutes, a closed system that yields only sensation and thoughts that are worthless; nothing is bound to the ultimate, to final cause, purpose, morals, the Divine—they are all out. It has, by its assumptions, declared its independence from eternal Reason. In this connection, Lewis wrote:

In so far as thought is merely human, merely a characteristic of one particular biological species, it does not explain our knowledge. Where thought is strictly rational it must be, in some odd sense, not ours, but cosmic or super-cosmic. It must be something not shut up inside our heads but already "out there"— in the universe or behind the universe: either as objective as material Nature or more objective still. Unless all that we take to be knowledge is an illusion, we must hold that in thinking we are not reading rationality into an irrational universe but responding to a rationality with which the universe has always been saturated. (2000: 268)

What is especially clear in Lewis's writing is the idea that the human mind in the act of knowing is inseparable from supernatural Reason. Lewis is, of course, well aware that physical Nature (the brain) conditions and modifies thought, but his point is that it is powerless to cause or originate it. For him, "A man's rational thinking is just so much of his share in eternal Reason as the state of his brain allows to become operative: it represents, so to speak, the bargain struck at the frontier fixed between Reason and Nature at that particular point" (Lewis 2001b: 62). His major concern was to show that "God pierces her [Nature] wherever there is a human mind" (p. 69). What matters here is the necessary understanding that we can only derive our ground for opinion and truth from the first principles of Reason, "which neither admit nor require argument to support them" (Lewis 2000: 252). This starting point can never be neglected. For knowledge has no meaning in the absence of an ultimate, objective standard. Without an absolute, without an eternally valid law of the universe, all meaning ceases to exist. It is almost impossible not to agree with Lewis when he said: "If nothing is self-evident, nothing can be proved. Similarly, if nothing is obligatory for its own sake, nothing is obligatory at all" (2001a: 40). Indeed, nothing seems more obvious than the fact that we cannot argue to these first principles, we can only argue from them.

Naturalism, Dewey, and the central offense of the Tao

If all knowledge is supernatural, if all institutions are supernatural (owing their existence to the First Cause: Reason), and if education is a knowledge institution, then education itself is supernatural. It is of some significance, then, which model of reality and which background idea of existence grounds conceptions of persons and their education. When a model of reality and background idea of existence inaccurately accounts for the human and our knowledge, or provides us an insufficient account, or pursues a self-contradictory or harmful account, and its conception or ground holds authority across society and its institutions, an unredeemable cost is levied against individuals, communities, and institutions. It is a cost manifest in all sorts of fallacies of category; the misapplication of means to ends, as for example the misapplication of a technical model to complex human reality. Errant, incomplete, or contradictory models of reality and humanity lead us to modify our educational ends, in turn leading to a confusion about processes and practices, ultimately leading to the diminishment of human capacities, the loss of human thriving in light of full reality, a general underdevelopment of the social welfare, and the loss of richer dimensions of freedom. We raise the specter of freedom again because, when liberty is taken on its deepest account, it is an essential characteristic to the prospect of human flourishing; it is a good of liberal education.

Dewey is a prominent foil (but no straw man) for our objection to the modern analysis of education and the elimination of markets. Dewey, on the one hand, believed that learning requires the development of self-directed and creative beings, students possessing significant degrees of freedom of choice in a dynamic environment for individual and social growth. This side of Dewey was interested in the dynamical properties of human learning (1980: 5). On the other hand, we have Dewey employing at full vigor principles of naturalism and scientism in order to efficiently organize social life, including most of all "the planned use of scientific techniques" (1973a: 396). This is the Dewey of rationalized planning sprung from naturalistic principles deployed across institutions, including most of all education.

But Dewey's road is not without considerable potholes. Seeing the human in naturalistic terms is a loss of information; it means (1) to suspend all value judgments about the human domain, (2) to ignore issues of final cause, and (3) to emphasize its quantitative aspects (Lewis 2001a: 69). And as we have seen, the reduction is the belief that human beings constitute the sum of their physical parts; that no immaterial, spirited element such as soul or mind or heart exists, or if granted existence they are seen as mere properties of the material self and will likewise be subject to progressive conditioning (the shaping of instinct).

A key intellectual challenge at the moment is to see that the reduction to physical object (the human as an aggregate of physical properties) is a necessary step for the trimming of the information base of institutions, necessary for the conditioning process, and a much easier pathway for control than, say, attempts to control a set of immaterial faculties whose recesses of private access, incalculability, and indeterminacy are more difficult to penetrate, factor, and predict. On terms of developmentalism, human beings are far more pliable to institutional influence when the perception of materialism holds, where transcendent values are thought absent, where reason cannot warn of impending harm. Dallas Willard (2000b: 45) notes that the "single unifying theme of all Naturalisms is *anti-transcendentalism*. Their steady point of reference is the visible world and whatever it contains, which is 'Nature' in extension. Nothing 'outside' it is to be allowed. This visible world is held to be self-existent, self-explanatory, self-operating and self-directing. Usually though not always it is thought to consist entirely of processes involving only blind force. But what 'Nature' is in intention has never been agreed upon among Naturalists."

On this line of thought reduction to brains and bodies is a rational way to proceed in education policy. The present ancestors of secular progressives (e.g., Dewey) and behaviorists (e.g., Skinner) have us understand that various instruments of order and conditioning operate in proportion to their fixation on the material. Dewey (1899/1980) was discussing the "New Education" with a group of parents, where, he argued, the "new" should match social changes, he vividly recognized that the power of the new models of thought, when triggered by technical growth, "is as much an effort to meet the needs of the new society that is forming, as are changes in modes of industry and commerce" (p. 6).

The change that comes first to mind, the one that overshadows and even controls all others, is the industrial one – the application of science resulting in the great inventions that have utilized the forces of nature on a vast and inexpensive scale: the growth of a world-wide market as the object of production, of vast manufacturing centres to supply this market, of cheap and rapid means of communication and distribution between all its parts. Even as to its feebler beginnings, this change is not much more than a century old; in many of its most important aspects it falls within the short span of those now living. One can hardly believe there has been a revolution in all history so rapid, so extensive, so complete. Through it the face of the earth is making over, even as to its physical forms; political boundaries are wiped out and moved about... population is hurriedly gathered into cities from the ends of the earth; habits of the living are altered with startling abruptness and thoroughness; the search for the truths of nature is infinitely stimulated and facilitated, and their application to life made not only practicable, but commercially necessary. Even our moral and religious ideas and interests, the most conservative because the deepest-lying things in our nature, are profoundly affected. That this revolution should not affect education in some other than a formal and superficial fashion is inconceivable. (pp. 6–7)

Dewey understood that naturalism has clear information advantages that make it impossible (or makes it less likely) that any entity but natural man is in charge of life's affairs. It is Protagoras's "man is the measure of all things" philosophy brought to modern terms: "In the dimension of describing and explaining the world, science is the measure of all things, of what is that is, and of what is not that is not" (Sellars 1963: 173).

Human education and progress on these terms makes society's institutions far *less* sensitive to human agency. Constraints (rules) act impersonally to narrow and continually reinforce roles, which constrain the decision making of agents (Becker 1962). Once the Tao is discounted and eliminated, nothing is stable. This is what the Conditioner and Straightener wants. Potential truth bearers—like beliefs, sentences, and propositions—are thought to become truth makers (the means of actual reality) without the step of matching up with the real, mind-independent reality. In its inflationary forms, social constructivism creates a virtual reality that blurs distinctions between brute truths of reality (Reason, mountains, molehills, and moral principles) with social truths (truths constructed around pragmatism and social consensus). In order to bring order and structure to the potential chaos of social constructivism, Nature becomes the proxy institution (replacing Reason) that grounds all estimation of human progress.

In the evolving power of its methods of inquiry and evident successes in the sciences, modernity gives the impression of an increasing power over Nature (see Chapter 3). It is the usual argument, seen now for over a century: that Nature may be rolled back, held at bay, set upon, manipulated and made to conform to human will. The consequence of this belief is that human beings are emancipated from the terrifying uncertainties of reality. Risk and fear are attenuated by a faith in scientism. New certainties have substituted for old certainties; the old ways have submitted to the new; scientific and political questions have replaced the metaphysical; the technocratic spirit over a religious one. After the closed ontology displaces the open, the closed view of reality has no final purpose, no outside teleological destination (Gunton 1993: 18–19). The void leads E.O. Wilson (2004: 3) to conclude: "The first dilemma, in a word, is that we have no particular place to go. The species [man] lacks any goal external to its own biological nature."

The naturalistic reduction moves Nature ahead of Reason, advancing it in four recognizable ways: (1) metaphysical questions are subordinated to epistemological ones; (2) an epistemic attitude puts social planning and human nature in a production disequilibrium; (3) rationality splits from reason and Reason's Tao; and (4) methods of social inquiry and production are bounded by principles of methodological positivism. Education as an institution is committed to all four reductions. All four help to tie education production to the growth solution. The four reductions have the practical effect of obscuring the moral law. For Reason to take its proper place in the minds of educationists, a reversal of order is required: epistemological questions are subsidiary to metaphysical ones; lucid conceptions of human nature find equilibrium with minimalist social planning; in the mature human being, rationality bonds to reason in ways that access the wider-information base of Reason and its basic moral framework; methods of social inquiry are confined to describing general social patterns, not precise prediction of individual phenomena (Hayek 1967: 22–42). A reversal of this order allows a clearer way to see and understand reality. Lewis's *Abolition* argument suggests that a good place to start is the recognition of the mind-independent moral law. For the developmentalist this is a heresy against human progress.

According to developmentalists like Dewey, public belief in the Tao raises a cost against social progress. The Tao continuously distracts the use of scarce resources (time, money, attention, ideas, energy, investment, etc.) that could otherwise be put to better, more efficient use by direction under a technical framework. The Tao is seen as constraining not enabling science and its methods from "completing its constructive potentialities" (Dewey 1998: 163).[9] Hence Dewey asks, "Does anyone believe that where this climate of opinion [about the moral law] prevails, scientific method and the conclusions reached by its use can do what they are capable of?" (167). Thus, the Tao reminds us that there exists an zone of reality beyond the technical scope and abstract space of the developmentalist's investigation; that an ideal and perceptible moral law superimposes or supervenes certain first principles onto humanity and its institutions, making these contingent to the objective reality. Inquiry here, in this complex sphere, requires nontechnical epistemologies. In fact, it is an environment open to the poet, the philosopher, storytellers like Shakespeare and Dickens, the musician, the historian, the theologian, and the artist as much as anyone else.

The split today in perception over human identity, a perception caused by what public vestiges of the Tao remain, seems to be continually obstructing the full use of science and its methods for producing knowledge and creating the new reality. If we can just let our scientism answer questions of human possibility we can settle all matters concerning social progress, we can allow material facts to speak for themselves without interference from values from an externality like the moral law. Dewey alleged that the extent to which this split in perception exists, where the resilient Tao somehow hangs on as a framework in the minds of many, it is a direct cause of "the division, confusion and conflict that is embodied in this half-way, mixed, unintegrated situation in respect to knowledge and attainment of truth" (163).

In effect, cosmic developmentalists allege that the central offense of the Tao and its followers is threefold. First, it prevents institutional integration necessary for material growth, thus hindering the pursuit of social progress. Second, it fails to assent to the new property rights structure and information blueprints obtained through rational planning. Third, the central apostasy is that the Tao fails to stand scrutiny to the scientific method: that data-driven legibility performed by quantity adjusters and social engineers must be extended to all domains of public knowledge for public and educational policy. To the technical theorist this constraint is resolved by shifting questions and categories of thought away from first principles of reality and toward issues about what counts as knowledge. Ontology is subordinated to epistemology; questions of *how* we know are elevated above questions about *what* we know.

The basis behind the avoidance of the first questions of ontology and epistemology has to do in significant part with the ideology of methodological scientism that shades one's own presuppositions to naturalism (Schumpeter 1949). W.H. Sheldon (1945: 256), like Lewis, supposes that another part of the reason lies in power: "it is power that the naturalist hopes by his scientific method to gain: power to ensure the arrival of things on the higher level by proper 'redistribution' of things on the lower." C.S. Lewis mentions "power" more than 30 times in the first several pages of the third chapter of the *Abolition*. Power is achieved by controlling method. As became evident in our earlier chapters, the developmentalist leads with his method, which, as Sheldon notes, becomes the critical issue for the naturalist: "We know well that for [Dewey] and for the other naturalists it is not so much the conclusions of science that they stress, as the method. That is for them all-important, the *sine qua non*, the one thing needful" (p. 258). We also know from Dewey's writings that the unity of method requires a developmentalist presupposition about human nature. In method there is great power to unite disparate factions. In a remarkable preface to a book, C.S. Lewis (1979: 9–10) takes up implications of this line of faith. Regarding methods of naturalism,

> The Subject becomes gorged, inflated, at the expense of the Object. But the matter does not rest there. The same method which has emptied the world now proceeds to empty ourselves. The masters of the method soon announce that we were just as mistaken (and mistaken in much the same way) when we attributed "souls," or "selves" or "minds" to human organisms, as we attributed Dryads to the trees.... And just as we have been broken of our bad habit of personifying trees, so we must now be broken of our bad habit of personifying men: a reform already effected in the political field.[10]

Over the last couple of centuries, the task of developmentalism has been to show up and make clear that any recognition of the Tao is escapist, an embarrassing belief to hold publicly, and clearly irrational. Rationality lies with naturalist method of developmentalism and its institutional consequences; it is the naturalist who has respect for the conclusions of natural science. In his 1943 essay, "Anti-naturalism in Extremis", Dewey has had enough and launches a frontal assault against the Tao and its followers (1998: 162–171). The line of argument proceeds thus. First, the Tao is itself a degrading view and a misread of the human situation. Human problems entail human solutions, not solutions informed by an extra-natural (mythical) source. Second, belief in the amelioration of human problems from within the Tao is an absurd perspective to hold in the age of science and high human thinking. The moral law produces unnecessary conflict; science settles conflict. Dewey (1998: 168) remarks that believers in the Tao "are aware of the conflict that exists between truths claiming ultimate and complete authority is the most fundamental kind of discord that can exist. Hence, their claim to supernatural guidance; and hence fanaticism in carrying on a campaign to wipe out heresies which are dangerous in the degree they claim to rest on possession of ultimate truths." In Dewey's view, the Tao and its adherents are a threat to the very fabric of the social contract. Because they propagate friction, they raise the price of collective rationality and joint action. It is when people finally assent to the empirical methods of science and its conclusions that human relations become more humane, just, genial, and liberal. Dewey (1981: 4) writes in the essay, Experience and Nature,

> I believe that the method of empirical naturalism presented in this volume provides the way, and the only way... by which one can freely accept the

standpoint and conclusions of modern science: the way by which we can be genuinely naturalistic and yet maintain cherished values, provided they are critically clarified and reinforced. The naturalistic method, when it is consistently followed, destroys many things once cherished; but it destroys them by revealing their inconsistency with the nature of things. . . . But its main purport is not destructive; empirical naturalism is rather a winnowing fan. Only chaff goes, though perhaps the chaff had once been treasured. An empirical method which remains true to nature does not "save"; it is not an insurance device nor a mechanical antiseptic. But it inspires the mind with courage and vitality to create new ideals and values in the face of the perplexities of a new world.

Humanity must control its own destiny and separate from old myths about supervening moral spheres originating from mystical externalities. Hence the social choice problem about how to allocate resources and which policies to implement is resolved through the public methods of science. It is not by accident that the U.S. No Child Left Behind Act mentions "scientifically based" over 100 times (Levine 2007).

Third, the optimistic tendency of methods of natural and social science cannot help the Tao to save humanity from its absurd pessimism about human nature. In Dewey's view, such pessimism artificially hinders what and how science can examine and create. The pessimism tends to reinforce a dystopia at odds with the reach for an earthly utopia. The developmentalist conviction is that the imperfect can be made perfect through technical, applied science (material growth), that human nature can evolve within conditions of growth, and that education does not include an initiation into the old, but is itself a process of social reconstruction, that is, a mechanism for reshaping humanity for social progress. Fourth, followers of the Tao possess lower intellectual standards than the progressive-minded followers of science, the latter having a broader, more liberal perspective about reality and humanity's central place in it. And fifth, the naturalist is concerned with the here and now, not an eternity. Improving living conditions for humanity's three score and ten years, into temporal posterity, is achievable if society and culture and institutions follow the authority of science. Only then can we collectively, that is, institutionally, align the new rules to achieve prescribed ends.

Dewey was correct to see that the moral law raised a cost against naturalism, developmentalism, scientism, and collectivism. Dewey was wrong to suppose that the moral law raised a corollary cost against the social welfare. It was Dewey's own faith that elevated costs against the social welfare. Institutional analysis allows one to see and understand how a neglect of the moral law over time raises costs against the social welfare.

Sidebar: The End of the Game: A New Unit of Analysis

One way to view this book is a call for a new way to analyze education. There are two issues to consider. The first is how to ground a complex social institution like education. Most of our book is about this first issue. A second issue comes in how to investigate education as an institution, including how to posture schools of education for doing just that. This second issue is the purpose of this sidebar.

Schools of education today are avidly tracking the performance and direction of the technical institution, where taking the pulse of a dying patient marks a scholar's career. This is an inadequate way for schools of education to proceed. Our case for an institutional framework of analysis for the modern system of education can be summarized in two ways. First, rules supporting the expansion are themselves evolving from a national market of education to the formation of regional and global (transnational) markets, particularly in higher education. This means that the rules that support the national market will themselves be called into question and shift as the market gets outside the box of a national rule system (just as occurred in the shift from local to national control). The risk for schools of education is that they will suffer a fate similar to what overtook the old Ed.D. (school planning) programs when schools of education at elite universities moved toward the social science model, the Ph.D., and the training of scholar-practitioners. In other words, the research arm of education could become centered in one or more of the academic disciplines (e.g., sociology, economics, political science, philosophy, or even urban studies) leaving schools of education as caretakers of practice. The University of Chicago's decision to close its storied school of education was predicated in part by the realization that other areas of the university (e.g., sociology and economics) could pick up much of the education research agenda.

Second, and this is the more important point, is that the institutional framework and unit of analysis, if adopted, would allow schools of education to address pressing strategic questions about education; questions that will undoubtedly become central as the national framework recedes in importance. Many of these questions will center on the information trade-off that

Sidebar (Continued)

the institution framework illuminates. A key problem for different cultures and nations will be to figure out how to optimize education production given the constraints of growth and information cost. The highly practical problem they will confront will be to identify what particular information, lodged within the individual human being and local culture, needs to be retained or put back into production given the (necessary) information loss that occurs under growth. The answer to these issues will vary somewhat from culture to culture and from one national circumstance to another. Thus, in many ways, the question of institutional design can become the central focus of schools of education under the development of this new market.

Consequently, the information trade-off under growth should be viewed strategically: What particular information would improve production? The application of universal (i.e., technical) information improves efficiency along a narrower path. The loss of particular information affects the quality of production. Both universal and particular information are needed for the production of the education good. The institutional perspective allows the leader or researcher to see the importance of both types of information. The organizational framework focuses mainly on conformity to the rules of the institution (e.g., Dimaggio and Powell 1983), not the impairment of production that occurs as a result of the loss of particular information. The choices about particular information are the more difficult to figure out because, as we have demonstrated, that type of information is inherently more expensive to introduce into production. Sorting this issue out is where the competitive advantage often lies. Sorting this issue out is an opportunity for a new direction of research.

As a practical illustration, one can recall the old Toyota advertisements where modern manufacturing production processes were emphasized (based on universal information), but what made their automobile special (higher in quality), particularly in contrast with American standardization, was their use of craftsmanship in production (based on particular information) (Womack et al. 1990; Lynn 2005). Not everything craftsmen once did could be injected back into production, because that would be too costly and they would lose out to manufacturing that relied on mass production techniques. But a competitive advantage could be obtained by figuring out precisely what particular information would make their production result in cars that had a qualitative edge in the market place. These will be the kinds of issues that will arise under globalization. The trade-off the United States made in joining the states was to homogenize virtually everything under a central authority. What was once the purview of individual states (particular information) is now regulated by a federal system (universal information). While this was no doubt necessary in certain instances (e.g., civil rights), we must not be blind to real trade-offs that affect individual or local freedom in the production of a complex good like education. If the European Union (EU) is to succeed it will need to figure out the issues of particular information. So will almost all the smaller countries and communities in the new global and transnational market. They will confront a similar competitive problem (postwar) Toyota faced: how to capture competitive advantage in a market where competitors possess greater (universal) resources. The fact that educational systems around the world are moving toward a condition of fewer qualitative distinctions makes this line of research particularly important.

As the market moves from a national to a global trading environment, the strategic problem now facing education is how to achieve competitive differentiation. Success on these terms will depend on finding some particular advantage that could be marshaled to find a qualitative and competitive edge. The particular attributes might involve an intimate understanding of the terrain of knowledge, or experience of the institutional climate, or the complexities of the single and nonrepeatable situation, but is understood as connected to the individual and local in complex and dynamic relation to the universal. More importantly, it is constituted upon those principles we have identified in this text.

It is the identification of this particular information (the recognition of its importance, the vision of how it could be utilized to keep at bay intrusive standardization) that makes the quality aspects of education potentially sustainable in the international press for standardization. One key to success for a people is figuring out "who we are." This is a cultural question, not a cosmopolitan one. That is how the trade-off of information under growth becomes a strategic question. Given that our thesis is correct—that within the technical growth phenomenon

Sidebar (Continued)

universal information displaces particular information and that this information loss impairs production of the education good—then one strategic question that arises for a nation-state is what kind of particular information needs to be preserved or reintroduced into production to give a community or country or a people a strategic advantage in competition under conditions of scarcity. Figuring this out is no easy task.

All the particular information that is being displaced cannot be put back without stalling growth (the upshot to our loss thesis). Leaving it all out impairs the production of the good. So the policy question is what should be kept or reintroduced in order to maximize competitive opportunity. For many countries and communities that will be the big question they will confront in the larger (global) education market. They will need to tap into some aspect of themselves as a people (their religion, their history, their culture, their philosophic traditions, their values)—something specific or particular to their own experience as a people. Trying to universalize information is not much help. That was tried in the United States by lowering class size, in the belief that more particular education would enter the education production process, or making schools themselves smaller. But this is simply another way of thinking about education as universal information under the technical system; it's another attempt to identify a standardized production function. It does not really address the problem of particular information; it looks for a universal (naturalistic) prescription, not one from Reason. Yet the triumph of a high-quality education system doesn't depend just on material resources (universal information) but on the intangibles of particular information—that willingness to struggle, that urgency of perception, that commitment to figuring out how to win.

As U.S. political, economic, and social institutions transition to and integrate with global markets of information (including the wider set of rules), the quality of its system of education will become increasingly important, especially if American economic power recedes (a very possible scenario). The Nation at Risk report (1983) correctly recognized that the quality of education production was central to the economic and political future of the United States and its people. But by adopting an organizational framework, its authors focused principally on universal information (standards, goals, accountability). By itself, this vision is incompatible with the nature of the education good. Shifting the unit of analysis in education to the institution will offer schools of education a pathway to engage a much broader range of new research and policy questions.

We suggest that one of the fundamental strategic questions for leaders of education moving forward is the question of what particular information needs preserving or reintroduced into production. Such questions are very difficult to answer within a decimated information environment and that by the time a society gets around to asking these types of questions it maybe too late. Perhaps the better set of questions center on finding (or re-discovering) the mechanism or entity that can make the combination of universal and particular information incentive-compatible. These are the larger questions of political philosophy: How do we lower the costs of preserving national sovereignty and jurisdictions? How do we lower the costs of increasing the flow of particular information? What gives the particular worth or value in the world? Is there a mechanism that can harness universal and particular information? Is there a way to counteract and constrain the process of information division and act to preserve the universal/particular relation under growth? From Lewis we know that the core of an answer involves maintaining our transcendent connection to the Tao—the moral law of God.

THE COLLECTIVE OR THE BODY: A REEVALUATION OF THE SOCIAL CONTRACT AND THE EDUCATION GOOD

The social contract and the education good are at present incompatible. The question for leaders and participants is how to align the two on a reliable foundation so they become more compatible. The social contract, whose success and intergenerational renewal is quite dependent upon the conditions of a society's education system, is today linked to conditions emerging from the philosophical presuppositions of naturalism, developmentalism, and scientism, in the code and measures of institutional enlargement and globalization, and in the collective (and collectivist) ordering of social goods: efficiency, social cooperation, reduction of risk, greater certainty of information and its direction, less friction (cost) in trade, standardization of rules, and flattened communication and evaluation systems. Educational organizations proceed on these assumptions as they continually make capital commitments to the expanding institution. And as we and Lewis have shown, these presuppositions inflict a heavy ontological tax relative to the individual and his or her learning, the development of one's reason, the ability to see reality as it is, and the enacting of one's native talents, abilities, and gifts. Such agency, when in proper function, entails the property of uncoerced choice in the set of life's potential realities. Constriction of choice and the thinning of potential realities imposed by collectives over individuals are meant by contract theorists and elites to avoid the chaotic condition.

The central mistake (intentional or unintentional) in the vision of Rousseau, Marx, and all the rest, up to Rawls and including Jurgen Habermas, is in the way they envisioned organizing and maintaining the interdependence of all human life. Their mistake was in formulating or reformulating the social contract as membership in a collective where the primary rule or organizing principle is flat equality of all data (including persons), where unity is coerced and choice curtailed, where freedom has no quarter in obedience, and where we necessarily fall short of full humanity. What the American founders did, by contrast, was to conceive of the social contract as membership in a body (no doubt owing to certain religious convictions), which is hierarchically ordered; it is an organic union that is committed to the particularity of persons and where self-identity and freedom are preserved. Genuine fellowship, freedom, and humanity in a body (the more concrete world of the family is the image of a body on the natural level) are impossible without inequality among the members. This is a remarkable observation in today's politically correct marketplace of information: inequality—or variation and diversity—properly understood is a necessary condition for individual freedom and valuable dimensions and health of social institutions. The thought originates from monotheism and the Greeks and is manifest in the political writings of early American founders such as Thomas Jefferson. It is also a commitment of C.S. Lewis.

Sidebar: Lewis on Equality

There are two citations from Lewis on equality that earn our consideration. The first is from the essay "Equality" (first published in August, 1943) and the second from the essay

"Membership" (read aloud in February and then published in June, 1945).

"Equality": I am a democrat because I believe in the Fall of Man. I think most people are democrats for the opposite reason. A great deal of democratic enthusiasm descends from the ideas of people like Rousseau, who believed in democracy because they thought mankind so wise and good that everyone deserved a share in the government. The danger of defending democracy on those grounds is that they're not true. And whenever their weakness is exposed, the people who prefer tyranny make capital out of the exposure. I find that they're not true without looking further than myself. I don't deserve a share in governing a hen-roost, much less a nation. Nor do most people—all the people who believe advertisements, and think in catchwords and spread rumours. The real reason for democracy is just the reverse. Mankind is so fallen that no man can be trusted with unchecked power over his fellows. Aristotle said that some people were only fit to be slaves. I do not contradict him. But I reject slavery because I see no men fit to be masters.

This introduces a view of equality rather different from that in which we have been trained. I do not think that equality is one of those things (like wisdom or happiness) which are good simply in themselves and for their own sakes. I think it is in the same class as medicine, which is good because we are ill, or clothes which are good because we are no longer innocent, I don't think the old authority in kings, priests, husbands, or fathers, and the old obedience in subjects, laymen, wives, and sons, was in itself a degrading or evil thing at all. I think it was intrinsically as good and beautiful as the nakedness of Adam and Eve. It was rightly taken away because men became bad and abused it. To attempt to restore it now would be the same error as that of the Nudists. Legal and economic equality are absolutely necessary remedies after the Fall, and protection against cruelty.

But medicine is not good. There is no spiritual sustenance in flat equality. It is a dim recognition of this fact which makes much of our political propaganda sound so thin. We are trying to be enraptured by something which is merely the negative condition of the good life. And that is why the imagination of people is so easily captured by appeals to the craving for inequality, whether in a romantic form of films about loyal courtiers or in the brutal form of Nazi ideology. The tempter always works on some real weakness in our own system of values: offers food to some need which we have starved.

When equality is treated not as a medicine or a safety-gadget but as an ideal we begin to breed that stunted and envious sort of mind which hates all superiority. That mind is the special disease of democracy, as

> **Sidebar (Continued)**
>
> cruelty and servility are the special diseases of privileged societies. It will kill us all if it grows unchecked.
> And that is why this whole question is of practical importance. Every intrusion of the sprit that says "I'm as good as you" into our personal and spiritual life is to be resisted just as jealously as every intrusion of democracy or privilege into our politics. Hierarchy within can alone preserve egalitarianism without. Romantic attacks on democracy will come again. We shall never be safe unless we already understand in our hearts all that the anti-democrats can say, and have provided for it better than they. Human nature will not permanently endure flat equality if it is extended from its proper political field into the more real, more concrete fields within. Let us WEAR equality; but let us undress every night. (Lewis, "Equality," *Present Concerns*, 1986: 17–22)
> "Membership": I believe in political equality. But there are two opposite reasons for being a democrat. You may think all men so good that they deserve a share in the government of the commonwealth, and so wise that the commonwealth needs their advice. That is, in my opinion, the false, romantic doctrine of democracy. On the other hand, you may believe fallen men to be so wicked that not one of them can be trusted with any irresponsible power over his fellows.
> That I believe to be the true ground of democracy. I do not believe that God created an egalitarian world. I believe the authority of parent over child, husband over wife, learned over simple to have been as much a part of the original plan as the authority of man over beast. I believe that if we had not fallen, Filmer would be right, and patriarchal monarchy would be the sole lawful government. But since we have learned sin, we have found, as Lord Acton says, that "all power corrupts, and absolute power corrupts absolutely." The only remedy has been to take away the powers and substitute a legal fiction of equality. The authority of father and husband has been rightly abolished on the legal plane, not because this authority is in itself bad (on the contrary, it is, I hold, divine in origin), but because fathers and husbands are bad. Theocracy has been rightly abolished not because it is bad that learned priests should govern ignorant laymen, but because priests are wicked men like the rest of us. Even the authority of man over beast has had to be interfered with because it is constantly abused. (Lewis, "Membership," *The Weight of Glory*, 2001c: 168
>
> Here, in these two pieces, Lewis launches a successive row against progressivist assumptions, emerging from Rousseau, Dewey, and others, that human nature is good (or tends to the good), and all that is required in the question of social choice

and certain conceptions of equality is a collective alignment on agreed purposes and aims, and the means to achieve them provided to the collective and its straighteners by scientism and the statistician, not "in subordination to alien institutional interests" of morality and religion, that is, the Tao.[11] Lewis has a realist view of human nature and of institutions; he knew that dispersed power and decentralized decision making—in other words, more individual freedom and less collectivism—would act as a hedge against the authoritarian and totalitarian personality and their abuse of power through social institutions. This was Lewis's second line of defense against the potential for injustice. The first was a recognition of and adherence to the Tao.

We know that institutions include the rules for collective behavior. But as scale rises, the institutional structure shifts from the rules that govern collective behavior to the rules that govern collectivism. The collective or group may retain an ultimate point of reference—a transcendent realm that gives us unity in our diversity and that defines meaning and existence (which is the idea in the U.S. Declaration of Independence and Constitution). But scale leads to the acceptance of collectivism as a working ideology in our culture. When we add "ism" to the collective it means the collective is all there is; it is the total reality and rational starting point for all explanation. In the final analysis, collectivism has no core outside of itself; it offers nothing that can bring harmony and coherence to bear. It offers diversity of a sort but no ultimate unity. There is no ultimate or absolute reference point for decisions or rights. Who or what provides the right? When all of the options have been laid on the table, it is based only on the preferences of those in power: right back to the Thrasymachan conception of justice (Book II of Plato's *Republic*). A view of toleration emerges in which—in its logically consistent form—all views are equally tolerable and equally valid. But this means that truth is impossible, values have no value, purposes have no purpose, rationality has no reason, truths have no truth.

The modern world is in full agreement and sympathy with the doctrine of collectivism. For it restricts the informational content to a specified social or aggregated context over which individuals exist and have conditioned preferences. This is a system in which the social alone has genuine significance and reality, in which the claims of progressive society are supreme. It is everybody except the individual. Thus, on the one hand, it increases the environment's capacity to carry universal (collective) information, and on the other, it marginalizes and rules out the use of particular information (the actual human being, the variety of human desires, and local culture and the like) in production and exchange. From this very move the priority of individual liberty becomes implausible, and the attempt to resolve the social choice individual – collective dilemma cannot but end in failure. Lewis, of course, saw the social problem with remarkable clarity. In a letter to Warfield Firor in December 1950, Lewis (2007a: 16–17) wrote in relevant part:

> For the good life as (I suppose) you and I conceive it—independence, calling one's house one's castle, saying "Mind your own business" to impertinent people, resisting bribes and threats *as a matter of course*, culture, honour, courtesy, un-assertiveness, the ease and elbow-room or the mind—all this is no natural endowment of the animal Man, the fine flower of a privileged class. And because it is so fine a flower it breeds, within the privileged class itself, a desire to equalize, a guilty conscience about their privileges. (At least I don't think the revolt from below has often succeeded, or even got going, without this help from above.)
>
> But then, the moment you try to spread this good life you find yourself removing the very conditions of it both from the few and from the many, in other words for all. (The simplest case of all is when you say "Here is beautiful solitude—let us bring charabanc-loads of the poor townsmen to enjoy it": i.e. let it cease to be beautiful solitude.) The many, merely by being the many, annihilate the goals as soon as they reach them: as in this case of education that I started with.
>
> Don't imagine that I am constructing a concealed argument in favour of a return to the old order. I know *that* is not the solution. But what is? Or are we assuming that there must be a solution? Perhaps in a fallen world the social problem can in fact never be solved and we must take more seriously—what Christians admit in theory—that our home is elsewhere.

To achieve a social choice possibility, the collectivist has devised a system geared to controllable forms of information, to chosen samples and similarities, and to the aims and interests of growth. Understanding this point is crucial to any effort to preserve freedom (and thereby optimize educational opportunity), chiefly because it involves a necessity in terms of expanding the public character of freedom to the diminution of its private character. In keeping with the logic of expansion under the technical model, the collectivist has created an order that turns away from the notion of freedom in its individual sense, which in his view is devoid of true liberating effects, and attaches freedom to a collective conceptual base.

The collective formula, across education, across politics and markets, adjusts human beings to nonindependence, to a distorted synthesis, and to a unity under the technical procedure that eliminates from consideration the greater part of what we know to be the human experience. The collective standard of rational action and thought reduces individual liberty and thereby raises the total sum of costs in the socioeconomic system, particularly within education systems. It does this, as we have shared, by dissolving the concrete individual into the abstraction of the class, by prescribing universal goals to all agents, by emphasizing collective rationality in the choice of ends. In so doing, it forces the individual and the individual's freedom into a model that is in conflict with our basic categories of thought and action, with reason and its moral framework, with our recognition of what it means to be a person. In this world, outside of the overarching institution of the moral law, human freedom is necessarily and only social; it is a procedure of aggregation, and the correct means of its attainment is through united public action, political effectiveness, and the integrative force of the State and its institutions.

By failing to provide safe harbor to particularity and aggregating identity to the collective, they only compound existing problems of rationality and freedom within social institutions. It is a movement of public achievement and power that extends the frontiers of the collective against the rightful claims of the individual or local community in which public authority progressively assumes central control over the context of public and private life, in which the ruling powers decide which freedoms will be respected and denied, in which individual actions will increasingly be by permission only. With enough effort, everything can be put in the service of a common cause and purpose. To do so, the Conditioners and Straighteners must thin the influence of the personal, the peculiar, the nonsocial; they dismantle the home of distinction and that which seeks independence and extend the category of the general interest that replaces private rule with public rule; they redefine the very meaning of freedom. Abraham Lincoln (1865: 253) understood better than most leaders the risk freedom faces when left to ambiguity:

The world has never had a good definition of the word liberty, and the American people, just now, are much in want of one. We all declare for liberty; but in using the same *word* we do not all mean the same *thing*. With some the word liberty may mean for each man to do as he pleases with himself, and the product of his labor; while with other the same word may mean for some men to do as they please with other men, and the product of other men's labor. Here are two, not only different but incompatible things, called by their same name, liberty. And it follows that each of the things is, by the respective parties, called by two different and incompatible name—liberty and tyranny.

The shepherd drives the wolf from the sheep's throat, for which the sheep thanks the shepherd as a *liberator*, while the wolf denounces him for the same act, as the destroyer of liberty, especially as the sheep was a black one. Plainly, the sheep and the wolf are not agreed upon a definition of the word liberty; and precisely the same difference prevails to-day among us human creatures, even in the North, and all professing to love liberty. Hence we behold the process by which thousands are daily passing from under the yoke of bondage hailed by some as the advance of liberty, and bewailed by others as the destruction of all liberty.

Grounding liberty within collectivism is not much help. The collectivist formula thus functions to bring forth an inadequate information base for the provision of social opportunity, for the proper function and full productivity of an education system, the social ordering of preferences, and sustained improvements in human liberty; it is a movement that deals with the class, with the chosen sample, the statistical mean, not the individual; it removes the independent self, the solitary will, the individual as separate from the continuum of the social nexus; it reduces the number of variables that must be taken into account and it destroys real freedom through aggregation. The individual and the collective are not just joined together; they become one.

By achieving fewer qualitative distinctions, society and its institutions achieve a state of greater coherence and more stability and control over the data, to achieve lesser levels of complexity. From a highly complex and personal order to a less complex, less personal order, each stage under the closed growth model facilitates a shift in both thought and action away from the individual and toward the collective, the larger whole—the group, race, state, culture, nation, and so on. This is a move in line with and sustained by the drive to direct from the center, to standardize, and to align the system of creation with the side of material gain (Nature). This is the direction of growth. It takes the rules of production out of a (higher-cost) personal frame and sets them on a (lower-cost) collective base.

There is a way out. To be rational and reasonable is to recognize that all life is, in various levels of complexity, interdependent. It is a basic human need to belong to some group, to find an acceptable place in society, to be meaningfully integrated into communal life. The group is a reality and in its political organization has a warranted claim to some part of our freedom. In other words, no man is an island; human identity and purpose possess both an individual and social component. If this is true, then the way we organize and maintain our interdependence has important implications for the possibility of freedom and the general welfare. Consider, in this regard, how membership in a collective differs from membership in a body in terms of structure, function, and dignity. Thus, collective membership entails the following elements:

- The structured position of the individual
- The homogeneous class
- Interchangeable units, specimens
- Unity of likes, commensurables
- An impersonal order
- Human beings are all the same
- This sameness is fit for service to the State
- It is a political orientation against the cruelty and exploitation of isolation
- Both can speak of unity, but one is an arithmetical unity while the other is an organic unity
- Collective unity is coerced
- Individual endeavors are normal, rational, and significant only in the path of the all-inclusive whole. The individual person has value only insofar as he is a sustainer of the sanctioned order
- All data modeled within it begin from equal status and are equally dependent on the total system
- The aim is not to achieve individual distinction but to achieve distinction by blending individual selves into a collective whole
- The collective begins and ends with the social whole
- The social contract precedes and trumps individual rights by nature
- The highest state of reality is the social whole
- The class precedes its form
- Collective instantiation precedes an individual one
- The collective or social whole is the most basic unit of analysis
- Equality is the rule

Now consider community membership; that is, a body of individual organs each striving for proper function within their unique purpose and design, and all contributing to an organic equilibrium. Their elements result in the following characteristics:

- Things essentially different from, and complementary to, one another, things differing not only in structure and function but also in dignity
- Members of one another

- Unity of unlikes, almost incommensurables
- There can be extreme differentiation yet real organic unity
- Is highly personal
- It is submission of the individual to the function of the head and members of the body
- It is a hierarchical world
- In a body you are called in and acknowledged
- Love binds members to a body
- Personality is preserved or is not lost
- Genuine fellowship in the body is impossible without inequality among the members
- Unity of the body is by means of love freely given
- Self-giving love makes unity of the body possible
- Body is a hierarchical union of reciprocal love
- A body is protective of the primacy of the individual member
- Does not believe in compensating groups for antecedent positions
- Body tends to evaluate and define equality in terms of opportunity for individuals.

As moderns presupposing the hidden assumptions of naturalism and developmentalism, many educationists are today devoted to the doctrine of collectivism. From the very beginning, their education and culture have trained them to embrace and defend its principles. This suggests that the doctrine of collectivism is a form of propaganda in the educationist's life that has yet to be deconstructed, evaluated, and critiqued; it exists as an unquestioned assumption. For example, it is a fundamental principle to collective thought that the State exists only to do us good or make us good, in spite of the many violations of human liberty throughout the centuries. To abide this belief requires the additional doctrine of State infallibility where the individual "ceases to be a person, subject to rights and duties, and becomes merely an object on which society can work.... If society can mend, remake, and unmake men at its pleasure, its pleasure may, of course, be humane or homicidal" (Lewis 1970: 313).

Conclusion

What are we to make of education as an institution? Well, for one, there are two types of sustainability available to us: one under the technical growth model (under Nature) and the other under an open and liberal system (under Reason). When we analyze the information economy of both models, the former leads to the abolition of man; the latter tends to lead to the liberation and flourishing of man. History has shown us the consequences of both models. Our project has been to partner with C.S. Lewis in order to evaluate the problem, understand the causes, and look for a plausible way out. Lewis had the answer, which he borrowed from the ancients. Rodica Albu (2006: 114), in a fine review of the *Abolition*, summarizes nicely a key part of Lewis's solution:

Re-discovering the "middle-element", the moral-affective centre of the human being ("Chest-Magnanimity-Sentiment"), in its correct relation to reason, means re-creating the balance between the "visceral man" and the "cerebral man" and, hence, reactivating the ability to intuitively establish the best hierarchies and priorities of values. This involves the full recognition of the fact that natural existence is holy and that free will is a universal right which involves immense responsibilities regarding the preservation of fundamental values. Thus, the itinerary of the human being in this world can be described as optimum as long as it evolves in harmony with the Natural Law.... This message, launched as a warning during the great world-wide conflagration in the early forties, has preserved its validity untouched.

Our argument moves the matter forward by constructing a deeper theory of social institutions, most especially education, based on sound principles of equilibrium between the individual person and that institution that simply must be maintained. The idea of proper function extends to the human and its institutions and is guided by a mind-independent, observer-independent institution called the moral or natural law. This law serves as the overarching institution; the standard of analysis that brings legitimate order to the universe of human affairs and relations. Without it, capricious rule is about all we have to work with. And the idea that evolutionary biology can get us to a moral or just situation is, once we have accounted for its main line of arguments, more than a little absurd. As we have seen, it involves a prior philosophical (nonevolutionary) commitment to cosmic developmentalism, which cannot sustain its own premises.

Do we have an education system today that will preserve democracy tomorrow? The answer is no, not at the moment. However, once reason and Reason have been restored to their proper spheres of influence—as reliable public umpires of reality—then and only then will formal components of an education system and the social contract that preceded it foster the institutional conditions necessary for human beings to flourish. This is the redemption of reason that will foster richer, non-eliminative information and knowledge environments across SIs; where rationality is married with reason, where the individual – community equilibrium is a just one, where choices and decisions occur appropriate to the range of decision making required, where particular information is not traded off for universal information, where knowledge itself receives proper warrant, where educational attainment serves as a reliable proxy for the actual possession of knowledge and skills, where the principle of substitution is held at bay, and where human freedom is made most responsible. All of this implies that education, as an institution, must be recalibrated on new (once old) terms. C.S. Lewis reminded us of how to do this and on what principles to do it on. The only question remaining is whether there is enough courage lingering amongst participants to do it.

NOTES

INTRODUCTION

1. Cited in Michael Travers, "The Abolition of Man: C.S. Lewis's Philosophy of History," in Bruce Edwards, ed., *C.S. Lewis: Life Works, and Legacy, Volume 3: Apologist, Philosopher, and Theologian* (Westport, CT: Praeger, 2007), p. 107.
2. Walter Hooper (ed.), *The Collected Letters of C.S. Lewis, Volume 3: Narnia, Cambridge, and Joy 1950–1963* (New York: HarperCollins, 2007), p. 567.
3. Letter to Dan Tucker, Bodleian Library, Oxford University, M.S. Eng. Lett. C. 220/1, fols. 193–9. The letter now may be found in *C.S. Lewis Collected Letters: Vol. 3*, edited by Walter Hooper.
4. William Lane Craig and J.P. Moreland (eds.), *Naturalism: A Critical Analysis* (London: Routledge, 2000).
5. Ontology is that branch of metaphysics concerned with the nature and status of existence; it is about what actually exists in reality.
6. There is often in debates of this kind a preoccupation on the nature and ground of knowledge (how we know) rather than on the nature and ground of reality and being itself (what we know). We side with the view that ontological (or metaphysical) questions are prior to epistemological ones. Questions about knowledge will be discussed in Chapter 2. As James Feibleman (1951: 16) noted some time ago, "ontology is inevitable; we may as well face up to it." Feibleman, *Ontology* (Baltimore: The Johns Hopkins Press, 1951).
7. Concerning intellectual models, Heilbroner (1999: 14) cited the great economist John Maynard Keynes: "The ideas of economists and political philosophers... both when they are right and when they are wrong, are more powerful than is commonly understood. Indeed the world is ruled by little else. Practical men, who believe themselves to be quite exempt from any intellectual influences, are usually the slaves of some defunct economist. Madmen in authority, who hear voices in the air, are distilling their frenzy from some academic scribbler of a few years back. I am sure that the power of vested interests is vastly exaggerated compared with the graded encroachment of ideas." Robert Heilbroner, *The Worldly Philosophers*. 7th ed. (New York: Simon and Schuster, 1999).
8. *The Discarded Image*. In this book we are raising new questions and giving new answers to old questions. Lewis, *The Discarded Image: An*

Introduction to Medieval and Renaissance Literature (Cambridge, UK: Cambridge University Press, 1964/2007).
9. Berlin, *The Sense of Reality* (New York: Farrar, Straus and Giroux, 1996).
10. Kenneth J. Arrow (2007) "Global Climate Change: A Challenge to Policy," *The Economists' Voice*, Vol. 4, No. 3, Article 2, p. 1. Available at: http://www.bepress.com/ev/vol4/iss3/art2
11. See, for example, Theodore Porter, "Life Insurance, Medical Testing, and the Management of Mortality," in Lorraine Daston, ed., *Biographies of Scientific Objects* (Chicago: The University of Chicago Press, 2000), pp. 226–246.
12. C.S. Lewis, "The Funeral of a Great Myth," in *Christian Reflections* (Grand Rapids, MI: Eerdmans Publishing Co., 1995), pp. 82–93.
13. Jacques Ellul, "The Technological Order," in *Technology and Culture*, Vol. 3, No. 4, Proceedings of the Encyclopaedia Britannica Conference on the Technological Order (Autumn, 1962), pp. 394–421.
14. Lewis, "Preface," in D.E. Harding, *The Hierarchy of Heaven and Earth* (Gainsville, FL: University of Florida, 1979).

Chapter 1

1. See Amundson and Lauder (1994). "Function Without Purpose: The Use of Causal Role Function in Evolutionary Biology," *Biology and Philosophy*, Vol. 9, pp. 443–469.
2. In educational theory, institutional study remains almost entirely off the research agenda.
3. As regards naturalism and materialism, Alvin Plantinga notes, "The first thing to see is that naturalists are also always or almost always materialists: they think human beings are material objects, with no immaterial or spiritual soul, or self. We just are our bodies, or perhaps some part of our bodies, such as our nervous systems, or brains, or perhaps part of our brains (the right or left hemisphere, for example), or perhaps some still smaller part. So let's think of naturalism as including materialism." Plantinga, "Evolution v. Naturalism." *Books and Culture*, Vol. 14, No. 4 (July-August 2008), p. 37.
4. John Rawls, "Two Concepts of Rules," *The Philosophical Review*, Vol. 64, No. 1 (January, 1955), pp. 3–32.
5. Plato, *The Laws*, Trevor Saunders, trans. (New York: Penguin Books, 1975).
6. In a letter to an interlocutor, Kenneth Brewer (June 12, 1962), Lewis sets shop on the problem: "Your view is that by a statistically improbable even C–E [cause and effect] trains of cerebral events happened in some brains to coincide with GC [ground consequent] chains of propositions. But *what* is this other connection with which they coincide? Another series of C–E events? If so, what and where? We can't simply mean that some of the CE trains led to a correct anticipation of some experiences,

because false reasoning from false premises can sometimes do that where sound reasoning from false premises can lead us astray" (Lewis 2007b: 1351).
7. Mayhew notes that on Habermas's account, "true *social* integration [requires] the new moral order that replaces mechanical solidarity must be founded on achieved consensus on postconventional norms." Leon Mayhew, *The New Public: Professional Communication and the Means of Social Influence* (Cambridge: Cambridge University Press, 1997), p. 82.
8. On this point, Dewey writes concerning the intellectual transformation of Darwinian, naturalistic logic: "Interest shifts from the wholesale essence of special changes back to the question of how special changes serve and defeat concrete purposes; shifts from an intelligence that shaped things once for all to the particular intelligences which things are even now shaping; shifts from an ultimate goal of good to the direct increments of justice and happiness that intelligent administration of existent conditions may beget and that present carelessness or stupidity will destroy or forego." John Dewey, *The Influence of Darwinism on Philosophy and Other Essays* (Amherst, NY: Prometheus Books, 1997), p. 15.
9. We show elsewhere that the problem of social choice as Kenneth Arrow framed it can be resolved without Arrow's dictator. See Arrow's framing of the social choice problem *Social Choice and Individual Values*, 2nd edition (New Haven: Yale University Press, 1963) and our contribution to the question in Jacob Rodriguez, Steven Loomis, and Joseph Weeres, *The Cost of Institutions: Information and Freedom in Expanding Economies* (New York: Palgrave Macmillan, 2007).
10. See Lewis, *That Hideous Strength* (New York: Scribner, 2003), p. 39.
11. Because Dewey so often had his pulse on the direction of American society, he deserves to be cited at some length. "In spite, then, of all the record of the past, the great scientific revolution is still to come. It will ensue when men collectively and cooperatively organize their knowledge for application to achieve and make secure social values; when they systematically use scientific procedures for the control of human relationships and the direction of social effects of our vast technological machinery. Great as have been the social changes of the last century, they are not to be compared with those which will emerge when our faith in scientific method is made manifest in social works. We are living in a period of depression. The intellectual function of trouble is to lead men to think. The depression is a small price to pay if it induces us to think about the cause of the disorder, confusion, and insecurity which are the outstanding traits of social life. If we do not go back to their cause, namely our half-way and accidental use of science, mankind will pass through depressions, for they are a graphic record of our unplanned social life. The story of the achievement of science in physical control is evidence of the possibility of control in social affairs. It is our human intelligence and human courage which are on trial; it is incredible that men

who have brought the technique of physical discovery, invention, and use to such a pitch of perfection will abdicate in the face of the infinitely more important problem [of social development]." John Dewey, "*Science and Society*," in Jo Ann Boydston, ed., *The Collected Works of John Dewey, 1882–1953, The Later Works 1925–1953, Vol. 6: 1931–1932, Essays* (Carbondale, IL: Southern Illinois Press, 1991), pp. 62–63.

12. North's comments are apposite: "Although I know of very few economists who really believe that the behavioral assumptions of economics accurately reflect human behavior, they do (mostly) believe that such assumptions are useful for building models of market behavior in economics and, though less useful, are still the best game in town for studying politics and the other social sciences." North, *Institutions, Institutional Change, and Economic Performance* (Cambridge: Cambridge University Press), p. 17.

13. Hacking, *The Taming of Chance* (Cambridge: Cambridge University Press, 1990), pp. vii, 6.

CHAPTER 2

1. Michael Loux, *Substance and Attribute* (London: D. Reidel Publishing Co., 1978).
2. One faction of public choice looks upon this inefficiency as a maladjustment, a problem potentially resolvable through the discovery of a superordinate set of constitutional rules that secures consensus. What this endeavor implies is that information is abundant, but for self-interest. Nudging this logic forward, it means that in the absence of self-interest (1) the rules could be written without bias, that they could retain neutrality among competing conceptions of the good; (2) that it could solve the problem of the identification of fair and cognizable public interest. This, in turn, leads to (3) that it is possible that competing values, such as justice and efficiency, can be united together under the umbrella of a neutral constitutional framework, that there would be no incompatibility or conflict between ultimate values in such a system.
3. By naturalism, we roughly mean the view that the physical (spatiotemporal) universe of entities advanced by ideal theories in the physical sciences is all there is. As Lewis implies, naturalism consists of physical properties and fields of force that operate on their own; it is the "the whole [physical] show." Lewis, *Miracles* (New York: HarperCollins, 2001b), pp. 5–9. Willard Quine suggests that naturalism "looks only to natural science, however fallible, for an account of what there is." W. Quine. 1992. "Structure and Nature," *Journal of Philosophy*, 89, pp. 5–9. For purposes of this chapter, naturalism will stand for physicalism and materialism, though there exist nuances not presently important to our study. J.P. Moreland identifies three key elements of scientific naturalism: "(1) different aspects of a naturalist epistemic attitude (e.g. a rejection of so-called first philosophy along with an acceptance of either weak or strong

scientism); (2) an etiological account of how all entities whatsoever have come to be, constituted by an event causal story (especially the atomic theory of matter and evolutionary biology) described in natural scientific terms; and (3) a general ontology in which the only entities allowed are ones that bear a relevant similarity to those thought to characterize a completed form of physics." Moreland, "The Ontological Status of Properties," in William Craig and J.P. Moreland, eds., *Naturalism: A Critical Analysis* (London: Routledge, 2000), p. 73.

4. Friedrich Hayek makes a similar "discarded image" point, though without the theological backdrop. "Against all this [Middle Ages' anthropomorphism] the persistent effort of modern Science has been to get down to 'objective facts', to cease studying what men thought about nature or regarding the given concepts as true images of the real world, and, above all, to discard all theories which pretended to explain phenomena by imputing to them a directing mind like our own. Instead, its main task became to revise and reconstruct the concepts formed from ordinary experience on the basis of a systematic testing of the phenomena, so as to be better able to recognize the particular as an instance of a general rule. In the course of this process not only the provisional classification which the commonly used concepts provided, but also the first distinctions between the different perceptions which our senses convey to us, had to give way to a completely new and different way in which we learned to order or classify the events of the external world." Hayek, *The Counter-revolution of Science: Studies in the Abuse of Reason* (New York: Macmillan, 1955), p. 18.

5. There is much ontological wisdom in Mark Goldberg's observation that "A year's or a semester's education is just too complex to reduce to a single test, and one test can't tell us much about a student." Goldberg, "Test Mess 2: Are We Doing Better a Year Later?" *Phi Delta Kappan* (January, 2005), p. 390.

6. As Jacques Barzun sardonically notes concerning the tested pupil, "But the tests continue to rain down: they measure the depth of information pumped into him, they try to predict medical, legal, engineering aptitude, they delve into emotions, characterize social and other background, classify political 'temperament', in short, attempt to decant personality into small bottles." Barzun, *Teacher in America* (Indianapolis, IN: Liberty Fund, 1981), p. 297.

7. John Dewey, *Human Nature* in Jo Ann Boydston, ed., *The Collected Works of John Dewey, 1882–1953, The Later Works 1925–1953, Vol. 6: 1931–1932, Essays* (Carbondale, IL: Southern Illinois Press, 1991), pp. 29–39.

8. See Ellen Lagemann, *An Elusive Science: The Troubling History of Education Research* (Chicago: The University of Chicago Press, 2000), esp. pp. 58–60.

9. It may or may not make greater sense for elementary educators to use the behavioral objectives model than secondary teachers and faculty in

higher learning. As students mature, the responsible exercise of the will and intellect moves the student deeper into the vital and dynamic role of coproducer of the education good. This requires a greater range of terrain for teacher and pupil in choice, decision making, spontaneity, and progressively unbounded activities, chiefly because the nature of the good increases in complexity as it grows nearer to the labor market and higher learning.

10. Joseph Dunne, *Back to the Rough Ground* (Notre Dame, IN: University of Notre Dame, 1993), p. 10.
11. Ethnic minorities in the United States and other countries are often confined by economic circumstances to large-scale urban school districts that often under-realize students' abilities and talents. As one example, see Richard Fry, "The High Schools Hispanics Attend: Size and Other Key Characteristics" (Washington, DC: Pew Hispanic Research Center, November 2005).
12. Created in 1988 by an act of Congress (Public Law 107–110), NAGB has a 26-member "independent, bipartisan" governing board "whose members include governors, state legislators, local and state school officials, educators, business representatives, and members of the general public. Members are appointed by the Secretary of Education but remain independent of the Department [of Education]." NAGB controls NAEP frameworks and test specifications. They select subject areas to be assessed, set appropriate student achievement levels, develop test objectives, design test methodologies, and develop standards for interstate, regional, and national comparisons. Because NAEP frameworks and tests set the information priorities and institutional incentives for what qualifies as good education, local bodies of education become "accountable" to these national priorities. <http://nces.ed.gov/nationsreportcard/about/nagb/>
13. Weber says that the calculability of decision making "is more fully realized the more bureaucracy 'depersonalizes' itself, i.e., the more completely it succeeds in achieving the exclusion of love, hatred, and every purely personal, especially irrational and incalculable, feeling from the execution of official tasks. In the place of the old-type ruler who is moved by sympathy, favor, grace and gratitude, modern culture requires for its sustaining external apparatus the emotionally detached, and hence rigorously 'professional' expert." Cited in Lewis Coser (1977: 230–231).
14. Like Scott (1998), Sowell (1980: 14) draws the helpful distinction between production complexities in a steel factory and agriculture. Agriculture production entails a far more complex production process because the variables of time, weather, environment, and price conditions all factor into decision making.
15. Ethics has no place in the activity of growth. Rothschild notes that the "'scientification' of economics...has led to a separation of economics from its ethical roots. The 'mainstream economics' of the 20th century

fully accepts this separation. Economic theory is seen as a positive science which has to analyse and to explain the mechanisms of economic processes.... Important as ethical valuation ('ought'-statements) may be, they should not form [any] part of the economist's research programme." K.W. Rothschild, *Ethics and Economic Theory* (Aldershot: Edward Elgar, 1993), p. 16.
16. Rodriguez, Loomis, and Weeres,. *The Cost of Institutions: Information and Freedom in Expanding Economies* (New York: Palgrave Macmillan, 2007), p. 162.
17. See Daniel Bell, "The Study of Man: Adjusting Men to Machines: Social Scientists Explore the World of the Factory," *Commentary* (January, 1947), pp. 79–88.
18. Thus growth is not itself an ontology, but has an ontology; it is not itself an epistemology, but it has an epistemology.
19. "Institutions are the humanly devised constraints that structure political, economic and social interaction. They consist of both formal constraints (sanctions, taboos, customs, traditions, and codes of conduct), and formal rules (constitutions, laws, property rights). Throughout history, institutions have been devised by human beings to create order and reduce uncertainty in exchange. Together with the standard constraints of economics they define the choice set and therefore determine transaction and production costs and hence the profitability and feasibility of exchanging in economic [and other human activities]." North, Douglass. *Institutions, Institutional Change, and Economic Performance* (Cambridge: Cambridge University Press, 1990), p. 97.
20. See James Carter, *Corporation as a Legal Entity* (Baltimore: M. Curlander, 1919).
21. See Bank of the United States *v.* Devaux, 9 U.S. (5 Cranch) 61, 86.

CHAPTER 3

1. For excellent accounts of this history see Ian Hacking's *The Taming of Chance* (Cambridge, UK: Cambridge University Press, 1990) and Alain Desrosières's *The Politics of Large Numbers: A History of Statistical Reasoning* (Cambridge, MA: Harvard University Press, 1998). As Desrosières noted, "All this involves the establishment of general forms, of categories of equivalence, and terminologies that transcend the singularities of individual situations" (p. 8).
2. Theodore M. Porter provides a detailed description of this worldwide trend toward measurement. See his *Trust in Numbers: The Pursuit of Objectivity in Science and Public Life* (Princeton: Princeton University Press, 1995).
3. Gigerenzer, et al. noted, "The law of errors had originally been used to describe such things as the distribution of repeated measurements of a

particular object or event. In applying the law of errors to human variation, Quetelet understood variation within species as something very akin to measurement error, or rather, replication error." Gigerenzer et al., *The Empire of Chance: How Probability Changed Science and Everyday Life* (Cambridge, UK: Cambridge University Press, 1989), p. 142.

4. See David Howie's *Interpreting Probability* (2002: 36). Here he describes how this view developed from science: "Where in the astronomical case the mean of the distribution represented the true value, and the scatter the errors of observation, so in the social case the mean must represent the human archetype, and the variation a sort of mistake due to perturbing factors." Howie, *Interpreting Probability: Controversies and Developments in the Early Twentieth Century* (Cambridge, UK: Cambridge University Press, 2002).

5. To quote Gigerenzer et al. (1989: 291), "...we have learned to think and argue in terms of averages, and to thus confer on them a reality greater than the sum of their parts—greater than the individuals they summarize."

6. "In all cases, their [statistics] function was a public one: to meld many minds or opinions into one, stopping short of force or fiat. Probability and statistics are the most versatile tools for generating the impersonal knowledge that Karl Pearson thought indispensable for a truly social existence" (Gigerenzer et al. 1989: 291).

7. Many scientists find this idea of a random universe very seductive, as this statement attributed to Anton Zeilinger shows: "I love this idea of intrinsic randomness for the same reason that I love the idea of natural selection in biology, because it and only it ensures that every possibility will be tried, every circumstance tested, every niche inhabited, every escape hatch explored. It's a prescription for novelty, and what more could you ask for if you want to hatch a fecund universe?" In Dennis Overbye, "The Laws of Nature", *New York Times* (December 18, 2007).

8. It is of course well known that Einstein believed in the concept of a causal universe. As Porter noted, Einstein believed "that statistical laws were based on causal assumptions and reflected a causal reality." Porter, *The Rise of Statistical Thinking 1820–1900* (Princeton: Princeton University Press, 1986), p. 218.

The behaviorist B.F. Skinner was obviously in complete agreement with the assumption of uniformity; he said: "It is a working assumption which must be adopted at the very start. We cannot apply the methods of science to a subject matter which is assumed to move about capriciously. Science not only describes, it predicts. It deals not only with the past but with the future.... If we are able to use the methods of science in the field of human affairs, we must assume that behavior is lawful and determined" (quoted in Cowles, *Statistics in Psychology: An Historical Perspective*, 2nd ed. Mahwah, NJ: Lawrence Erlbaum Associates, 2001, p. 24; Skinner 1953: 6).

9. "By the end of the twentieth century, almost all of science had shifted to using statistical methods," noted David Salsburg in *The Lady Tasting Tea: How Statistics Revolutionized Science in the Twentieth Century* (New York: Henry Holt and Company, 2001).
10. For example, see Berlin's *Four Essays On Liberty* (Oxford: Oxford University Press, 1969), *The Crooked Timber of Humanity* (Princeton: Princeton University Press, 1990), and *The Power of Ideas* (Princeton: Princeton University Press, 2000).
11. For detailed history on the rise of the testing industry, please see Nicholas Lemann, *The Big Test: The Secret History of the American Meritocracy* (New York: Farrar, Straus and Giroux, 1999). See also, Peter Sacks's *Standardized Minds: The High Price of America's Testing Culture and What We Can Do to Change It* (New York: Perseus Publishing, 2001).
12. Cited in Lemann (1999: 68). For primary source documents, see Henry Chauncey Papers, Box 95, Folder 1068, Frame 00310.
13. Lemann (1999: 68–69). See also Henry Chauncey Papers, Box 95, Folder 1069, Frame 00338.
14. Howard Bowen, Burton Clark, Clark Kerr, Brian MacArthur, and John Millett, *12 Systems of Higher Education: 6 Divisive Issues* (New York: International Council for Education Development, 1978), p. 7.
15. Carol Dwyer, Catherine Millett, and David Payne, *A Culture of Evidence: Postsecondary Assessment and Learning Outcomes* (Princeton, NJ: Educational Testing Service, 2006).
16. Commission on the Future of Higher Education, Report Draft (August 9, 2006), p. 15: "Despite increased attention to student learning results by colleges and universities and accreditation agencies, parents and students have no solid evidence, comparable across institutions, of how much students learn in colleges or whether they learn more at one college than another. Similarly, policy makers need more comprehensive data to help them decide whether the national investment in higher education is paying off and how taxpayer dollars could be used more effectively." Sam Dillon, "Panel's Report Urges Higher Education Shake-Up," *The New York Times* (August 11, 2006); Kelly Field, "Higher-Education Leaders Debate a Testing Service's Proposal for Accountability Testing," *The Chronicle of Higher Education* (August 8, 2006). See the Spellings Commission Report, U.S. Department of Education, "A Test of Leadership: Charting the Future of Higher Education," Washington, DC, 2006.
17. Richard Ingersoll, *Who Controls Teachers' Work?* (Cambridge, MA: Harvard University Press, 2006).
18. Jurgen Habermas, *On the Logic of the Social Sciences*, S.W. Nicholsen and J. Stark, trans. (Cambridge, MA: MIT Press, 1988), p. 96.
19. The originator of TQM is William Deming (1900–1993). Two of his works are worth noting: *Out of the Crisis* (Cambridge, MA: MIT Press, 1986) and *The New Economics for Industry, Government, Education*, 2nd ed. (Cambridge, MA: MIT Press, 2000).

20. Robert Kaplan and David Norton, "The Balanced Scorecard: Measures That Drive Performance," *Harvard Business Review* (January–February, 1992), pp. 71–80; Kaplan and Norton, *The Balanced Scorecard: Translating Strategy into Action* (Cambridge, MA: Harvard Business School Press, 1996).
21. Behaviorism may manifest in different sectors of the education market but it usually entails a reductionism. James McClellan testifies to its application to pedagogy: "Reductionism is thriving because of its fusion with the vilest form of behaviorism, pedagogical behaviorism: the doctrine that teaching can be defined and described in terms which are purely behavioral in reference. The political strength of pedagogical behaviorism lies in a complex of bureaucrats and testers who understand education as something that can be predicted, measured, and controlled through mechanisms of political power. The dangers as well as conceptual confusion inherent in pedagogical behaviorism are obviously enormous." McClellan, *Philosophy of Education* (Englewood Cliffs, NJ: Prentice-Hall, Inc., 1976), p. 8.
22. Jacques Monod said it this way: "The cornerstone of the scientific method is the systematic denial that 'true' knowledge can be got at by interpreting phenomena in terms of final causes—that is to say, of 'purpose' " (quoted in Huston Smith's *Why Religion Matters: The Fate of the Human Spirit in an Age of Disbelief* [New York: HarperCollins, 2001], p. 55).
23. We may know the exact value of the parameters of the probability distribution but be completely uncertain about the actual or future value of an observable. The statistical equations can appear precise and methodologically rigorous, but investigators are very often unsuccessful in making causal inferences from associational data. David Freedman of Berkeley provided this insight: "Stringent assumptions are needed to determine significance from the data. Even if significance can be determined and the null hypothesis rejected or accepted, there is a much deeper problem. To make causal inferences, it must in essence be assumed that equations are invariant under proposed interventions" (see Freedman, "From Association to Causation: Some Remarks on the History of Statistics", Statistics Department, University of California, Berkeley, CA. Technical Report 521 (January, 2002), p. 8.
24. "At best, statistics—the stat life, as it figures in these pages—puts before us a plausible reproduction at the remove from reality," said the historian Jacques Barzun in *From Dawn to Decadence: 500 Years of Western Cultural Life (1500 to the Present)* (New York: HarperCollins 2000), p. 767.
25. About one year after this sidebar was originally developed (Fall 2007), *The Chronicle of Higher Education* posted an interview conducted by Jeffrey Young or Alex Pentland of the Massachusetts Institute of Technology. Pentland developed a "sociometer," which digitally

measures and quantifies aspects of face-to-face interactions. See Young, "Learning from Digital Measurements of Face-to-Face Interactions," *The Chronicle of Higher Education*, Vol. 55, No. 15 (December 5, 2008) (http://chronicle.com/free/v55/i15/15a01301.htm on December 5, 2008).

Chapter 4

1. In the first few pages of his work *Hard Times*, Charles Dickens initiates the reader to a frightening educational reality within industrial England of the 1850s. The essentialism that drew Dickens's indignation is familiar in the rationalized form of schooling today. " 'Now, what I want is, Facts. Teach these boys and girls nothing but Facts. Facts alone are wanted in life. Plant nothing else, and root out everything else. You can only form the minds of reasoning animals upon Facts: nothing else will ever be of any service to them. This is the principle on which I bring up my own children, and this is the principle on which I bring up these children. Stick to the Facts, Sir! ... In this life, we want nothing but Facts, Sir; nothing but Facts!' The speaker [one Thomas Gradgrind, a man ready to weigh and measure any parcel of human nature], and the schoolmaster, and the third grown person present, all backed up a little, and swept with their eyes the inclined plane of little vessels then and there arranged in order, ready to have imperial gallons of facts poured into them until they were full to the brim."
2. "Different conceptions of human nature lead to different views about what we ought to do and how we can do it. If an all-powerful and supremely good God made us, then it is His purpose that defines what we can be and what we ought to be, and we must look to Him for help. If, on the other hand, we are the products of society, and if we find our lives are unsatisfactory, then there can be no real solution until human society is transformed. If we are radically free and can never escape the necessity of individual choice, then we have to accept this and make our choices with full awareness of what we are doing. If our biological nature predisposes or determines us to think, feel, and act in certain ways, then we must take realistic account of that." Leslie Stevenson and David Haberman, *Ten Theories of Human Nature* (Oxford, UK: Oxford University Press, 1998), p. 4.
3. As Callahan observes, "The procedure for bringing about a more businesslike organization and operation of the schools was fairly well standardized from 1900 to 1925. It consisted of making unfavorable comparisons between the schools and business enterprise, of applying business-industrial criteria (e.g., economy and efficiency) to education, and of suggesting that business and industrial practices be adopted by

educators." Raymond Callahan, *Education and the Cult of Efficiency* (Chicago: The University of Chicago Press, 1962), p. 6.
4. McCall went so far as to claim a set of theses, including these: (1) whatever exists at all, exists in some amount; (2) anything that exists in amount can be measured; (3) measurement in education is the general the same as measurement in the physical sciences. William McCall, *How to Measure in Education* (New York: Macmillan, 1922), pp. 3–6.
5. Reinhold Niebuhr, *Human Nature*, vol. of *Nature and Destiny of Man* (New York: Scribner's Sons, 1964).
6. J.P. Moreland, *Consciousness and the Existence of God* (London: Routledge, 2008).
7. Choice, says Arrow (1983: 56), in the rational model "has the following well-known form: an individual is assumed to rank all alternative logically possible [choices] in order of preference; in any given situation, only some of the logically possible alternatives are in fact available, due to budgetary or other limitations, and the individual is assumed to choose among alternatives available that one which is highest on his ranking.... [T]he more important part of the content of a rational model of choice in any particular context lies in the specification of the range of alternatives actually available, and, it might be added, in more specific hypotheses about the underlying ordering."
8. Brian Skyrms, *Evolution of the Social Contract* (Cambridge, UK: Cambridge University Press, 1996).
9. James D. Hunter, *The Death of Character* (New York: Basic Books, 2000), p. xv. Emphasis added.
10. R.W. Burchfield, ed., *The Compact Oxford English Dictionary*, new ed. (Oxford, UK: Clarendon Press, 1998), p. 1521, III.10.a., "reason".
11. Meilander makes an important distinction between self-evidency and obviousness. The former does not entail the latter in moral matters. Meilander, *The Taste for the Other: The Social and Ethical Thought of C.S. Lewis* (Grand Rapids, MI: William B. Eerdmans, 1998), p. 200.
12. Uppercase "R" Reason is Lewis's device to represent God. "The supernatural Reason enters my natural being not like a weapon—more like a beam of light which illuminates or a principle of organization which unifies and develops" (Lewis 2001b). Small "r" reason is "the intellectual faculty of natural man...employed in practical judgment, capable of being good or evil, and of being regenerated, the mind, the reason, the reasoning faculty" (Lewis 2007b). Lewis, *Miracles* (New York: HarperCollins, 2001b), p. 48, *The Collected Letters of C.S. Lewis: Narnia, Cambridge, and Joy 1950–1963* (San Francisco: Harper, 2007), p. 1005.
13. G.J. Warnock, "Reason," Paul Edwards, ed., *The Encyclopedia of Philosophy*, Vol. 7 (New York: Macmillan Publishing Inc., 1967), pp. 83–85.
14. Buber 2000; in contrast to a richer view of relations found in an I – Thou situation. Lewis (1982: 78) adds, "Nothing but a *Thou* can be loved and a *Thou* can exist only for an *I*. A society in which no one was conscious

of himself as a person over against other persons, where none could say 'I love you', would, indeed, be free from selfishness, but not through love. It would be 'unselfish' as a bucket of water is unselfish." Lewis, *On Stories* (New York: Harcourt, 1982).
15. What did the expansion of education result in from the 1950s to today? It widened the gap between knowledge and skills and attainment. Basically, it imposed a cost on the individual's access to knowledge and skills.
16. There is no limitation that we know of to the amount of information that can go into a production process. However, production processes are limited by the kinds of information that can be effectively utilized in production.
17. Theodore Porter, "Life Insurance, Medical Testing, and the Management of Mortality," in Lorraine Daston, ed., *Biographies of Scientific Objects* (Chicago: The University of Chicago Press, 2000), pp. 226–246.
18. We should note that the great sinologist Joseph Needham argued that, in China, the natural law (as Tao, not Li) meant order, and system and pattern were visualized as running through the whole of nature, "philosophical principles neither of which had juristic content." Needham, *Science and Civilization in China: Vol. 2: History of Scientific Thought* (Cambridge: Cambridge University Press, 1956), p. 579.
19. We define a fact as a true proposition; a state of affairs that obtains. See Roderick Chisholm, *A Realistic Theory of Categories: An Essay in Ontology* (Cambridge: Cambridge University Press, 1996), p. 25.

CHAPTER 5

1. Quoted in Peter G. Klein, "Biography F.A. Hayek (1899–1992)," Ludwig Von Mises Institute, November 1, 2008.
2. See Lewis's essay "De Futilitate" *C. S. Lewis Essay Collection: Literature, Philosophy and Short Stories*, Lesley Walmsley, ed. (London: HarperCollins, 2002), p. 273.
3. See C. Camerer, G. Loewenstein, and D. Prelec, "Neuroeconomics: Why Economics Needs Brains," *Scandinavian Journal of Economics*, Vol. 106, No. 3 (September 2004), pp. 555–579.
4. See, for example, the chapter "Psychology as Engineering" by Thomas Hardy Leahey in *The Mind as a Scientific Object*, C.E. Erneling and D.M. Johnson, eds (Oxford, UK: Oxford University Press, 2005).
5. See Camerer, Loewenstein, and Prelec, "Neuroeconomics: How Neuroscience Can Inform Economics," *Journal of Economic Literature*, Vol. XLIII (March 2005), pp. 9–64.
6. On the subject of measurement see Joel Michell, *Measurement in Psychology: A Critical History of a Methodological Concept* (Cambridge, UK: Cambridge University Press, 1999).

7. C.S. Lewis is that wise man. The book is *Miracles* (New York: Harper-Collins, 2001), p. 11.
8. John Dewey, "Reconstruction," *The Bulletin*, Vol. 15 (May 1894), quoted in Marsden, *The Soul of the American University: From Protestant Establishment to Established Nonbelief* (Oxford, UK: Oxford University Press, 1994), p. 179.
9. John Dewey, "Anti-naturalism in Extremis," *The Essential Dewey, Vol. I.* Larry Hickman and Thomas Alexander (eds.) (Bloomington, IN: Indiana University Press, 1998).
10. C.S. Lewis, "Preface," *The Hierarchy of Heaven and Earth*, D.E. Harding, ed. (London: Faber and Faber, Ltd, 1952; Gainesville, FL: University of Florida, 1979), pp. 9–10.
11. Dewey, "Liberating the Social Scientist," in *The Later Works of John Dewey, Vol. 15, 1942–1948*, pp. 224–238, citation at p. 229.

Bibliography

Abella, Alex. 2008. *Soldiers of Reason*. Orlando, FL: Houghton Mifflin Harcourt.
Adler, M. 1940. "God and the Professors." A paper given at the First Conference on Science, Philosophy and Religion, September: Science, Philosophy and Religion: A Symposium on Science, Philosophy and Religion in Their Relation to the Democratic Way of Life. New York.
Aeschliman, Michael. 1998. *The Restitution of Man*. Grand Rapids, MI: William B. Eerdman.
Albu, Rodica. 2006. A Review of The Abolition of Man. *Journal for the Study of Religions and Ideologies*. No. 15, Winter, 110–116.
Alchian, Armen. 1950. "Uncertainty, Evolution, and Economic Theory." *The Journal of Political Economy*, Vol. 58, No. 3, June, 211–221.
Alston, William. 1997. *A Realist Conception of Truth*. Ithaca, NY: Cornell University Press.
Amundson, Ron and George Lauder. 1994. "Function without Purpose: The use of Causal Role Function in Evolutionary Biology." *Biology and Philosophy*, Vol. 9, 443–469.
Aquinas, Thomas. 1988. *Summa Theologiae*. Dominican Fathers (trans.). New York: Continuum International Publishing Group.
Arrow, Kenneth. 1950. "A Difficulty in the Concept of Social Welfare." *The Journal of Political Economy*, Vol. 58, No. 4, August, 328–346.
———. 1963. *Social Choice and Individual Values*. 2nd edition. New York: Wiley.
———. 1974. *The Limits of Organization*. New York: W.W. Norton.
———. 1981. "Introduction: The Social Choice Perspective." Symposium: The Implications of Social Choice Theory for Legal Decision Making. *Hofstra Law Review* Vol. 9, No. 5, 1373–1380.
———. 1983. "Utilities, Attitudes, Choices." *Collected Papers of Kenneth Arrow: Individual Choice under Certainty and Uncertainty*. Cambridge, MA: The Belknap Press of Harvard University Press.
———. 2007. "Global Climate Change: A Challenge to Policy." *The Economists' Voice*, Vol. 4, No. 3, Art. 2. Accessed on September 8, 2008: http://www.bepress.com/ev/vol4/iss3/art2.
Audi, Robert. 2000. *Religious Commitment and Secular Reason*. Cambridge, UK: Cambridge University Press.

Audi, Robert and Nicholas Wolterstorff. 1996. *Religion in the Public Square: The Price of Religious Convictions in Political Debate.* New York: Rowman and Littlefield.

Barzun, Jacques. 1981. *Teacher in America.* Indianapolis, IN: Liberty Fund.

———. 2000. *From Dawn to Decadence: 500 Years of Western Cultural Life (1500 to the Present).* New York: HarperCollins.

Bastiat, Frederick. 2004. *The Law.* Whitefish, MT: Kessinger Publishing.

Becker, Gary. 1962. "Irrational Behavior and Economic Theory." *Journal of Political Economy*, Vol. 70, No. 1, February, 1–13.

———. 1964. *Human Capital: A Theoretical and Empirical Analysis, with Special Reference to Education.* 3rd edition. Chicago: The University of Chicago Press.

———. 1976. *The Economic Approach to Human Behavior.* Chicago: The University of Chicago Press.

Beinhocker, Eric. 2007. *The Origin of Wealth.* Boston: Harvard Business School Press.

Bell, Daniel. 1947. "The Study of Man: Adjusting Men to Machines: Social Scientists Explore the World of the Factory." *Commentary*, January, 79–88.

Berlin, Isaiah. 1969. *Four Essays on Liberty.* Oxford, UK: Oxford University Press.

———. 1990. *The Crooked Timber of Humanity.* Henry Hardy (ed.). Princeton, NJ: Princeton University Press.

———. 1996. *The Sense of Reality.* New York: Farrar, Straus, and Giroux.

———. 1999. *Concepts and Categories.* Henry Hardy (ed.). Princeton, NJ: Princeton University Press.

———. 2000. *The Power of Ideas.* Henry Hardy (ed.). Princeton, NJ: Princeton University Press.

———. 2002. *Liberty.* Henry Hardy (ed.). New York: Oxford University Press.

Bloom, Benjamin. 1956. *The Taxonomy of Educational Objectives, Handbook I: The Cognitive Domain.* New York: David McKay Company, Inc.

Bowen, Howard, Burton Clark, Clark Kerr, Brian MacArthur, and John Millet. 1978. *12 Systems of Higher Education: 6 Divisive Issues.* New York: International Council for Education Development.

Bowles, Samuel. 2003. *Microeconomics: Behavior, Institutions, and Evolution.* Princeton: Princeton University Press.

Buber, Martin. 2000. *I and Thou.* Ronald Smith (trans.). New York: Simon and Schuster.

Buchanan, James, and Gordon Tullock. 1962. *The Calculus of Consent.* Ann Arbor, MI: University of Michigan Press.

Burchfield, R.W. (ed.) 1998. *The Compact Oxford English Dictionary.* Oxford, UK: Clarendon Press.

Caldwell, Bruce. 1982. *Beyond Positivism: Economic Method in the Twentieth Century.* Boston, MA: Allen and Unwin.

Callahan, Raymond, E. 1962. *Education and the Cult of Efficiency.* Chicago: University of Chicago Press.
Camerer, C., G. Loewenstein, and D. Prelec. 2004. "Neuroeconomics: Why Economics Needs Brains." *Scandinavian Journal of Economics,* Vol. 106, No. 3, September, 555–579.
———. 2005. "Neuroeconomics: How Neuroscience Can Inform Economics." *Journal of Economic Literature,* Vol XLIII, March, 9–64.
Carnoy, Martin and Henry Levin. 1976. *The Limits of Educational Reform.* New York: D. McKay Company.
Carter, James. 1919. *Corporation as a Legal Entity.* Baltimore, MD: M. Curlander.
Charter, David. 2006. "Schools Told It's No Longer Necessary to Teach Right from Wrong." *London Times* at http://timesonline.co.uk on July 31, 2006.
Chisholm, Roderick. 1996. *A Realistic Theory of Categories: An Essay in Ontology.* Cambridge, UK: Cambridge University Press.
Chubb, John and Terry Moe. 1990. *Politics, Markets, and America's Schools.* Washington, DC: Brookings Institution.
Cohen, Jonathan. 1993. "Rationality." Jonathan Dancy and Ernest Sosa (eds.). *A Companion to Epistemology.* Oxford, UK: Blackwell.
Collins, Randall. 1998. *The Sociology of Philosophies: A Global Theory of Intellectual Change.* Cambridge, MA: The Belknap Press of Harvard University Press.
Coser, Lewis. 1977. *Masters of Sociological Thought.* 2nd edition. New York: Harcourt Brace Jovanovich.
Cowles, Michael. 2001. *Statistics in Psychology: An Historical Perspective.* 2nd edition. Mahwah, NJ: Lawrence Erlbaum Associates.
Craig, William Lane. 2000. "Naturalism and Cosmology." *Naturalism: A Critical Analysis.* London: Routledge.
Crosby, Alfred. 1997. *The Measure of Reality: Quantification and Western Society, 1250–1600.* Cambridge, UK: Cambridge University Press.
Cuban, Larry. 2004. "Looking through the Rearview Mirror at School Accountability." K. Sirotnik (ed.). *Holding Accountability Accountable.* New York: Teachers College Press.
David, Naugle. 2002. *Worldview: The History of a Concept.* Grand Rapids, MI: Wm. B. Eerdmans Publishing Company.
Deming, William. 1986. *Out of the Crisis.* Cambridge, MA: MIT Press.
———. 2000. *The New Economics for Industry, Government, Education.* 2nd edition. Cambridge, MA: MIT Press.
Denison, E.F. 1962. *The Sources of Economic Growth in the United States and the Alternatives before Us.* New York: Committee for Economic Development.
Desrosières, Alain. 1998. *The Politics of Large Numbers: A History of Statistical Reasoning.* Cambridge, MA: Harvard University Press.
Dewey, John. 1991. *A Common Faith.* New Haven, CT: Yale University Press.

———. 1920. *Reconstruction in Philosophy.* New York: Henry Holt and Company.

———. 1936. "Rationality in Education." *The Social Frontier*, Vol. III, No. 21, December, 71–73.

———. 1973a. "Philosophy and Civilization." *The Philosophy of John Dewey: Volumes I and II.* John McDermott (ed.). Chicago: The University of Chicago Press.

———. 1979. *The Collected Works of John Dewey, 1882–1952: The Middle Works, 1899–1924, Volume 7: 1899–1924: Essays on Philosophy and Psychology, 1912–1914.* Jo Ann Boydston (ed.). Carbondale, IL: Southern Illinois University Press.

———. 1991. *The Collected Works of John Dewey, 1882–1952: The Later Works, 1925–1953, Volume 6: 1931–1932, Essays.* Jo Ann Boydston (ed.). Carbondale, IL: Southern Illinois Press.

———. 1997. *The Influence of Darwinism on Philosophy and Other Essays.* Amherst, NY: Prometheus Books.

———. 1998. *The Essential Dewey: Volume I.* Bloomington, IN: Indiana University Press.

———. 2008. *The Collected Works of John Dewey, 1882–1952: The Middle Works, 1899–1924, Volume 3: Journal Articles, Book Reviews, and Miscellany in the 1903–1906 Period.* Jo Ann Boydston (ed.). Carbondale, IL: Southern Illinois University Press.

Diagnostic and Statistical Manual IV. 1994. Arlington, VA: American Psychiatric Publishing, Inc.

Dillon, Sam. 2006. "Panel's Report Urges Higher Education Shake-Up." *The New York Times.* August 11.

Dimaggio, Paul, and Powell, Walter. 1983. "The Iron Cage Revisited: Institutional Isomorphism and Collective Rationality in Organizational Fields." *American Sociological Review*, Vol. 48, No. 2., April, 147–160.

Dunne, Joseph. 1993. *Back to the Rough Ground.* Notre Dame, IN: University of Notre Dame Press.

Dwyer, Carol, Catherine Millet, and David Payne. 2006. *A Culture of Evidence: Postsecondary Assessment and Learning Outcomes.* Princeton, NJ: Educational Testing Service.

Earman, John. 2000. *Hume's Abject Failure: The Argument Against Miracles.* Oxford: Oxford University Press.

Eliade, Mircea. 1987. *The Sacred and the Profane: The Nature of Religion.* New York: Harcourt.

Ellul, Jacques. 1962. "The Technological Order." *Technology and Culture*, Vol. 3, No. 4, 394–421.

———. 1964. *The Technological Society.* John Wilkinson (trans.). New York: Vintage Books.

Elshtain, Jean. 2008. "C.S. Lewis's Prescience Concerning Things to Come." David Baggett, Gary Habermas, and Jerry Walls (eds.). *C.S. Lewis as Philosopher: Truth, Goodness, and Beauty.* Downers Grove, IL: InterVarsity Press.

Field, Kelly. 2006. "Higher-Education Leaders Debate a Testing Service's Proposal for Accountability Teasting." *The Chronicle of Higher Education.* August 8.
Freedman, David. 2002. "From Association to Causation: Some Remarks on the History of Statistics." *University of California, Berkeley, Statistics Department.* Technical Report 521, January.
Friedman, Milton. 1966. "The Methodology of Positive Economics." *Essays in Positive Economics.* Chicago: The University of Chicago Press.
Fry, Richard. 2005. "The High Schools Hispanics Attend: Size and Other Key Characteristics." Washington, DC: Pew Hispanic Research Center.
George, Robert. 2001a. *The Clash of Orthodoxies: Law, Religion, and Morality in Crisis.* Wilmington, DE: ISI Books.
———. 2001b. *In Defense of Natural Law.* Oxford: Oxford University Press.
Gigerenzer, Gerd, Zeno Swijtink, Lorraine Daston, Theodore Porter, Lorenz Kruger, and John Beatty. 1989. *The Empire of Chance: How Probability Changed Science and Everyday Life.* Cambridge, UK: Cambridge University Press.
Gleick, James. 1992. *Genius: The Life and Science of Richard Feynman.* New York: Vintage Books.
Goetz, Stewart. 2000. "Naturalism and Libertarian Agency." *Naturalism: A Critical Analysis.* William Lane Craig and JP Moreland (eds). London: Routledge, 156–186.
Goldberg, Mark. 2005. "Test Mess 2: Are We Doing Better a Year Later?" *Phi Delta Kappan.* January, 390.
Gunton, Colin. 1993. *The One, the Three, and the Many.* Cambridge, UK: Cambridge University Press.
Habermas, Jurgen. 1988. *On the Logic of the Social Sciences.* S.W. Nicholsen and J. Stark (trans.). Cambridge, MA: MIT Press.
Hacking, Ian. 1990. *The Taming of Chance.* Cambridge, UK: Cambridge University Press.
Hare, John. 2000. "Naturalism and Morality." *Naturalism: A Critical Analysis.* William Lane Craig and JP Moreland (eds). London: Routledge, 189–212.
Hayek, Fredrich. 1940. "The Socialist Calculation: The Competitive 'Solution'." *Economica*, Vol. 7, No. 26, May, 125–149.
———. 1945. "The Use of Knowledge in Society." *The American Economic Review*, Vol. 35, No. 4, September, 519–530.
———. 1955. *The Counter-Revolution of Science: Studies on the Abuse of Reason.* New York: Free Press of Glencoe.
———. 1967. "The Theory of Complex Phenomena." *Studies in Philosophy, Politics, and Economics.* Chicago: University of Chicago Press.
Heilbroner, Robert. 1999. *The Worldly Philosophers.* 7th edition. New York: Simon and Schuster.
Hodgson, Geoffrey. 2003. "The Hidden Persuaders: Institutions and Individuals in Economic Theory." *Cambridge Journal of Economics*, Vol. 27, 159–175.

———. 2006. "What Are Institutions?" *Journal of Economic Issues*, Vol. XL, No. 1, March, 1–25.

Hooper, Walter. 1996. *C.S. Lewis: Companion and Guide*. New York: Harper Collins.

———. 2007. *The Collected Letters of C.S. Lewis, Volume III: Narnia, Cambridge, and Joy 1950–1963*. New York: Harper Collins.

Howie, David. 2002. *Interpreting Probability: Controversies and Developments in the Early Twentieth Century*. Cambridge, UK: Cambridge University Press.

Hunter, James. 2000. *The Death of Character*. New York: Basic Books.

Ingersoll, Richard. 2006. *Who Controls Teachers' Work?* Cambridge, MA: Harvard University Press.

Kaplan, Robert, and David Norton. 1992. "The Balanced Scorecard: Measures That Drive Performance." *Harvard Business Review*. January–February, 71–80.

———. 1996. *The Balanced Scorecard: Translating Strategy into Action*. Cambridge, MA: Harvard Business School Press.

Kilby, Clyde. 1964. *The Christian World of C.S. Lewis*. Grand Rapids, MI: William B. Eerdmans.

Klein, Peter G. 2008. "Biography F. A. Hayek (1899–1992)." Ludwig Von Mises Institute. http://mises.org/resources/3234 (accessed November 1, 2008).

Krathwohl, David, Benjamin Bloom, and Bertram Masia. 1956. *The Taxonomy of Educational Objectives, Handbook II: The Affective Domain*. New York: David McKay Company, Inc.

Lagemann, Ellen. 2000. *An Elusive Science: The Troubling History of Education Research*. Chicago: The University of Chicago Press.

Leahey, Thomas Hardy. 2005. "Psychology as Engineering." C.E. Erneling and D.M. Johnson (eds.). *The Mind as a Scientific Object*. Oxford, UK: Oxford University Press.

Lemann, Nicholas. 1999. *The Big Test: The Secret History of the American Meritocracy*. New York: Farrar, Straus, and Giroux.

Levine, Robert. 1984. "Properties of Culture: An Ethnographic View." Richard Shweder and Robert Levine (eds.). *Culture Theory: Essays on Mind, Self, and Emotion*. Cambridge, UK: Cambridge University Press.

Lewis, C.S. 1939. *Rehabilitations and Other Essays*. Oxford: Oxford University Press.

———. 1962. "De Descriptione Temporum." *They Asked for a Paper*. London: Geoffrey Bles.

———. 1964/2007. *The Discarded Image: An Introduction to Medieval and Renaissance Literature*. Cambridge: Cambridge University Press.

———. 1970. *God in the Dock*. Walter Hooper (ed.). Grand Rapids, MI: William B. Eerdmans.

———. 1973. *The Great Divorce*. New York: HarperCollins.

———. 1979. "Preface." D.E. Harding (ed.). *The Hierarchy of Heaven and Earth*. Gainsville, FL: University of Florida Press.

———. 1982. *On Stories*. New York: Harcourt.
———. 1986. *Present Concerns*. New York: Harcourt.
———. 1995. *Christian Reflections*. Grand Rapids, MI: William B. Eerdmans.
———. 1996. *The Essential C.S. Lewis*. Lyle W. Dorsett (ed.). New York: Touchstone.
———. 2000. *C. S. Lewis Essay Collection: Literature, Philosophy and Short Stories*. Lesley Walmsley (ed.). London: HarperCollins.
———. 2001a. *The Abolition of Man*. New York: HarperCollins.
———. 2001b. *Miracles*. New York: HarperCollins.
———. 2001c. *The Weight of Glory*. New York: HarperCollins.
———. 2001d. *Mere Christianity*. New York: HarperCollins.
———. 2001e. "Screwtape Proposes a Toast." *The Screwtape Letters*. New York: HarperCollins.
———. 2002. *C. S. Lewis Selected Books*. London: HarperCollins.
———. 2003. *That Hideous Strength*. New York: Scribner.
———. 2004a. *The Collected Letters of C.S. Lewis, Volume 1: Family Letters 1905–1932*. New York: HarperCollins.
———. 2004b. *The Collected Letters of C.S. Lewis, Volume 2: Books, Broadcasts, and the War, 1931–1949*. New York: HarperCollins.
———. 2007. *The Collected Letters of C.S. Lewis, Volume 3: Narnia, Cambridge, and Joy, 1950–1963*. New York: HarperCollins.
Loux, Michael. 1978. *Substance and Attribute*. London: D. Reidel Publishing Company.
———. 2006. *Metaphysics: A Contemporary Introduction*. London: Routledge.
Loveless, Tom. 1998. "Uneasy Allies: The Evolving Relationship of School and State." *Educational Evaluation and Policy Analysis*, Vol. 20, No. 1, 1–8.
Lynn, Barry. 2005. *End of the Line*. New York: Doubleday.
MacIntyre, Alasdair. 1999. "Social Structures and Their Threat to Moral Agency." *Philosophy*, Vol. 73, No. 3, 311–329.
Marsden, George M. 1994. *The Soul of the American University: From Protestant Establishment to Established Nonbelief*. Oxford, UK: Oxford University Press.
———. 1997. *The Outrageous Idea of Christian Scholarship*. Oxford, UK: Oxford University Press.
Mayhew, Leon. 1968. "Society." D. Sills (ed.). *International Encyclopedia of the Social Sciences*. New York: Macmillan.
———. 1997. *The New Public: Professional Communication and the Means of Social Influence*. Cambridge: Cambridge University Press.
McCall, William. 1922. *How to Measure in Education*. New York: Macmillan.
McClellan, James. 1976. *Philosophy of Education*. Englewood Cliffs, NJ: Prentice-Hall, Inc.
McGinn, Colin. 2000. *The Mysterious Flame*. New York: Basic Books.

Meilander, Gilbert. 1998. *The Taste for the Other: The Social and Ethical Thought of C.S. Lewis*. Grand Rapids, MI: William B. Eerdmans.

Mincer, J. 1958. *The Illusion of Equality: The Effect of Education on Opportunity, Inequality, and Social Conflict*. 1st edition. San Francisco: Jossey-Bass, Inc.

Michell, Joel. 1999. *Measurement in Psychology: A Critical History of a Methodological Concept*. Cambridge: Cambridge University Press.

Moreland, J.P. 2000. "Naturalism and the Ontological Status of Properties." *Naturalism: A Critical Analysis*. William Lane Craig and J.P. Moreland (eds). London: Routledge, 67–109.

———. 2008. *Consciousness and the Existence of God*. London: Routledge.

Moreland, J.P., and William Lane Craig. 2003. *Philosophical Foundation for a Christian Worldview*. Downers Grove, IL: InterVarsity Press.

Meyer, John, and Brian Rowan. 1977. "Institutionalized Organizations: Formal Structure as Myth and Ceremony." *American Journal of Sociology*, Vol. 83, No. 2, September, 340–363.

Naugle, David. 2002. *Worldview: The history of a concept*. Grand Rapids, MI: William B. Eerdmans.

Needham, Joseph. 1956. *Science and Civilization in China: Volume 2: History of Scientific Thought*. Cambridge, UK: Cambridge University Press.

Nelson, Richard. 2005. *Technology, Institutions, and Economic Growth*. Cambridge, MA: Harvard University Press.

Neylan, Julian. 2005. "Quantifying Social Entities: An Historical-Sociological Critique." *Journal of Sociology and Social Welfare*, Vol. 32, No. 4, December, 23–40.

Niebuhr, Reihold. 1964. *Human Nature*. New York: Scribner's Sons.

North, Douglass. 1990. *Institutions, Institutional Change, and Economic Performance*. Cambridge: Cambridge University Press.

———. 1991. "Institutions." *Journal of Economics Perspectives*, Vol. 5, No. 1, Winter, 97–112.

Olson, Mancur. 1971. *The Logic of Collective Action: Public Goods and the Theory of Groups*. Cambridge, MA: Harvard University Press.

Overbye, Dennis. 2007. "The Laws of Nature." *New York Times*, December 18.

Pareto, Vilfredo. 1906/1971. *Manual of Political Economy*. Ann Schwier (trans.). Fairfield, NJ: A.M. Kelley.

Pearcey, Nancy R., and Charles B. Thaxton. 1994. *The Soul of Science: Christian Faith and Natural Philosophy*. Wheaton, IL: Crossway Books.

Plantinga, Alvin. 1993. *Warrant and Proper Function*. Oxford, UK: Oxford University Press.

———. 1996. "Methodological Naturalism?" J.M. van der Meer (ed.). *Facets of Faith and Science: Vol. 1: Historiography and Modes of Interaction*. New York: University Press of America, Inc.

———. 2008. "Evolution v. Naturalism." *Books and Culture*, Vol. 14, No. 4, July–August, 37.

Plato. 1975. *The Laws*. Trevor Saunders (trans.). New York: Penguin Books.
———. 1986. *The Republic*. Benjamin Jowett (trans.). New York: Prometheus Books.
Popham, James. 1965. *The New Teacher: The Teacher-Empiricist*. Los Angeles: Tinnon-Brown.
Porter, Theodore M. 1986. *The Rise of Statistical Thinking 1820–1900*. Princeton, NJ: Princeton University Press.
———. 1995. *Trust in Numbers: The Pursuit of Objectivity in Science and Public Life*. Princeton, NJ: Princeton University Press.
———. 2000. "Life Insurance, Medical Testing, and the Management of Mortality." Lorraine Daston (ed.). *Biographies of Scientific Objects*. Chicago: The University of Chicago Press.
Rader, Melvin. 1941. "New Wine and Old Bottles: The Anatomy of the World Crisis." *The Antioch Review*, Vol. 1, No. 2, Summer, 156–174.
Quine, Willard. 1992. "Structure and Nature." *Journal of Philosophy*, Vol. 89, 5–9.
Rawls, John. 1971. *A Theory of Justice*. Cambridge, MA: Harvard University Press.
———. 1955. "Two Concepts of Rules." *The Philosophical Review*, Vol. 64, No. 1, January, 3–32.
Reppert, Victor. 2003. *C.S. Lewis's Dangerous Idea: In Defense of the Argument from Reason*. Downer's Grove, IL: InterVarsity Press.
Richter, M. 1971. "Rational Choice." J.S. Chipman (ed.). *Preference, Utility, and Demand*. New York: Harcourt Brace Jovanovich.
Rodriguez, Jacob P., Steven R. Loomis, and Joseph G. Weeres. 2007. *The Cost of Institutions: Information and Freedom in Expanding Economies*. New York: Palgrave Macmillan.
Romer, Paul. 1990. "Endogenous Technological Change." *Journal of Political Economy*, Vol. 98, No. 5, 71–102.
———. 1994. "New Goods, Old Theory, and the Welfare Costs of Trade Restrictions." *Journal of Development Economics*, Vol. 43, 5–38.
Rosenberg, Alex. 2005. "Lessons from Biology for Philosophy of the Human Sciences." *Philosophy of the Social Sciences*, Vol. 35, No. 1, March, 3–19.
Rothschild, K.W. 1993. *Ethics and Economic Theory*. North Hampton, MA: Edward Elgar.
Rutherford, Paul. 2000. *Endless Propaganda: The Advertising of Public Goods*. Toronto: University of Toronto Press.
Ryle, Gilbert. 1949/2000. *The Concept of Mind*. Chicago: The University of Chicago Press.
Sacks, Peter. 2001. *Standardized Minds: The High Price of America's Testing Culture and What We Can Do to Change It*. New York: Perseus.
Salsburg, David. 2001. *The Lady Tasting Tea: How Statistics Revolutionized Science in the Twentieth Century*. New York: Henry Holt and Company.
Samuelson, Paul. 1955. *The Foundations of Economics*. Cambridge, MA: Harvard University Press.

Satz, Debra and John Ferejohn. 1971. "Rational Choice." J.S. Chipman et al. (eds.). *Preference, Utility, and Demand Theory: A Minnesota Symposium.* New York: Harcourt Brace Jovanovich.

———.1994. "Rational Choice and Social Theory." *Journal of Philosophy.* Vol. 91, No. 2, Feb. pp. 71–87.

Sayers, Dorothy. 1947/2007. "The Lost Tools of Learning." Richard Gamble (ed.) *The Great Tradition.* Wilmington, DE: ISI Books.

Searle, John. 1995. *The Construction of Social Reality.* New York: The Free Press.

———. 2005. "What is an Institution?" *Journal of Institutional Economics*, Vol. 1, No. 1, 1–22.

Sellars, Wilfrid. 1963. *Science, Perception, and Reality.* London: Routledge and Kegan Paul.

Sen, Amartya. 1977. "Rational Fools: A Critique of the Behavioral Foundations of Economic Theory." *Philosophy and Public Affairs*, Vol. 6, No. 4, September, 317–344.

Sheldon, W.H. 1945. "Critique of Naturalism." *The Journal of Philosophy*, Vol. 42, No. 10, May, 258.

Schultz, T.W. 1961. "Investment in Human Capital." *American Economic Review*, Vol. 51, No. 1, March, 1–17.

Schumpeter, Joseph. 1949. "Science and Ideology." *The American Economic Review*, Vol. 39, No. 2, March, 346–359.

Scott, James. 1990. "A Mechanism for Social Selection and Successful Altruism." *Science* Vol. 250, No. 4988, December 21, 1665–1668.

———. 1998. *Seeing Like a State: How Certain Schemes to Improve the Human Condition Have Failed.* New Haven, CT: Yale University Press.

Simon, Herbert. 1983. *Reason in Human Affairs.* Stanford, CA: Stanford University Press.

Skinner, B.F. 1953. *Science and Human Behavior.* New York: Macmillan.

Skyrms, Brain. 1996. *Evolution of the Social Contract.* Cambridge, UK: Cambridge University Press.

Sloan, Douglas. 1994. *Faith and Knowledge: Mainline Protestantism and American Higher Education.* Louisville, KY: Westminster John Knox Press.

Smith, Houston. 2001. *Why Religion Matters: The Fate of the Human Spirit in an Age of Disbelief.* New York: HarperCollins.

Sowell, Thomas. 1980. *Knowledge and Decisions.* New York: Basic Books.

———. 2002. *A Conflict in Visions.* New York: Basic Books.

Spellings Commission Report. 2006. "A Test of Leadership: Charting the Future of Higher Education." Washington, DC: Department of Education.

Stevenson, Leslie, and David Haberman. 1998. *Ten Theories of Human Nature.* Oxford: Oxford University Press.

Taliaferro, Charles. 2000 "Naturalism and the Mind." *Naturalism: A Critical Analysis.* William Lane Craig and JP Moreland (eds). London: Routledge, 135–155.

Taylor, Charles. 1989. *Sources of the Self: The Making of Modern Identity.* Cambridge: Harvard University Press.

———. 2007. *A Secular Age.* Cambridge, MA: Belknap Press of Harvard University Press.
Thaler, Richard and Cass Sunstein. 2007. *Nudge: Improving Decisions about Health, Wealth, and Happiness.* New Haven, CT: Yale University Press.
Thurow, Lester. 1975. *Generating Inequality: Mechanisms of Distribution in the U.S. Economy.* New York: Basic Books.
Tinbergen, Jan. 1987. "The Optimum Order Revisited." George Feiwel (ed.). *Arrow and the Foundations of the Theory of Economic Policy.* New York: New York University Press.
Tomas, George, Lisa Peck, and Channin Dehaan. 2003. "Reforming Education, Transforming Religion." Christian Smith (ed.). *Power, Interests, and Conflict in American Public Life.* Berkeley, CA: University of California Press.
Travers, Michael. 2007. "The Abolition of Man: C.S. Lewis's Philosophy of History." Bruce Edwards (ed.). *C.S. Lewis: Life, Works, and Legacy, Volume 3: Apologist, Philosopher, and Theologian.* Westport, CT: Praeger.
Trigg, Roger. 1993. *Rationality and Science: Can Science Explain Everything?* London: Wiley-Blackwell.
Trow, Martin. 1970. "Reflections on the Transition from Mass to Universal Higher Education." *Daedalus.* Vol. 99, No. 1, The Embattled University, Winter, 1–42.
Tyack, David. 1974. *The One Best System.* Cambridge, MA: Harvard University Press.
Tyler, Ralph. 1949. *Basic Principles of Curriculum and Instruction.* Chicago: The University of Chicago Press, 1949.
Warnock, G.J. 1967. "Reason." Paul Edwards (ed.). *The Encyclopedia of Philosophy: Volume Seven.* New York: Macmillan Publishing Inc.
White, William. 1968. "The Image of Man in C.S. Lewis." Evanston, IL: Northwestern University, Unpublished dissertation.
Willard, Dallas. 1998. "Truth in the Fire: C. S. Lewis and Pursuit of Truth Today." For the C. S. Lewis Centennial, Oxford, July 21. http://dwillard.org/articles/artview.asp?artID=68 (accessed September 23, 2007).
———. 2000a. "How Reason Can Survive the Modern University: The Moral Foundations of Rationality." For the American Maritain Association meeting at Notre Dame, IN, October 19–22. http://dwillard.org/articles/artview.asp?artID=33 (accessed September 23, 2007).
———. 2000b. "Knowledge and Naturalism." *Naturalism: A Critical Analysis.* William Lane Craig and JP Moreland (eds). London: Routledge. 24–48.
———. 2006. "Knowledge and Naturalism." Research Article for the Independent Institute. http://www.independent.org/printer.asp?page=%2Fpublications%2Farticle%2Easp?id=1725 (accessed May 5, 2007).
Williamson, Oliver. 1987. *The Economic Institutions of Capitalism: Firms, Markets, Relational Contracting.* New York: Collier Macmillan.

Wilson, E.O. 2004. *On Human Nature*. 2nd edition. Cambridge, MA: Harvard University Press.

Womack, James, Daniel Jones, and Daniel Roos. 2001. *The Machine that Changed the world*. New York: Free Press.

Young, Jeffrey. 2008. "Learning from Digital Measurements of Face-to-Face Interactions." *The Chronicle of Higher Education*, Vol. 55, No. 15, December 5.

Veblen, Thorstein. 1950. *The Portable Veblen*. Max Learner (ed.). New York: Viking Press.

Index

Abella, Alex, 135
Adequate Yearly Progress (AYP) score, 84
Albu, Rodica, 194–5
Alchian, Armen, 148
Amundson, Ron, 36
anima, 89
aptitude tests, 81, 86, 116–17
Aristotle, 36, 40–1, 102, 139, 187
Army General Classification Test, 116
Arrow, Kenneth, 31, 38–9, 45, 51, 54, 56, 59, 97, 132, 134n9, 208n7
assessment, educational, 80–4, 93, 116–19, 121–2
Audi, Robert, 128
authority, 56–7, 85

Bacon, Francis, 92
balanced scorecard business model, 119
Barzun, Jacques, 201n6, 206n4
Bastiat, Frederick, 37
Bayes, Thomas, 106
Becker, Gary, 135, 152, 176
behavioral objectives model of education, 81–3, 201–2n9
behaviorism, 81, 119, 175n8, 206n21
Beinhocker, Eric, 134
beliefs
   coherence of, 133, 164
   compatibility of, 55
   costs of, 70
   education and, 131–8

   false, 54, 96, 166
   formation of, 47, 54–5, 60, 97, 102, 131, 140, 144, 161–2
   justification of, 145, 169
   social, 140
   target (aim) for, 55
   see also disbelief
Bell curve, 107
Bell, Daniel, 129
Bentham, Jeremy, 45, 143
Berlin, Isaiah, 114, 123, 161
Bernoulli, Daniel, 106
biotechnology, 89
bloodless institutions, 47, 53
Bloom, Benjamin, 81
Bowen, Howard, 73
Bowles, Samuel, 47
Buber, Martin, 44, 146
Buchanan, James, 73
bureaucracy, 59, 65, 83, 85, 150n13, 206n21
business models applied to education, 119, 207–8n3

Caldwell, Bruce, 55
Callahan, Raymond, 89, 93, 129, 207–8n3
Carnoy, Martin, 150
Chauncey, Henry, 117
Chisholm, Roderick, 97, 209n19
choice, 90, 132–5
Christianity, 34–5, 123, 144, 169–71, 190
Chubb, John, 73
Classical Education, 53, 84
Cohen, Jonathan, 144–5

coherentism, 145
collective intentionality, 43
collectives and collectivism
  as propaganda, 194
  closed model of growth and, 74
  democracy and, 32
  education and, 147, 154, 185–94
  emphasis on in modern world, 31, 35, 51
  expanding social institutions and, 54, 56
  freedom and, 65
  individual choices relative to, 31
  information and, 51
  law and, 37
  Lewis on, 32
  liberty and, 65, 87
  magician's bargain and, 89
  membership, 192–3
  modern world and, 189
  reality and, 128
  screwtape and, 32
  social choice and, 73
  social progress and, 31
  social theory and, 35, 45, 87, 128
  statistical method and, 107
  valuations of, 51, 56, 130
  see also individual-collective problem
collectivism, definition of, 189
College Board, 116–17
Commission on the Future of Higher Education, 118, 206n16
community membership, 193–4
compartmentalization, 41, 45
complex good(s), 38, 41, 59
Comte, Auguste, 92
Conditioners, 42, 75, 88, 91, 128, 141, 176, 191
conformity, 32, 72
Confucius, 157

conscience, 34, 41, 61, 142
Craig, William, 132
Crosby, Alfred, 55
Cuban, Larry, 86

Darwin, Charles, 42, 72, 79n8
decision-making
  brain research and, 166
  bureaucracy and, 85, 202n13
  calculability of, 202n13
  choice *vs.*, 131–5
  collectivism and, 89, 99, 188
  constraints on, 176
  emotions and, 166
  growth and, 56
  information and, 80–5, 145, 152
  knowledge and, 47, 160
  SI proper function and, 38, 41
  Weber on, 202n13
decision-sets, 57, 145
democracy, 32, 49, 52, 85, 150, 160, 186–8, 195
De Moivre, Abraham, 106
Denison, E. F., 152
Desrosières, Alain, 106–7, 203n1
developmentalism, cosmic, 50, 62–3, 76, 78, 87–8, 128, 178, 195
Dewey, John
  compartmentalized as usefulness, 45
  on Darwinian, naturalistic logic, 199n8
  on displacing philosophy, 87–8
  on education, 174–6
  on empirical naturalism, 179–80
  on moral law, 177–80
  on naturalism, 58, 63, 79, 92, 169, 174–6
  on New Education, 175
  on philosophy, 87
  on religion, 169
  on scientific revolution, 199–200n11

scientism and, 60, 63, 78–9, 81, 178
substitutions/displacements of, 58, 60, 81, 87
Dickens, Charles, 177, 207n1
dictatorships, 32, 39, 54, 60, 65
Dimaggio, Paul, 148, 182
disbelief, 111, 163
disequilibrium, 33–4, 40, 52, 104, 177
doctrine of objective value, 99, 137–8
Donne, John, 47

economic efficiency, 42, 73
economic growth
  economists on, 104
  information and, 145
  rationalism and, 137
  social welfare and, 40, 45, 57, 61, 63, 69, 89–91, 130, 155, 157
economic independence, 58
economics
  choices and decisions in, 132–6
  dehumanizing of, 76
  education and, 73–4, 150
  human behavior model of, 134, 143–5, 200n12
  institutions and, 46–57, 69–74, 77, 98
  Keynesian, 32
  markets and, 159
  naturalism and, 77, 89
  non-teleological study of institutions in, 42–4
  scientification of, 202–3n15
  socialism and, 159
  statistics and, 154
economists, 44, 94–5, 104, 117, 129, 132, 138, 154, 159n7, 200n12
education
  accountability movement in, 82–4, 118
  analysis of, 181–5

  as an institution, 33, 45–6, 50
  as a production activity, 73–4, 148–52, 177, 182–5
  as conditioning, 59, 62
  as inferior to the individual human being, 35
  assessment of, 80–4, 93, 116–19, 121–2
  as supernatural, 173
  behavioral objectives model of, 81–3, 201–2n9
  behaviorism and, 206n21
  beliefs and, 131–8
  bureaucracy and, 59
  business models applied to, 119, 207–8n3
  collectivity and, 147, 154, 185–94
  comprehensive high school, 81
  definition of, 50
  democracy and, 195
  Dewey on, 58, 63
  economics and, 73–4, 117–18, 150, 181–3, 206n21
  ethnic minorities and, 202n11
  expanding of, 51
  freedom and, 33, 162, 174, 183
  higher quality, 51–2
  individual-collective problem in, 54–5
  Lewis on, 33–5, 59
  markets, 117–18, 181–3, 206n21
  models of thought and, 40
  moral, 35
  Nature and, 62–3
  No Child Left Behind Act, 84, 180
  power of, 68
  private *vs.* public, 74
  proper functioning, 137, 147
  purpose of, 49, 52
  reductionism and, 206n21
  sameness and, 63
  scientific management of, 53
  standardization of, 51–2

education – *continued*
  sustainability of, 73, 75, 93, 127, 132, 147–55, 194
  Tao and, 35
  tending toward optimization, 38, 51–2
  testing in, 80–4, 84, 86, 116–22
  see also miseducation
Educational Testing Service (ETS), 116–18
efficiency movement, 93, 119, 129, 150–2
Einstein, Albert, 204n8
Elshtain, Jean, 89
Enlightenment, 63, 67
equality, 32, 49, 150–1, 186–8, 193–4
equilibrium, 34, 37–40, 49, 52, 78, 104–5, 177, 193–5
essentialism, 81, 133n1
ethics, 47, 61, 87, 89, 117, 129, 171, 202–3n15
evolution, Darwin's theory of, 42, 148
excellence, 32
external realism, 69
extra-Nature, 58

fact, definition of, 209n19
Ferejohn, John, 135
Feuerbach, Ludwig Andreas, 92
Firor, Warfield, 189
Freedman, David, 206n23
freedom, *see* liberty

game theory, 39, 55
Gaussian distribution, 107
George, Robert, 34, 129
Gigerenzer, Gerd, 203–4n3, 204n5–6
Gleick, James, 109
Goldberg, Mark, 201n5
Great Myth (evolution as a philosophical position), 76, 148

growth
  as a model of thought, 54, 56, 72–3, 75–81
  as an attribute of social institutions, 56, 72, 93–9
  as a solution to social problems, 57
  as neutral, 40
  closed (technical) model of, 41, 57–60, 64–5, 68, 70, 72, 74–5, 80–93, 135, 140–5, 192–4
  constrained by first principles, 40
  decision making and, 56
  definition of, 40
  education and, 73, 80–1, 102, 125, 155, 164, 177
  ethics and, 202n15
  information and, 68, 73, 85, 145, 182–4
  knowledge and, 102–3, 164
  liberty and, 90, 160–1
  modern environment of, 46, 160
  naturalism and, 54, 63, 92, 160
  nature's variability and, 106–7, 116
  open model of, 40, 60, 74–5
  power and, 101–4, 125
  production and, 105
  progress and, 104–5, 159
  similarity and, 104
  social choice and, 73
  social institutions and, 56, 72, 93–9
  spiritual, 122–3
  Tao and, 40, 57–8, 72, 152–5, 157–8, 163
  see also economic growth
guide, definition of, 57
Gunton, Colin, 61, 78

Haberman, David, 207
Habermas, Jurgen, 39, 64, 118, 185–6, 199n7
Hacking, Ian, 64, 67–8

happiness, 35, 58
Hayek, Friedrich A., 55, 134, 154, 159n4
Heilbroner, Robert, 76, 197n7
Heisenberg uncertainty principle, 109
Hobbes, Thomas, 91
Hodgson, Geoffrey, 40, 47, 70, 95, 98, 144
Howie, David, 108, 204n4
humanism, 50, 58
human nature, 64, 67–8, 81, 117, 130, 134, 165, 177–80, 187–8, 207n2
Hume, David, 45, 54, 92, 143
Huxley, Aldous, 32

I–It/Them relation, 44, 61, 146
imago Dei (image of God), 40
immortality, 33–5
individual-collective problem, 34, 40, 47, 49, 54–5, 59, 128, 189, 194–5
individuals and individualism
  abstractions against, 75
  agency and, 34, 99, 132
  as criterion for evaluation, 44
  choice and, 31, 38–9, 51, 90
  collective membership and, 192–3
  community membership and, 193–4
  costs against, 89–91, 162, 174
  decision making and, 85, 104, 134, 145, 160
  democracy and, 32
  education and, 147–54
  harm to, 41, 52–3
  human relationships and, 130
  immortality and, 31, 34–5
  institutions' dependence on, 98–9
  Lewis on, 112, 131, 146
  liberty and, 31, 39, 89–90, 130, 137, 160, 186–90
  natural rights and, 160
  Screwtape and, 32
  substitutions against, 68
  teleological relation between social institutions and, 48
  underdevelopment of, 80
  valuation of, 44, 51
Industrial Revolution, 67–8, 92, 105, 150
information
  collectivism and, 51
  costs of, 43, 55, 73, 76, 79, 85, 88, 92, 104, 108, 145, 148, 154, 184
  decision making and, 80–5, 145, 152
  division of, 39, 41, 47, 51, 54–9
  economic growth and, 145
  loss of, 84
  malfunction or distortion of, 38, 93
  markets, 116, 136, 181–3
institutional expansion, *see* growth
institutions, *see* social institutions (SIs)
intellectus, 55, 91, 142–3
Intelligence Quotient (I.Q.) tests, 81, 86, 116
intentionality, 43, 97
International Baccalaureate programs, 84
intuition, 41, 57
isomorphism, 71, 148
I–Thou relation, 44, 61n14

Jefferson, Thomas, 186
justice, moral law necessary for, 34

Kerr, Clark, 117
Keynesian economics, 32, 197n7
Keynes, John Maynard, 197n7
Kilby, Clyde, 146, 157
knowledge, 38, 47, 163–73
Krathwohl, David, 81

Laplace, Pierre Simon, 106
Lauder, George, 36
law of the instrument, 84–5

Levin, Henry, 150
Lewis, Clive Staples
  and conformity, 32
  and democracy, 32, 186–8
  and education, 33, 51–2, 137
  and reason, 34, 139
  and social choice, 31
  as an educator, 33
  magician's bargain of, 89–91, 103–4
  on Chest-Magnanimity-Sentiment, 131, 195
  on collectivism, 32
  on decision making, 85
  on economic independence, 58
  on equality, 32, 186–8
  on happiness, 58
  on human reason, 112, 139, 143–4
  on individualism, 31–2
  on naturalism, 163–5, 179
  on Nature, 36
  on "ordinary people", 34–5
  on philosophy, 54
  on reason's unsymmetrical relationship to Nature, 138
  on social institutions and moral law, 31–5
  on Tao (moral law), 31–5, 43–4, 71, 75, 177
  on the "average man", 107
  on the good life, 189–90
  on the model, 46
  on thought, 173
  on uniformity, 112
  suspicion of collectives, 32
Lewis, Clive Staples, works of
  De Futilitate, 139
  "Equality", 186
  "Learning in War-Time", 54
  "Membership", 33, 187–8
  Mere Christianity, 33, 78
  Miracles, 44, 65, 71, 112, 138
  "On Living in an Atomic Age", 163–4
  "Our English Syllabus", 50
  "Screwtape Proposes a Toast", 32
  That Hideous Strength, 141, 144
  The Abolition of Man
    abstraction man in, 75
    categories of reality in, 128
    chest (heart) of man in, 131, 194–5
    conquest of Nature in, 103
    information theory in, 54
    integrated theory of SIs and, 46
    ontological correspondence in, 155
    "power" mentioned in, 178
    proper functioning education system in, 137, 147
    reductionist rationality in, 141
    sustainability in, 155
    Tao (moral law) in, 33, 43–4, 71, 75, 177
    technical model of growth in, 65–6
  The Discarded Image, 46, 76, 197–8n8
  The Great Divorce, 86
  The Screwtape Letters, 32
  The Weight of Glory, 34–5, 158, 186–8
liberty
  academic, 118
  American founders and, 186
  antecedent questions regarding, 65
  as a good of education, 174
  collectivism and, 32, 87, 130, 190–2
  decision making and, 38, 41
  definition of, 191
  democracy and, 32
  Dewey on, 174
  education and, 162, 174, 183
  game theories and, 39
  growth and, 90, 160–1

inequality and, 186
Lewis on, 58, 89
Lincoln on, 191
loss of, 39, 65, 72, 80, 89–91, 161, 174
Plato on, 49
public, 90
rationality and, 137, 189–90
social institutions and, 33–4, 38–9, 41, 190–2
social problem and, 189
Weber on, 85
Lincoln, Abraham, 191
Loomis, Steven, 39, 46–7, 63, 72, 104, 115, 133, 149
Loux, Michael, 69, 129
Loveless, 150
Lucretius, 92

McCall, William, 129, 208n4
McClellan, James, 206n21
McGinn, Colin, 132
Machiavelli, Niccolo, 52
MacIntyre, Alasdair, 52, 61, 90, 93, 98, 130
magician's bargain, 89–91, 103–4
Mann, Horace, 151
markets
  behavior of, 42, 200n12
  definition of, 159
  education, 117–18, 181–3, 206n21
  elimination of, 159–60, 174
  expansion of, 85, 89, 102, 104–5, 115, 124, 136–7, 147, 159–60, 175
  global, 175, 181–3, 184
  information, 116, 136, 181–3
  labor, 202n9
  rules and procedures in, 46
Marsden, George, 169
Marshall, John, 95
Marx, Karl, 92, 185
mass production, 105, 148, 182
materialism, *see* naturalism

Mayhew, Leon, 59, 199n7
mean, Aristotelian, 36
Meilaender, Gilbert, 62, 146n11
metaphysics, 42–4, 61, 129n5
Meyer, John W., 73
Mill, John Stuart, 45
Mincer, J., 152
miseducation, 58–9
models of thought, 40, 46, 53–6, 72, 75–93, 175
Moe, Terry, 73
Monod, Jacques, 206n22
Montaigne, 58
moral law, *see* Tao (moral law)
moral responsibility, 90–1
Moreland, J. P., 132, 200–1n3

Nation at Risk report, 184
National Assessment Governing Board (NAGB), 84, 202n12
National Assessment of Educational Progress (NAEP), 84, 202n12
naturalism (materialism)
  as anti-transcendentalist, 175
  as a philosophical position, 138
  belief and, 96
  Darwin and, 79
  definition of, 200–1n3
  Dewey on, 58, 63, 79, 92, 169, 174–6, 179–80
  economics and, 77, 88–9
  growth and, 54, 63, 92, 160
  history of, 75–6, 79, 153
  in education, 63, 88, 117, 129–30, 153, 158, 161–2, 169, 184, 194
  information cost and, 154, 174
  in science, 62, 76, 154, 161, 169, 171–2, 178–80
  in social institutions, 63, 76, 79, 95, 103, 129–30, 161–2, 169, 184, 194
  knowledge and, 88, 163–5, 169, 171–2
  Lewis on, 61, 124, 163–5

naturalism (materialism) – *continued*
  logical inconsistencies of, 88, 135, 156, 161, 163–5, 168
  magician's bargain and, 91
  Moreland on, 200–1n3
  Plantinga on, 96, 198n3
  Plato on, 49, 91–2
  power and, 178–9
  progress and, 76, 153
  rationality allied with, 63, 136, 143
  reductionism and, 148, 176–7
  sameness and, 63
  Searle and, 42–4, 95–6
  subjectivism and, 161
  Tao and, 61–3, 128–30, 148, 153, 158, 167, 180
  technical image of, 109–15
  theologians and, 171
  use of the term, 200n3
natural selection, 79, 148n7
Nature
  as all there is, 35
  as mortal, 36
  as nonrational, 135, 170
  as proxy institution, 176
  as the "first sketch", 36
  definition of, 36
  Dewey on, 58
  education and, 62–3, 87, 125
  God and, 167–8
  Great Myth and, 77
  growth and, 75, 78, 89
  Lewis on, 36, 54, 62, 66, 103, 112, 135–6, 163–4, 168, 173
  magician's bargain and, 89–91
  man's conquest of, 103, 176
  models of thought and, 76
  position in relation to social institutions, 36, 38, 41, 62–3
  proper function and, 36
  quest to master, 33, 62, 66
  rationality and, 43, 63
  Reason's relationship to, 45, 71–2, 138, 167–73, 176
  reductionism and, 148, 155, 176
  rules and, 96–7
  science and, 172
  Searle on, 43–4
  social institutions reduced to, 43
  spatiotemporal, 38, 65
  Tao and, 130
  technical model and, 54, 64–6
  the self and, 61
  thought and, 163–4
  uniformity and, 112
Needham, Joseph, 209n18
Nietzsche, Friedrich, 92
No Child Left Behind Act, 84, 180
normal distribution, 36, 107
North, Douglass, 42, 47, 52, 70, 149, 153n12

objective value, doctrine of, 99, 137–8
Olson, Mancur, 52, 63
ontological correspondence, principle of, 48–50, 155
ontology, definition of, 197n5
Orwell, George, 32, 110

Pareto, Vilfredo, 129–30
Pascal's wager, 91
Pearcey, Nancy R., 109–11
Pearson, Karl, 204n6
pessimism, 180
philosophy, 37, 44, 52–4, 58, 60
phronesis, 83
physical imperative, 165, 167
physicalism, *see* naturalism
Plantinga, Alvin, 36–7, 50, 96, 139, 141n3
Plato, 48–50, 85, 90–2, 102, 189
poiesis, 83–4
Popham, James, 81
Porter, Theodore, 106–7, 203n2, 204n8
positivism, 55, 117, 128, 177
Powell, Walter, 148, 182

power
  collectivism and, 87, 191
  cosmic developmentalism and, 62
  decision making and, 85, 160
  Dewey on, 87
  growth and, 101–4, 125
  Lewis on, 53–4, 66, 89–91, 103–4, 178–9, 186–8
  Machiavelli on, 52
  naturalism and, 178–9
  of education, 68
  of institutions, 68–9, 71, 85, 188
  of the SI, 31
  over nature, 103, 110, 176
  Plato on, 49
  soul traded for (magician's bargain), 89–91, 103–4
practice, 68–9
pragmatism, 39, 60
praxis, 83–4
private sphere, 41, 65
probability, 67–8, 80, 106–13, 120, 145, 166n6, 206n23
progress, 58–63, 67, 76–8, 87–8, 94, 102–5, 150–62, 176–7
  see also social progress
propaganda, 40, 60, 141, 194
proper function
  agency and, 185
  choice and, 39
  criteria for, 37–41
  definition of, 36–9
  equilibrium and, 38–40
  law and, 37
  liberty and, 174
  moral agency and, 97
  Nature and, 36
  of collective membership, 192–3
  of community membership, 193–4
  of education, 50, 137, 147, 192
  of social institutions, 37, 48, 52, 140, 163, 192–5
  philosophy and, 37–8
  "proper" in, 37
  reason and rationality in, 139–41, 145
  science and, 36–8
  state S and, 38
  Tao and, 74, 97
  the mean and, 36
  used in the biological sciences, 36–7
  use of the term "proper" in, 37
Protagoras, 92, 176
Public Choice, 73
public sphere, 41, 64–5

quantum theory, 109–11
Quetelet, Adolphe, 106–7, 204n3
Quine, W., 200n3

randomness, 67, 72n7
random universe, idea of, 204n7
ratio, 55, 91, 142–3
rational choice theory, 134–7, 208n4
rationalism, extreme, 141
rationality
  as insufficient, 55
  consistency (coherence) of, 43
  deontological, 140–1
  individual liberty and, 137
  meanings of, 139–41, 144–5
  means-ends, 140
  Nature wedded to, 63
  reason divided from, 40–1, 55–6, 72, 91–3, 138–47
  Stalin and, 55–6
rational soul, 142–3
Rawls, John, 39, 185
reality, categories of, 128
reality principle, 146
reality substitution, principle of, 59–62
Reason
  as divine, 144
  as self-existent, 145, 165, 168
  belief in, 168
  cosmic developmentalism and, 78

Reason – *continued*
  first principles of, 70, 79, 163, 173
  knowing and, 173
  Lewis on, 139, 144, 168, 172
  Lewis's use of the upper case "R" term, 55, 91n12
  mutiny against, 92
  relationship to Nature, 45, 71–2, 136–9, 168, 173, 176–7
  relationship to reason, 34
  social institutions and, 70–1, 141–2, 163, 195
  Tao and, 49, 137, 157, 163, 177
reason, Lewis's use of the lower case "r" term, 91, 208n12
reductionism, 54, 94, 135, 141, 148n21
Reppert, Victor, 71
Richter, M. K., 45
Rodriguez, Jacob, 39, 46–7, 63, 72, 104, 115, 133, 149
Romer, Paul, 72
Rosenberg, Alex, 148
Rothschild, K. W., 202–3n15
Rousseau, Jean-Jacques, 185–6, 188
Rowan, Brian, 73
Rutherford, 64
Ryle, Gilbert, 156

Saint-Simon, Henri de, 92
Salsburg, David, 205n9
sameness, 32, 63, 193
Satz, Debra, 135
Sayers, Dorothy, 53
Scholastic Aptitude Test (SAT), 81, 116–17
Schultz, T. W., 152
Schumpeter, 178
science
  birth of, 61
  Dewey on, 58–9, 87, 169, 178–80, 199n11
  education based on methods of, 125, 180
  faith and, 169–70
  incomplete knowledge of, 53
  knowledge and, 172
  Lewis on, 61–3, 77, 79, 112, 143, 164, 172
  naturalism in, 62, 76, 154, 161, 169, 171–2, 178–80
  proper function and, 36–8
  social, 37, 55, 67, 81, 110, 117–21, 134–5, 138, 143, 154, 181
  subjectivity and, 109
  Tao and, 177
  theologians and, 170–1
scientific method, 79, 108, 112, 120, 123, 142–3, 177–8, 199n11, 206n22
scientific positivism, *see* positivism
scientism, 61, 87, 174, 176, 178, 180, 185, 188, 200–1n3
Scott, James, 80, 147n14
Searle, John, 42–4, 47, 68, 95–6, 98–9
secularism and secular humanism, 50, 62, 63–5
self-interest, 45, 99, 143n2
Sellars, Wilfrid, 176
Sen, Amartya, 136, 143
sentiment, 43, 89, 91, 102, 111, 131, 137
Sheldon, W. H., 178
Simon, Herbert, 136, 138
Skinner, B. F., 175, 204n8
Skyrms, Brian, 135
slavery, 41, 187
Sloan, Douglass, 169–71
Smith, Adam, 45, 159
Smith, Huston, 170
social choice
  allocation of resources and, 180
  Arrow and, 54, 199n9
  collectivism and, 188–90
  division of information and, 54, 85
  external authority and, 49

Great Myth and, 78
  growth and, 73
  individual–collective problem and, 45, 59, 128, 189
  knowledge and, 87
  Lewis and, 31, 33, 39
  rationality and, 78, 145
social cooperation, 45
social coordination, 63
social institutions (SIs)
  as agent of equality, 32
  as an impersonal authority, 56
  as hidden persuaders, 47
  as human dependent, 42
  as nonnatural phenomena, 41, 44–5, 95–8
  as producers of happiness, 35
  as "rules of the game", 94–5
  attributes of, 69
  bloodless, 47, 53
  collectivism and, 54, 56
  creative capacities of, 40
  distortions in, 52–4
  education as, 33, 45–6, 50
  equilibrium and, 38
  first-order, 31
  goods and, 48, 51
  growth and, 56, 72, 93–9
  happiness and, 35
  harm done by suboptimal, 52–3
  human immortality and, 33–5
  human nature and, 67–8
  importance to Lewis, 31–5
  in disequilibrium, 33
  individuals and, 48
  in state S, 38
  integrated theory of, 46, 65
  kinds of, 69
  Lewis on, 31–5
  liberty and, 33–4, 38–9, 41, 190–2
  models of thought and, 46–7
  naturalism and, 63, 76, 79, 95, 103, 129–30, 161–2, 169, 184, 194
  nature and, 36, 38, 41, 62–3
  necessity of, 52
  non-teleological study of, 42–5
  parameters for, 34
  position in relation to Nature, 36, 38, 41
  proper function of, 37, 48, 52, 140, 163, 192–5
  properties of, 69–70
  Reason and, 70–1, 141–2, 163, 195
  relations of, 69
  resources of, 51
  rules and conventions of, 47
  second-tier, 31
  stewardship of, 34
  teleology of, 42–5, 48
  traffic cop analogy of, 56–7
social mechanisms, 130–1
social progress, 31, 57–8, 63, 68, 136, 154–8, 177–8, 180
social sciences, rise of, 55
social unification, 60, 63–5
social welfare, 34, 40, 45–6, 52, 57, 61, 69, 78, 89–93, 129–30, 134, 146, 155, 174, 180
Solzhenitsyn, Alexandr, 127
Sowell, Thomas, 86, 202n14
Spencer, Herbert, 45
Stalin, Joseph, 55–6, 127
Standards movement, 73, 93, 133, 184
statistical mean, 36, 44, 107, 192
statistics, 106–11, 114–15, 120n6, 204n8, 205n9, 206n23, 206n24
Stevenson, Leslie, 207n2
straighteners, 176, 188, 191
subjectivism, 43, 55, 71, 97, 101, 120, 128, 137, 140, 160–1
substitution, principle of, 58–62, 78–9, 85, 89, 92, 104, 115, 136, 140, 148, 195
Sunstein, Cass, 132–3, 135

supernaturalism, 60, 62, 148, 161, 165, 168–73, 179n12
sustainability, educational, 73, 75, 93, 127, 132, 147–55, 194
sustainability, meanings of, 147

Tao (moral law)
  as a governing institution, 43
  as constraining institution, 33
  as enabling institution, 33
  as independent from human beings, 43
  as mind independent, 157
  authority and, 43, 49
  correspondence and, 50
  definition of, 33–4
  developmentalists' objections to, 177–9
  education and, 35
  growth and, 40
  justice and, 34
  Lewis on, 31–5, 43–4, 71, 75, 177
  moral education and, 35
  naturalism and, 61–3, 128–30, 148, 153, 158, 167, 180
  Reason and, 49, 137, 157, 163, 177
  rebellion against, 60
  social institutions' proper function criteria and, 34, 36–42
  target of, 157
  compared to a Sherpa, 33–4
Taylor, Charles, 41, 46, 61, 76, 156
teaching to the test, 84
techne, 83–4, 157
teleology of institutions, 42–5, 48
telos, 37, 72
testing industry, 80, 205n11
  see also assessment, educational
tests, aptitude, 81, 86, 116–17
Thaler, Richard, 132–3, 135
Thaxton, Charles B., 109–11
theologians, 169–72, 177

Thorndike, Edward, 81
Thurow, Lester, 150
total quality management (TQM), 119, 205n19
tracking, curricular, 81
Trigg, Roger, 136, 221
Trow, Martin, 149
truth, twofold theory of, 170
Tullock, Gordon, 73
Tyack, David, 73, 89, 129
Tyler, Ralph, 81

uniformity, 61, 65, 80, 105–9, 111–13, 120, 154, 169n8
U. S. Constitution, 189
U. S. Declaration of Independence, 189
utilitarianism, 143
utility analysis, 143
utility maximization, 35
  see also happiness

validity, descriptive *vs.* normative, 36
variation, 32, 67, 85–7, 105–7, 116, 166, 186n3
Veblen, Thorstein, 45

Warnock, G. J., 144
Weber, Max, 59, 85, 91, 143n13
Weeres, Joseph, 39, 46–7, 63, 72, 104, 115, 133, 149
Wells, H. G., 108
Whitehead, Alfred, 134
White, William, 71–2
Willard, Dallas, 88, 102, 123–4, 175
Wilson, E. O., 148, 176
Wolterstorff, Nicholas, 128
worldviews, 46, 50, 53, 60, 62, 65, 75–9, 87, 92, 94, 111, 153, 169–70

Yerkes, Robert, 116

Zeilinger, Anton, 204n7

GPSR Compliance

The European Union's (EU) General Product Safety Regulation (GPSR) is a set of rules that requires consumer products to be safe and our obligations to ensure this.

If you have any concerns about our products, you can contact us on

ProductSafety@springernature.com

In case Publisher is established outside the EU, the EU authorized representative is:

Springer Nature Customer Service Center GmbH
Europaplatz 3
69115 Heidelberg, Germany

www.ingramcontent.com/pod-product-compliance
Lightning Source LLC
LaVergne TN
LVHW011814060526
838200LV00053B/3775